THE BOUNDARIES OF ANCIENT TRADE

THE

BOUNDARIES OF
ANCIENT TRADE

Kings, Commoners, and the Aksumite Salt Trade of Ethiopia

Helina Solomon Woldekiros

UNIVERSITY PRESS OF COLORADO
Denver

© 2023 by University Press of Colorado

Published by University Press of Colorado
1624 Market Street, Suite 226
PMB 39883
Denver, Colorado 80202

 The University Press of Colorado is a proud member of
the Association of University Presses.

The University Press of Colorado is a cooperative publishing enterprise supported, in part, by Adams State University, Colorado State University, Fort Lewis College, Metropolitan State University of Denver, University of Alaska Fairbanks, University of Colorado, University of Denver, University of Northern Colorado, University of Wyoming, Utah State University, and Western Colorado University.

∞ This paper meets the requirements of the ANSI/NISO Z39.48–1992 (Permanence of Paper).

ISBN: 978-1-64642-472-6 (hardcover)
ISBN: 978-1-64642-473-3 (ebook)
https://doi.org/10.5876/9781646424733

Library of Congress Cataloging-in-Publication Data

Names: Solomon-Woldekiros, Helina, author.
Title: The boundaries of ancient trade : kings, commoners, and the Aksumite salt trade of Ethiopia / Helina Solomon Woldekiros.
Description: Denver : University Press of Colorado, [2023] | Includes bibliographical references and index.
Identifiers: LCCN 2023012994 (print) | LCCN 2023012995 (ebook) | ISBN 9781646424726 (hardcover) | ISBN 9781646424733 (ebook)
Subjects: LCSH: Salt industry and trade—Aksum (Kingdom) | Salt industry and trade—Ethiopia—History. | Trade routes—Africa. | Afar (African people)—Antiquities. | Ethiopia—Antiquities. | Aksum (Kingdom)—Antiquities.
Classification: LCC HD9213.A3 S656 2023 (print) | LCC HD9213.A3 (ebook) | DDC 338.2/763209634—dc23/eng/20230509
LC record available at https://lccn.loc.gov/2023012994
LC ebook record available at https://lccn.loc.gov/2023012995

Cover photograph by Helina S. Woldekiros

CONTENTS

FIGURES

TABLES

ACKNOWLEDGMENTS

Throughout my journey of writing this book, I was helped by various mentors, friends, colleagues, and family members—similar to the experience of the Arho (caravanners) in this book. The individuals and groups that make this work possible are too many to list, but I would be derelict if I did not acknowledge a few of them here.

First, I want to thank the caravanners of northern Ethiopia for sharing their stories with me and for allowing me to take this incredible journey on the Afar trail with them. Without the support and help of the Arho, this book would not have been possible.

I am grateful for numerous colleagues and friends who kindly read and commented on the book. As always, I am deeply grateful to Fiona Marshall for tirelessly reading various iterations of this book and providing valuable comments and edits. Her mentorship has guided me for more than fourteen years, from supporting my ambitious project on the Afar trade route to reviewing several versions of the manuscript. I appreciate her comments and suggestions, which helped improve the work. I also want to thank Dr. Steven Brandt of the University of Florida for his mentorship and for introducing me to Fiona Marshall and making my dream of becoming an Africanist archaeologist a reality. I also thank Mary Wertsch and my sisters Kelem Solomon and Tihitna Solomon for their constant help and support and for editing and commenting on versions of the manuscript.

I also owe my intellectual inspiration to several colleagues at Washington University in St. Louis: TR Kidder, Michael Frachetti, Gayle Fritz, David Freidel, David Browman, and John Kelly. The Department of Anthropology at Washington University in St. Louis is a first-class program. I am forever grateful for being exposed to this rich intellectual atmosphere. I want to also thank Kathleen Cook, Elaine Beffa, and Kirsten Jacobsen for their constant encouragement, support, and friendship throughout my fieldwork in Ethiopia.

At Washington University in St. Louis, I have benefited from the collegiality of individuals such as Adrienne Davis, Rachel Reid, Steven Goldstein, Alex Rivas, Jing Xu, James Wertsch, Shanti Parikh, Geof Childs, Mungai Mutonya, Emily Wroblewski, and Xinyi Liu. A special thank-you to Diana Montano for her consistent encouragement and support, as well as for the opportunity to learn from her experience and expertise in the field of academic book writing.

Several institutions funded this research. The ethnoarchaeological and archaeological research on the Afar Salt Caravan Route was funded by the National Science Foundation (NSF Grant #BCS 0939891, the Wenner-Gren Foundation Grant #8175) and the Fulbright Hays Research Abroad award 2010–2011. The Department of Anthropology at Washington University in St. Louis has also provided institutional support for further research agenda.

My thanks also to members of the Eastern Tigrai Archaeological Project; Authority for Research and Conservation of Cultural Heritage (ARCCH), Addis Ababa; and Culture and Tourism Agency, Mekelle, for their constant support through all phases of my work. All projects were carried out with the cooperation of the ARCCH office in Addis Ababa, Ethiopia. I also thank Dr. Habtamu Taddesse of Aksum University and his students for tirelessly accompanying me on surveys and excavations in northern Ethiopia and helping me run an efficient project. Special thanks to Catherine D'Andrea, Simon Fraser University in Canada, who has been a colleague and a friend throughout my fieldwork in northern Ethiopia. *Ameseginalehu!*

THE BOUNDARIES OF ANCIENT TRADE

1

INTRODUCTION

Rethinking Trade and Power in Archaeology

DUST AND DONKEYS' TAILS

Legendary salt, obsidian, and gold trade routes and extensive commodity exchanges structured relationships, created wealth, and drove political reorganization across the ancient world. We have extensive evidence suggesting that elite or state control of long-distance and regional trade routes has led to the development of hierarchical societies and centralized political institutions in Egypt and China. We know less about trade and exchange that was conducted outside the boundaries of the state; the role of flexible trade and exchange conducted by non-elites, the middle class, multiple agents, regional groups, and non-centralized or heterarchical political institutions in ancient trade routes; or their role in the development of internally differentiated polities. Decisions about local or regional trade or politics were not always limited to the state or charismatic leaders. Despite a history that lauds the power and grandeur of ancient kings, it is now clear that flatter, more varied, and more egalitarian or heterarchical power structures existed in many ancient cities and states globally, like those of Bronze Age Europe or Jenne-Jeno in West Africa (Atici 2014;

https://doi.org/10.5876/9781646424733.c001

Crumley 1995; Cumming 2016; Dueppen 2014; Frachetti et al. 2012; McIntosh 1999; Saitta and McGuire 1998; Wengrow and Graeber 2015).

Understanding ways of life along ancient trade routes helps us fathom these varied political power structures; still, we are hampered by an incomplete picture of the array of participants and the social and physical context of trade. Who were the participants or non-elite agents on trade routes? A better idea of the role of local players in ancient trade and wealth generation has become increasingly central to appreciating competition for resources and commodities in ancient states and to insights into ways hierarchical power and more diffuse egalitarian organization functioned in the ancient world (Brumfiel 1995; Frachetti et al. 2012; McIntosh 1999). Ethnoarchaeological studies of caravan trade can contribute to this pursuit, as they are one of the few areas where archaeologists have investigated specific mechanisms that led to the involvement of multiple agents in ancient trade (Biginagwa 2012; Franklin and Boak 2019; Hopkins 2008; Levi 1999; Nielsen 2001; Tripcevich 2007). I will return to this topic in chapter 2.

Africa has great potential to further our grasp of circumstances in which multiple power structures operated side by side: it has produced powerful Egyptian and Aksumite kings, one of the world's earliest states, egalitarian ancient pastoralists, and internally differentiated Swahili trading communities as well as Sahelian trading cities with diffuse power structures. To critically examine the development of early polities in sub-Saharan Africa, we need to know more about how each agent or element participated in wealth-generating trade systems. We need to understand both the social and geographic boundaries of trade. How did the location of resources determine the participation of and relationships among different traders? Was participation independent? Was it mutually cooperative? Discerning the social relationships among participants in ancient trade and how those relationships connect to power will help reveal the mechanisms that fueled these diverse political systems in Africa and elsewhere.

In *The Boundaries of Ancient Trade*, I challenge conceptions of highly centralized sociopolitical and economic organization and trade in the early Aksumite state in the Horn of Africa. I argue here that there was not just one form of Aksumite social structure—hierarchy—but concurrent structures that were flatter, more complex, and spatially and temporally varied. The Aksumite elite gained wealth and power through their domination of trade in the Red Sea, which connected Africa and Asia, between 450 BCE and 900 CE. This domination of trade helped transform the Aksumite Empire into one of the most powerful complex societies in sub-Saharan Africa (Fattovich 1990, 2010b; Finneran 2007; Munro-Hay 1991; D. Phillipson 2012; Phillipson, Phillips, and Tarekegn 2000). Recent research documents a flourishing rural and urban pre-Aksumite and Aksumite elite with agricultural and trade-based wealth (Harrower and D'Andrea 2014; Harrower, McCorriston, and D'Andrea 2010). However, little is known about the people

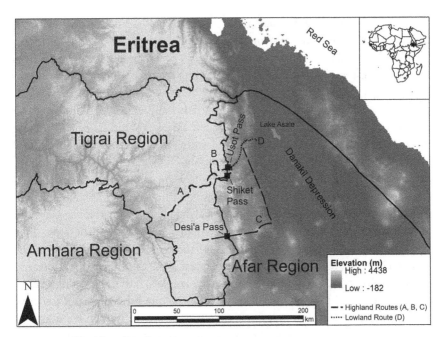

FIGURE 1.1. *The Afar salt trade route*

and power structures involved in Aksumite trade routes. In this book, I demonstrate how an essential comestible—salt—involved commoners as well as kings in Aksumite trade, drawing on integrated ethnographic and archaeological information from the Afar salt trail in northern Ethiopia (figure 1.1).

This legendary salt route is one of the last economically significant caravan-based trade routes in the world. Tigray farmers and Afar pastoralists run caravans of nearly a quarter of a million people and pack animals a year and walk the 132- to 220-km round-trip carrying all the salt for Ethiopia. The trail is extreme, moving from cool high-altitude farmlands of up to 3,000 m in the northern highlands to one of the hottest and most dramatic desert volcanic terrains on earth. Salt is mined from Lake Asale, which lies below sea level in the Afar Rift (figure 1.1)—a place where temperatures often reach 65°C (150°F) by mid-afternoon.

To investigate the organization of salt trade on the Afar salt route, I formed my own donkey and camel caravan train and walked over 130 km following salt trading groups between 2009 and 2012. Mine was the first ethnoarchaeological and archaeological research on the Afar salt route. I documented the route itself, its organization, and its participants. I also recorded three previously unreported Aksumite-period trading towns with churches and caravan campsites. Based on my findings, I argue that the ancient Aksumite salt trade route provides evidence for state intervention and control of salt trading far from the centers of power. There is also evidence that a complex network of other traders and non-elites existed around this state-centered trade, leading to complex, cooperative power relationships along the trade route. I describe the organization of present-day trade along the route in detail, offering a culturally informed framework for interpreting the organization of the ancient salt route and its role in linking the Aksumite state, rural highland agricultural, and lowland mobile pastoralist populations. The environmental conditions—volcanic terrain, temperature, climate—have not changed over thousands of years, and neither have the methods of caravan travel and salt collection (though caravanners today are linked to global networks). These ethnoarchaeological data help create a *middle-range* conceptual framework that facilitates relational analogies (*sensu* Wylie 1985, 2002). These analogies compare relevant aspects of the present to similar facets of the past and help create hypotheses that we can test using the archaeological record.

I use analogies in this book as "comparative models, rather than as illustrative devices" (see Stahl 1993, 253; 2001). Archaeologists often use analogies to derive meaning from the archaeological record in the absence of written records; however, the approach is not without critics. One such criticism of analogy is the direct historical approach that assumes that people do not change over time (Cunningham and McGeough 2018; Fewster 2006; Lyons and David 2019; Stahl 1993, 2001). The aim of this study, however, was not to show similarities between the past and the present but instead to document history in the making. The book looks at how the organization of the salt trade functioned within the broader socioeconomic and political framework of northern Ethiopia during different periods: the Aksumite period, the medieval/historical period, and the modern day. To do that, I rely on the intersection of various sources: ethnoarchaeology, archaeology, historical texts, and oral history. I move back and forth in time to show not only a partial view of history making by the contemporary Afar pastoralists and Tigray agriculturalists but also "the fragmentary glimpses of culture-making practices in the past" (*sensu* Stahl 2001, 40). I make clear distinctions between the source side (ethnographic, chapters 4 and 5) and the subject side (archaeological, chapter 6) so as not to conflate temporalizations (Cunningham and McGeough 2018; Stahl 1993, 2001).

Carole L. Crumley (1995, 4) argued nearly three decades ago that hierarchical-heterarchical relationships could be flexible in both time and space—the salt trade and practice of caravan organization in Aksumite polities illuminates this in northern Ethiopian landscapes, where cooperative local relationships and the centralized state operated simultaneously. As such, it contributes to our comprehension of flexible political configurations worldwide. The salt trade is also a compelling setting in which to investigate the organization of ancient trade because salt holds a unique position as a nutritionally essential food for people and animals as well as a valued and symbolic trade commodity worldwide (Brigand and Weller 2015; Flad 2011; Muller 1984; Parsons 2001). Despite this significance, daily activities related to salt procurement and distribution have not been as widely studied as trade itself (Good 1972). To address this gap, we must first recognize the factors that influence the scale of the salt trade in the remote and extreme Afar region: the availability of drovers, the participants at each node of the trade route, and the supply of pack animals. These factors form a system that empirically demonstrates direct and indirect trade and exchange, the matrix of participants, and the large-scale political control required to support this complex and far-reaching industry.

While the Afar trail is still economically significant in Ethiopia, study of the pack animal route is timely. The heat and terrain have long precluded construction, but roads are now being built for commercial exploitation of the Afar region. Although much about this caravan route at the time I conducted this study differed from the past—modern military enforcement of security, for example—other aspects such as the location of the major passes, physical challenges, and use of pack animals were similar to conditions in medieval and earlier periods. The logistics of local farming and distribution of water also influence seasonal participation in the salt trade by salt caravanners and the location of settlements in ways that help model ancient processes.

Although the Aksumites are well-known for their control of trade in the Red Sea ca. 450 BCE–900 CE and for their wealthy and powerful kings who minted their own currency and erected monumental stelae, we know little about the generation of wealth and the role of centralized hierarchical versus more diffuse power structures in ancient trade in the northern Horn of Africa. Chapter 5 describes a salt-oriented niche economy in northern Ethiopia today that provides rich material for understanding these mechanisms. Niche economies—diversified economic survival strategies developed where political or other conditions are unpredictable (Guyer 1997)—are well-known in Africa. On the salt route today, highland farmers and lowland herders secure a stable livelihood through the salt caravan and other trade, pack animal rental, construction and salt mine labor, redistribution or wholesale of salt and agricultural products, and reciprocity with extended family units and clans in the lowlands. Today's niche economy is affected by variables such as an individual's farmland size, physical strength, entrepreneurship, and social ties like membership in community associations. The central government also influences the economy through taxation and market location. This niche economic aspect of the modern Afar salt trade sheds light on the participation of multiple agents in the formation of early polities.

Ethnoarchaeological data reveal mechanisms that involved multiple agents in the salt trade and suggest models for interpreting archaeological data from this region and elsewhere. Today, in addition to the caravanners, varied participants are found at each node of the trade route: salt miners, warehouse owners, shop owners, water sack makers, tax collectors, and logistic providers. Through participant observation, I also documented the route itself, the landscape, and the material culture characteristics of caravan groups. Round stones used by caravanners for baking bread were revealed as previously unconsidered indicators of the camping spots of mobile and otherwise ephemeral salt caravans. The presence of these distinctive stones in cooking features allowed me to identify ancient caravan campsites.

Survey uncovered a suite of archaeological sites that revealed the role of participants on the salt route during Aksumite times. These include newly recorded ancient trader towns at Agula and Samra at the edge of the highlands and ancient border towns at Usot and Desi'a on the lower reaches of the salt route. The presence of a ruined Aksumite church clearly demonstrated an Aksumite presence on this section of the trail. Important Aksumite and pre-Aksumite elite funerary and ritual sites in higher-elevation towns at Atsbi and Wukro also indicate the participation of the Aksumite polity on the salt route far from the center of state power in Aksum.

Excavation on the perimeter of trader towns allowed me to examine the organization of ancient trade. Ancient caravan camps were situated in locales similar to those used today. Non-elite stone structures, Aksumite highland pottery, and obsidian tools distinctive of the Afar reflect the participation of foothill and lowland groups in ancient trade. Radiocarbon data and ceramic and lithic artifacts provided information on chronology and demonstrated the exchange of commodities such as salt and obsidian from the Afar lowlands to the northern Ethiopian plateau as early as the Aksumite period (450 BCE–900 CE). Data on subsistence strategies indicated that ancient traders relied on wheat, barley, and te'f, supplemented with small amounts of meat. This diet was a major signature of settlements that provided logistical support and caravan campsites.

Ultimately, the Aksumites' exploitation of the lowland salt basin and organization of the salt trade resulted in towns and settlements located far from the center of the Aksumite polity along local trails leading to the salt flats and in transition zones between the highlands and lowlands. Based on the strategic location of settlements in the highlands and eco-tonal areas close to the route, the presence of elite and non-elite architecture, and the distinctive artifacts of trading towns in the borderlands between the highlands and the lowlands, I argue that during the Aksumite period, elite Aksumites organized large-scale trade on the Afar route to meet the demand for salt in urban areas. Significantly, the location of foothill towns and the presence of non-elite architecture and ceramics from many regions demonstrate that small-scale farmers and traders moved closer to key trade routes and transition zones to participate in annual trade. The state stood to benefit from trade in a variety of ways, not least of which was taxation. Through their participation in trade, state actors also provisioned highlanders with salt, which was dietarily significant as well as politically desirable. In return, state traders obtained obsidian, a crucial raw material for producing leather for international trade. Accumulation of wealth by members of the elite who participated in organizing trade caravans may have played a role in the expansion of the Aksumite state. Small-scale farmers and pastoralists also benefited from their participation in the trade by obtaining salt for their herds, households, and villages and the ability to supplement their livelihoods through exchange.

This case study provides insight into the logistics of pack animal–based trade and the complexities of central and regional organization to inform thinking about complex societies globally. What follows is an in-depth exploration of trade and the Aksumite state, contextualization of the research area, data sets, and broader implications of the study.

AKSUMITE ARCHAEOLOGY

The questions driving this research—those surrounding the generation of wealth and the role of centralized hierarchical versus more diffuse power structures in ancient trade in the northern Horn of Africa—are situated in a pivotal period during which the pre-Aksumites (> 800–450 BCE) and Aksumites (450 BCE–900 CE) developed mixed agricultural systems dependent on domestic livestock and Asian and African crops and pulses. During the pre-Aksumite period of early state formation in the Horn of Africa, there is evidence of regional variation in pottery and lithics, access to copper, monumental architecture, and a writing system using Sabean, a South Semitic language. By contrast, the Aksumite period correlates with the establishment of the Aksumite state. At the peak of their power, the Aksumites engaged in extensive long-distance trade over the Red Sea and the Indian Ocean and controlled territory as far away as Yemen and Meroe in the Sudan (Fattovich 1990, 2010b; Finneran 2007; D. Phillipson 2012; Phillipson, Phillips, and Tarekegn 2000). They also enjoyed economic and political contact with the Romans and states and empires in the Mediterranean, the Nile Valley, and South Arabia. Goods from as far away as India and China were shipped through the port of Adulis and northern highland cities, including Cohaito, Matara, Yeha, and the capital Aksum (Fattovich 2010a; Finneran 2007; Munro-Hay 1991; D. Phillipson 2012).

The wealth of the Aksumite kings and elite and the development and expansion of the state have been tied to trade in commodities such as gold and ivory (Kobishchanov 1966). Texts from the sixth century CE also mention the existence of salt trade during Aksumite times, which could have constituted a source of local wealth (Kobishchanov 1966; Munro-Hay 1991; Pankhurst 1968) (I discuss this in more detail in chapter 3). Today, the Afar lowlands adjacent to the

Aksumite highlands are the only source of salt in the region. The rugged Afar salt route is still defined today by the location of passes from the lowlands to the highlands (Wilson 1976; Woldekiros 2014, 2019). This project was the first archaeological examination of whether an ancient trade existed on this route and the significance of local trade on the salt route from the southern lowlands of the Afar Depression to the eastern highlands during the Aksumite period. In the following section, I contextualize highland and lowland geographic and cultural areas through which the Afar salt trade (both modern and ancient) passes and describe my data collection methods.

METHODOLOGY

I conducted my research in two ecological zones in northern Ethiopia: the Afar Desert and the north Ethiopian highlands. The Afar Desert is currently occupied by mobile Afar pastoralists who make a living from their herds and the salt trade. The adjacent highlands receive abundant rainfall and support productive agricultural systems but lack salt sources. The variation in altitude, ecology, and distribution of resources, along with the organizational requirements of the Afar salt route, would have presented early agriculturalists and pastoralists with a unique set of options for trade as well as significant geographic constraints.

The evidence for this book is derived from nineteen months of fieldwork I carried out between 2009 and 2012. With my own camel train, I joined the caravanners and followed them for 90 km in the highlands and 72 km in the lowlands: the entire portion of the route that lacks roads even today. I used interviews and participant observation to collect data from 152 caravanners as well as from salt miners, salt cutters, warehouse owners, intermediaries (brokers), shop owners, residents of salt villages, and leather water bottle makers (between 3 and 30 of each). The Afar salt trail begins at the lowland salt source of Lake Asale in the northern Afar Desert and runs from the Afar Depression to the Ethiopian plateau. It travels 3,000 m up a precipitous escarpment following the few available water sources and mountain passes. From Lake Asale, the 162-km route runs through the towns of Hamed Ela and Berhaile to the major highland town Mekelle.

I followed up the ethnographic portion of my study with archaeological research, which led to the documentation of at least three significant and previously unrecorded ancient archaeological sites along the route. During excavation on the perimeter of these sites, I found ancient caravan camps in locales similar to those used today. I also identified Aksumite churches, nonelite stone structures, Aksumite highland pottery, and obsidian distinctive of the Afar. Radiocarbon dates and attributes of ceramic and lithic artifacts provided information on chronology and site use. Ancient activity on the Afar salt route revealed regional exchange in commodities from the Afar lowlands to the northern Ethiopian plateau from as early as the Aksumite period.

SIGNIFICANCE

Until recently, Aksumite archaeology has focused almost entirely on the elite. Scholars have argued for top-down elite control of ancient trade in Aksumite and other ancient polities, in part because of the history of research on monumental architecture and ancient writing (Blanton 2010; Blanton et al. 1996; Brumfiel 1995; Earle 2002; Oka and Kusimba 2008; Wheatley 1975). Data on the ancient Afar salt route suggest that informal economies and local power brokers played a role in regional trade and ultimately in maintaining the state's power. These data contribute to a more complex picture of ancient Aksumite society and current theoretical discussions regarding concurrent roles for hierarchy and more diffuse power structures in ancient states worldwide (more on this in chapter 2).

The varied environmental and social contexts of ancient sub-Saharan Africa can help illustrate and clarify variability in the organization of complex economies and societies, and the Ethiopian setting represents a compelling case. My ethnoarchaeological and archaeological research in the eastern highlands of Ethiopia and the Afar lowlands moves the discussion to different parts of the kingdom and populations than those of previous research, which has mainly focused on the northern highlands. It is clear that relationships between pastoralists and agriculturalists and between highlanders and lowlanders should not be viewed simply in terms of power relations between the dominant elite and non-elite but also in the context of cooperation and interdependence among participants in the salt trade. These perspectives allow us to depart from the dominant theories of the last 100 years that emphasize vertically controlled hierarchies and to explore new evidence from the region.

This study also contributes to documenting the rich cultural heritage of the salt trade in northern Ethiopia, where for thousands of years, the salt trade has functioned as a sustainable economic strategy. This practice is not only a significant cultural heritage but also reflects indigenous knowledge of the environment and pack animal use passed from generation to generation (Gebreab et al. 2005; Wilson 1991). In many parts of the world, pack animal–based caravans are being replaced by trucks and modern roads; this project may help preserve this ancient tradition of northern Ethiopia.

OUTLINE OF THE BOOK

In chapter 2, I problematize past conceptions of highly centralized and stratified polities and discuss how we can use trade and exchange in everyday commodities such as salt to unravel more complex and internally varied cultural processes. By doing this, I show the importance of using a synthetic approach that employs insights from anthropology, ethnoarchaeology, and archaeology to understand the effects of trade and exchange in consumable goods like salt in human history.

Chapter 3 provides the intellectual framework for my study of the Afar salt caravan trade in Aksumite archaeology. Here, I introduce the people, towns, and political structures of the Aksumite state. I discuss the emergence of Aksumite society; its social, political, and economic organization; and its settlements and towns. Finally, I outline archaeological and textual evidence for the role of the church, ancient trade routes, and the organization of Aksumite long-distance trade in the context of highland geography.

In chapter 4, I introduce the ethnoarchaeological research and the diverse social and ecological settings under which past and present local salt trade networks functioned and still function. I then situate salt provisioning within the socioeconomic and political landscape of the Aksumite state. Identifying the Aksumite socioeconomic and political landscape will indicate why the north Ethiopian and Eritrean highlands were major consumers of salt from the Afar Depression.

Chapter 5 looks at the pattern and organization of the salt trade cross-culturally and regionally. Using the ethnographic case study of the Afar salt trade, I focus on the principle of caravan organization, its participants (including traders), and the distribution of salt. This includes a discussion of caravan members, load preparation, and the journey. I also describe the concept of niche economies in northern Ethiopia, the role of caravanners within the system, and the potential for heterarchical and horizontal peer network connections. In the second part of this chapter, I focus on campsites and material residues of caravans and provide information on the functional and social aspects of long- and short-term campsites, the arrangement of camps, and the towns and villages visited on both outbound and return trips. The section concludes with a detailed consideration of the archaeological implications of the salt trade in the landscape.

Chapter 6 provides archaeological data that speak directly to the organization of the ancient Afar salt trade. It includes discussion and analysis of archaeological features, caravan campsites, churches on the route, and settlement areas near it. I also present archaeological remains that relate to the diet and identity of traders.

The final chapter of the book offers a nuanced view of the role local trade played in the economic organization of early complex societies in the northern Horn of Africa. Here I integrate the environmental, ethnoarchaeological, and archaeological data presented in earlier chapters and consider practices that shaped the organization of the Afar salt trade. I also focus on the relative roles of individuals, local traders, the Aksumite elite, and the ancient state—reflecting on their implications in interpreting the Aksumite political economy and social structure. I conclude by discussing the contributions of this study to Ethiopian archaeology and cultural heritage as well as perspectives offered by the organization of the Aksumite salt trail for understanding variability in ancient political structures globally.

2

HIERARCHIES, HETERARCHIES, PEER NETWORKS, TRADE, AND ETHNOARCHAEOLOGY OF CARAVANS

Interpretive Frameworks for the Study of the Salt Trade

While we know a great deal about the role of ancient trade routes in economic specialization and political reorganization, much less is understood about how trade was internally organized and differentiated. We also know very little about how hierarchy, heterarchy, or cooperative power functioned within trade organizations. Until recently, scholars have categorized early social and political systems in different parts of the world as either hierarchical—where a ruler and central administration exercise vertical control of power under the leadership of influential individuals—or egalitarian. Dissatisfaction with this binary has led to the introduction of the term *heterarchy*, as well as concepts such as horizontal, segmentary network (peer-to-peer), and corporate political systems (Blanton et al. 1996; Crumley 1995; Cumming 2016; McIntosh 1999; Rogers 1995; Southall 1988, 1999; C. Spencer 1994; White 1995). Carole L. Crumley (1979, 144) defines the concept of heterarchy as "the relation of elements to one another when they are unranked or when they possess the potential for being ranked in a number of different ways." These terms allow us to distinguish societies with power structures that did not fit into linear hierarchy models. They also offer an

https://doi.org/10.5876/9781646424733.c002

opportunity to reevaluate societies that were previously considered hierarchical. In light of this, I have framed this book to incorporate new concepts into pre-existing paradigms of the social and political organization of the Aksumites of the north Ethiopian and Eritrean highlands. The Aksumites function as a cogent example of the complexity and variability of early social and political systems and facilitate exploration of the concepts of trade, salt, and caravan archaeology.

HIERARCHIES, HETERARCHIES, PEER NETWORKS, AND CORPORATE SOCIETIES

Archaeologists' early perspectives on prehistoric and historical societies' political and social structures were influenced by evolutionary theories that viewed culture change in a linear way: from simple egalitarian level to mid-level chiefdom to a state-level society. It is now clear that early political systems were fairly complex, and scholars have called for new models to evaluate them (Dueppen 2014; Fargher and Espinoza 2016; LaViolette and Fleisher 2009, 2018; McIntosh 1999; Saitta and McGuire 1998; Southall 1988; Wengrow and Graeber 2015). Prehistoric political and social systems included diverse structures that sometimes operated side by side. A society could have dual political systems with elements that were hierarchical and heterarchical at the same time. A hierarchical system could also become heterarchical through time (Brumfiel 1995; Crumley 1995; White 1995).

Popular imagination and even scholarship have held onto the idea that all societies were structured in a nested hierarchy with top-down control. Archaeologists have typically categorized societies according to two hierarchical models: scalar hierarchy and control hierarchy (Crumley 1995). In a scalar hierarchy, any level within the system can affect any other (2). In control hierarchies, decisions at higher levels affect lower levels (2). It has become clear, however, that vertical and centered power was not universal in early societies and that even in places where it was present, it did not stay the same through time and across space (see Blanton et al. 1996; Crumley 1995; White 1995). These models also failed to account for societies that had complex, specialized economic systems but were not regulated by powerful individuals or settlements at the state's core. In light of shortcomings like this, the concept of heterarchy has gained traction (Blanton et al. 1996; Brumfiel 1995; Crumley 1995; Dueppen 2014; McIntosh 1999; White 1995).

Heterarchy recognizes the presence of multiple organizing principles in a system (Davies 2009). Scholars have identified counterpoised power even in strongly hierarchical systems where power was shared between a charismatic leader and coalitions of federations (Cumming 2016; Crumley 1995; McIntosh 1999). In many African segmentary states, both kings and associations held power. These associations included secret societies or cultures with titled elders as well as councils of lineage heads (McIntosh 1999, 15; Southall 1988, 1999). Susan Keech McIntosh (1999) argued more than twenty years ago that scholars who apply heterarchy models had failed to exploit this type of rich African data. Moreover, Aidan Southall proposed sixty-six years ago that segmentary state structures were found in many pre- and postcolonial African countries and that we could use these cases to study ancient and pre-colonial states outside Africa. The Alur of Africa and many better-known ancient African polities, including the Bunyoro-Kitara, Ufipa, Suku, and Amhara, were closer to segmentary states than unitary states (Southall 1956, 1988). Following Southall's proposal, similar arguments have been presented for Asian states such as Rajput and Cola (see Stein 1971).

The question becomes: what were segmentary states, and how were they different from unitary states with their centralized governments? First, it is important to note that segmentary states differed from stateless segmentary lineage systems, which were divided into local, territorial groups that exercised political authority within their jurisdictions. Southall (1988, 80) defined a segmentary state as "one in which political sovereignty was narrowly circumscribed, and ritual suzerainty much more widely spread" (ritual power had the potential to transcend political boundaries). It is not just a designation for specialized groups such as pastoralists or agriculturalists—the concept comprises more than economic elements. It seems to "require some kind of autonomy," whether in the form of a merchant guild, as in the case of West African states (Mali, Niger); localized lineages, as with the Alur (Uganda, Congo) and Rajput (Asia); or various kinship and other local institutions, as with the Cola (Asia) (McIntosh 1999; Southall 1956; Stein 1971). Both African and Asian case studies emphasize the ritual aspect of segmentary state leaders, who juggled the duties of political officials and clergy on a regular basis. Their ancestors were frequently linked to demigods in terms of genealogical ranking. Segmentary states had several levels of political segmentation and managed their own day-to-day affairs rather than being managed by a central government (Southall 1988, 61). Essentially, segmentary states were more than their unitary counterparts, serving to bring equal benefits to all stakeholders.

Southall (1988, 79) argued that segmentary states formed in gradual rather than evolutionary stages. As his case study of the Alur society indicates, the Atyak—their ruling clan—were initially "just a cluster of segmentary lineages, linked by overlapping chains of complementary opposition, highly egalitarian, disposing of no strictly political authority and only respecting the ritual-supernatural authority of their leaders" (58). In this initial stage, subordination to the lineage leader by other Alur or non-Alur groups was not a result of coercion but rather of peaceful acceptance of a powerful leader who was beneficial to the community. Community members believed these leaders had potent power that protected against natural disasters and outside enemies. They were able to bring food, fertility, and prosperity to the community in the form of livestock, agriculture, and metallurgy for farming and weaponry.

Political elements usually entered society in the second stage of segmentary state formation. People or communities receiving the benefit of ritual service were expected to reciprocate, and these acts of reciprocity gave rise to political order. At this stage, subjects were included in a political order. Once local people and other lineage groups were incorporated into the system, the process of polity formation began. In the case of the Atyak, their relationship with other members of the Alur society was equal and reciprocal. Other relationships were unequal: for example, the Lendu, a non-Alur group, paid the Alur with labor (Southall 1956, 1988).

The next stage in the formation of segmentary states was the development of segmentary polities. The Atyak formed segmentary polities as a result of the "offshoot" of "various kings' sons from the central line in successive generations" (Southall 1988, 61). Each hived-off lineage or secondary group established a new localized segmentary state that had ritual power over other lineage or non-lineage groups. Offshoot segmentary polities were not uniform in strength, size, demography, or wealth. Not all Atyak offshoot polities were economically, politically, and demographically successful. Some were replaced by other offshoot lineages, while others reverted to commoners. While collaboration was not necessary for the survival of the segmentary state, it was possible to achieve it. Collaboration was difficult for scattered polities in hard-to-navigate landscapes, but there was potential for it to exist between closely situated polities (Southall 1956, 1988). Segmentary states continued until the nineteenth century in Africa and elsewhere, even after the emergence of the centralized state with its effective central bureaucratic administration.

African history provides examples of societies that help us understand various ancient political systems worldwide. There need not be a connection between economic specialization and political hierarchy; societies can achieve industrialization, large-scale production, and distribution of commodities—especially staple goods—without a single political power or hierarchy administering economic and political functions (Brumfiel 1995, 126; McIntosh 1999). Ethnoarchaeological evidence from the Afar salt trade route demonstrates the participation of many independent groups and stakeholders in the trade. Today, a specialized group of workers handles salt mining. The villages from which the miners and caravanners came also show some level of community specialization. Store and shop owners, water sack (*sar*) makers, and others (villages and settlements) participated in the trade. Archaeological evidence likewise reveals participation by elite individuals as well as by towns and villages found along the route. Some of these findings include state-controlled Aksumite churches and other religious institutions built specifically along the trade route that confirm state participation.

One of the reasons ancient trade had such power to transform societies is that it linked diverse groups (Appadurai 1988; Dillian and White 2010, 7; Renfrew 1984; Renfrew, Cann, and Dixon 1965; Sahlins 1972). While according to the *Cambridge Dictionary* trade refers to the buying and selling of goods and services, the concept of exchange examines these transfers of goods from individual to individual and from society to society, with a known source and patterned spatial distribution (Bray 2005; Earle 1982, 1994, 2002; Goldstein 2000; Odess 1998; Wilk and Cliggett 2007). Because ancient trade (and the exchange it engendered) so profoundly impacted the people it linked, we often categorize it based on the people who drove it: their organization, organizers, and infrastructure. Accordingly, the Afar salt trade is named after the people who organized it.

The concept of a complex economy is also central to this inquiry. Timothy K. Earle (2002) suggested that we observe economic complexity through evidence that someone has indirectly transferred a commodity from a source, be it a village or an urban center. In a direct distribution system, by contrast, an individual or a group travels to the source of a commodity and acquires it for themselves. Concepts of trade, exchange, and complex economies are not straightforward, however, and have been part of formalist-substantivist and primitivist-modernist dichotomies and debates since the early 1960s (Adams 1992; Finley 1985; Oka and Kusimba 2008; Polanyi 1947; Polanyi, Arensberg, and Pearson 1957; Schneider, Herskovits, and LeClair 1968).

In Africa, as in many parts of the world, archaeological studies of trade and exchange have focused on long-distance trade, elite control of trade, and trade in luxury and prestige goods. Less studied have been local trade, participation of the non-elite or multiple agents in trade, and trade in consumable goods. In addition, studies of African trade have focused more on power, wealth, and legitimization of power than on obtaining food on a subsistence scale. Earlier historical and classical anthropologically oriented studies emphasized the social aspects of trade, but more recent syntheses have emphasized the economic aspects of trade in the development of complex institutions in Africa (Helm et al. 2012; Kessy 2003; Kusimba 1999; Kusimba and Kusimba 2003). Subscribers to the substantivist-primitivist paradigm have long argued that the concepts of markets and marketplaces were nonexistent in Africa prior to contact with European colonial economies. Paul Bohannan and George Dalton (1962), Abner Cohen (1966), and Ronald Cohen (1965) argued that prior to European interaction, trade in both African states and stateless societies was either reciprocal and redistributive or an administered rather than market-based exchange. The Western capitalist perspective on the African economy in general and its local economies in particular has contributed to the patchiness of trade and exchange studies in

Africa. Although many still argue for administrated or reciprocal exchange, an increasing amount of archaeological and historical data has provided evidence for complex interregional trade relations in Africa (see Biginagwa 2012; Insoll and Shaw 1997; Kessy 2003; Oka and Kusimba 2008; Vansina 1962; Wright 1993; Zarins 1990; Zarins and Reade 1996).

The mechanism of exchange, however, was not the same everywhere. Although trade studies have tended to focus on elite prestige objects and the most archaeologically visible trade routes, there has been some recognition of different mechanisms at work in different regions. In Great Zimbabwe and the Aksumites' case, scholars have concentrated on trade in gold, control of trade by the elite, and ties to the Arab and Roman worlds (Connah 2001; Kobishchanov 1979; Munro-Hay 1991). Trade studies in Jenne-Jeno and on the Swahili coast, in contrast, have focused on the role of intermediaries and small autonomous towns (Abungu and Mutoro 1993; Alagoa 1970). In the Swahili case, however, greater emphasis was placed on elite goods than in Jenne-Jeno (Curtis 2008; LaViolette and Fleisher 2005; McIntosh 1999; Wright 1993).

Earlier scholarship heavily emphasized the role of the elite and the state at the expense of mediators and trade specialists. While I have not dismissed the part played by elites, I have consigned it to specific realms, such as provisioning secure trade networks for traders and collecting tax and tribute in urban trade (Barfield 2001; Ferman, Henry, and Hoyman 1987; Oka and Kusimba 2008). I also join Rahul Oka and Chapurukha M. Kusimba (2008) in recognizing a less public role of the powerful elite in trade—offering protection and tax discounts to participants on trade routes in exchange for bribes.

WHY ENERGETIC AND NON-ENERGETIC COSTS OF TRADE GOODS MATTER

Some of the more formalist approaches I have found useful track the changing value of goods as they are exchanged farther and farther away from their place of origin. The value of an object increases the farther away it is exchanged from its original location (Hughes 1978; Santone 1997). The worth of the object is typically determined by looking at both the energetic and non-energetic costs associated with it. The operational costs, such as labor and time or hours worked, are included in the energetic costs. The mechanism used to transfer goods—whether pack animal or human—and the time and energy expended in the transfer also determine value (Appadurai 1988; Hughes 1978; Marx [1867] 1977; Renfrew, Cann, and Dixon 1965). All expenditures that are not directly related to operations, such as capital, are included in non-energetic costs (e.g., pack animals and water sack rental). I have tried to strike a balance in my consideration both of trade as an economic *versus* a socially and politically motivated activity and of the roles of non-elite intermediaries versus elites. Thus, in the following section, I return to the political and social landscapes for trade and the role of trade in structuring interactions within and between regions (Dillian and White 2010, 12). Finally, I address the question of methods employed for studying ancient trade in Africa and the importance of ethnographic data for understanding the totality of concerns in trading relationships, particularly when examining a resource such as salt that is difficult to find in the archaeological record.

INTRAREGIONAL AND INTERREGIONAL INTERACTION AND POLITICAL LANDSCAPES

Current approaches to intraregional and interregional interactions through trade provide valuable perspectives for understanding the salt trade. We have identified economic and political systems controlled and operated by multiple political, economic, and religious institutions in ancient societies around the globe (Barfield 2001; Cowgill 1997; Frachetti et al. 2012; Khazanov and Wink 2001; LaViolette and Fleisher 2009; Wright 1972). Anthropological studies have used interregional interaction to examine the exchange of ideas and goods between distinct regions and to understand how social interactions among groups with different socioeconomic and political organizations affected the structure of those systems (Curtin 1984; Earle and Ericson 1977; Frachetti et al. 2012; Freidel and Reilly 2010; Fry 1980; Hirth 1984). Michael D. Frachetti et al. (2012), for example, argued that while Eurasian pastoralists of the late fourth and third millennia BCE played a significant role in wide-scale regional interaction and economic development, they also managed to maintain their political autonomy and social identity. Interregional studies have also documented the creation of market centers and other specialized places. In some cases, the exchange and sharing of food created special zones, such as markets trading towns or middle zones (Adams 1975, 1992; Flannery 1968, 1972; Ford 1972; Freidel and Reilly 2010).

Interregional interaction through food exchange is especially significant in structuring relationships between culturally distinct groups and providing incentive for the emergence of specialist groups to facilitate those relationships (Ford 1972; Freidel and Reilly 2010; Frison 1972; Oka and Kusimba 2008). This is particularly relevant for the ancient Afar salt trade. Traders are vital in mediating exchanges between groups with drastically different socioeconomic and political structures, such as settled agriculturalists and mobile pastoralists. The Nubians, for example, connected distinct social groups over a wide area of Africa and are considered a prototype for intermediaries in regional trade (Edwards 1998; Hafsaas-Tsakos 2009). They were the primary movers of Egyptian goods and commodities from south of the Nile to Ethiopia and of traded goods that had come from as far as central Africa and the Sahara. Nubian traders also moved trade items in ways that connected with the Bronze Age world system (Hafsaas-Tsakos 2009). The beginning of the Bronze Age coincides with the rise of complex and strong city-states all over the world. These city-states were in fierce competition with one another for valuable resources and for economic relations with traders from both their own region and from outside. This need was filled by the Nubians, who supplied materials that are uncommon and hard to come by in other regions of the world.

Resource-motivated trade is also seen in Africa and is a key aspect of my consideration of the Afar salt route. Although the Egyptians had successful agriculture and innovation, they lacked many natural resources. In addition to gold—the Egyptians' most valued commodity—exotics such as elephant ivory, leopard skins, hardwood, ostrich eggshells and feathers, precious stones, aromatic resins, herbs, and spices were provided by the Nubians (Edwards 1998; Hafsaas-Tsakos 2009; Kendall 1997).

From a functional perspective, exchange tends to occur where resources are unevenly or patchily distributed or where there are political constraints on travel (Dillian and White 2010, 8). For example, David Freidel and F. Kent Reilly III (2010) argue that the Olmec and Lowland Maya exchanged with diverse social groups in the lowlands and highlands through elaborate and extensive trade networks to avoid the danger of dependency on a risk-prone crop such as maize. The Lowland Maya had maize, but crop failures could result in shortages for the general public, so food had to come from regions near and far (2010). Freidel and Reilly (640) also argue that this process eventually led to the development of a network of market centers oriented toward moving commodities between and within regions.

NICHE ECONOMIES

We often force pre- and postcolonial African and Asian market systems to fit Western capitalist economic models without due consideration of their own unique characteristics. Accordingly, and in conjunction with other Africanist scholars who study ancient and extant African economies, I use the concept of niche economy as proposed by Jane I. Guyer (1997) (see Barrett-Gaines 2004; Berry 2004; Chalfin 2004; Clark 2004; McDougall 2004; Wolff 2004). Guyer (1997) turned the dictionary and ecological meaning of the term *niche* upside down and came up with a way to understand the diversity of ancient as well as extant economic systems. She defined niche not as a "pre-existing space attracting suitable people" but as a space created by people "for themselves" (see also McDougall 2004, 155). Guyer's use of the concept is also different from the initial use of the term in economic studies of the *niche market*. Her notion of the niche economy emphasizes the flexibility of both people and niches. There will be times that a niche might gain some stability when "people move in and out of it." In other cases, "it is the niche itself that is transformed to fit the needs and abilities of the people," to the extent that it fades away (155). What makes Guyer's adoption of the term *niche economy* useful is the way it focuses attention on "a special area of production (of a commodity) rather than [on] demand" (155), as in neoclassical economic models. In this concept of the niche economy, "production and producers are front and center." The market, in contrast, "responds as it sees fit" (156).

Guyer and Africanist scholars who study the development of African economies adopted the concept of the niche economy to compensate for the shortcomings inherent to neoclassical economic models. The main problem with neoclassical economic models is the way they measure growth. Traditionally, we have assumed that growth occurs when there is "specialization and exchange" and that niche activity does not technically constitute specialization. Moreover, under the neoclassical assumption, the normal way to secure change is through commodity prices (McDougall 2004, 162–163). In this approach, individuals and society are not given agency. Guyer's (1997) seminal work, which looked at the social and agricultural history and various producers of the postcolonial Yoruba community of Ibadan, challenges this assumption. In this Yoruba community, people specialize in not one but several economic activities. They occupy niches seasonally and modify them at times. Guyer (1997) proposes that to measure change in this type of economic context, the movement of people and commodities from one form of economic activity to the next must be followed (McDougall 2004). In a niche economy, growth occurs as new economic niches are created, reorganized, or abandoned (Berry 2004; Clark 2004). Social networks, individuals, and cultural norms are also important aspects of the niche economy.

The concept of the niche economy, therefore, lends itself to the discussion of different "economic orders" (Chalfin 2004). It can be used to talk about local niche economies such as the production and sale of *Babban Riga*, embroidered robes in Zaria, Nigeria (Renne 2016); regional niche economies such as the salt industry of the Katwe of the Great Lakes (Barrett-Gaines 2004); and global niche economies like the global market demand for African arts and crafts such as Ghanaian wood-carved fertility dolls (Wolff 2004). Guyer's conceptualization of the niche economy is not exclusively applicable to an African economy; we can use it to investigate other economic systems globally. For example, we can observe seasonality in the Andean archipelagoes in South America, where people move up and down the different altitudes to exploit economic niches available at certain times of year (Capriles and Tripcevich 2016). A flexible economy is also constantly observed in the capitalist global market system (McDougall 2004). Exporting African resources like shea butter and then importing them in different forms, such as cosmetic or food products, exemplifies a capitalist economy reinventing itself (Chalfin 2004).

The most important aspect of the niche economy is its ability to "thrive [amid] instability, insecurity, and vulnerability" (McDougall 2004, 160). Niche economies provide a buffer and flexibility in the face of internal and external variables such as war, environmental change, pandemic, loss of agricultural land or livestock, and changes in government policy, taxation, or ideology. I return to this concept in chapter 5 in conjunction with the niche economy of northern Ethiopia.

SALT

Salt is a nutritionally essential food for people and animals and a valued trade and symbolic commodity worldwide (Brigand and Weller 2015; Flad 2011; Muller 1984; Parsons 2001). Daily activities related to salt procurement and distribution have not been as widely studied as trade itself (Good 1972), but there is a need to do so. Information on these processes allows empirical demonstration of direct and indirect trade and exchange, the matrix of participants, and estimations of value. It also reveals other factors affecting trade. For example, the availability of pack animals, donkeys, and camels influences the scale of the salt trade in the remote, extreme Afar region.

Salt has had economic, political, and symbolic value since ancient times. Availability of salt is limited, as sources are dispersed and not consistently found in every region. Its portability and status as a necessary element for human physiology have generated a widespread demand among consumers. As a result, salt has influenced the settlement patterns and socioeconomic organization in many regions (Alexander 1982; Andrews 1980; Denton 1984; De Villiers and Hirtle 2007; Harding 2013; Kurlansky 2002; McKillop 2002). Scholars argue that the patchy production and distribution of salt has affected local, regional, and interregional relationships and contributed to complex socioeconomic organization from China to Mesoamerica (Batterson and Boddie 1972; Flad 2011; Parsons 2001; Potts 1984; Yoshida 1993).

Despite salt's economic and symbolic importance, anthropological and historical studies have focused primarily on its role in influencing ritual activities, settlement patterns, monetary transactions, and political relations (Harding 2013; Muller 1984; Parsons 2001). Although we have previously ascribed minor importance to the daily activities related to salt procurement and distribution (Brigand and Weller 2015), it is now clear that the study of these activities can contribute to a more detailed understanding of local and regional trade.

The emergence of agriculture has increased our dependence on pure salt (Alexander 1982; Denton 1984; Parsons 2001). Scholars argue that a lack of sodium in plant-based diets pushed people to seek external sources of salt, probably starting from the Neolithic and even before (Andrews 1980; Weller 2015). Others suggest that salt use increased throughout human history because of its ability to make food palatable, increasing the variety of plants humans could consume. The required dietary salt intake varies from region to region and from one individual to another; too little or too much sodium can be problematic.

Scientists suggest that individuals ingest 0.7 to 20 g of salt daily, depending on diet and lifestyle (see Alexander 1993; Denton 1984; Parsons 2001). Nonetheless, there is still a debate about the exact amount of salt appropriate for the human body (Kurlansky 2002). People who live in hot areas, for example, require more salt because they tend to lose it through perspiration. Salt is also essential for livestock, and pastoralists will travel a long way to obtain it.

In addition to its role as a condiment, people have long used salt in symbolic rituals and religious ceremonies. The ancient Egyptians placed salt on coffins to ensure life after death for the deceased (Denton 1984). Numerous cultures have used salt in dyeing cloth and preserving meat, fish, and leather (Alexander 1993; Alexianu and Weller 2009; Parsons 2001). Today, we continue to use salt in a wide range of settings.

Although salt has several dimensions, its importance here is as a highly valued commodity in trade and exchange. Unlike exotic and luxury goods, which formed the bases of ancient trade and exchange, salt was in equal demand by the elite and the non-elite, for whom it was a basic commodity. Although ancient states successfully distributed salt en masse to a wide array of consumers, the natural occurrence of sources was as limited then as it is today. Consequently, control and distribution of this essential resource contributed to major social, political, and economic changes in most parts of the world.

Depending on the location of salt sources, at least two salt trading zones have been identified (Alexander 1993; Birmingham and Gray 1970). They include short-range zones, which lie within a 100-km radius of a source, and long-range zones, which are 1,000 km or further from a salt source (Alexander 1993). In the case of towns, villages, and cities located in the short-range zone, salt can be acquired from local markets or directly from the source (Birmingham and Gray 1970). In areas where the salt source is 1,000 or more km away, organized long- and medium-range trading caravans are required (Cohen 2018; Vansina 1962). These caravans require good logistical support, overnight rest areas, and social relations en route. I elaborate on this topic of caravan organization later in the caravan section in this chapter and in chapters 5 and 6, where I discuss caravan organization on the Afar salt route.

SALT INDUSTRIES OF AFRICA

Salt Trade and Exchange

In African areas where salt is a critical resource, its production, distribution, and long-distance trade have shaped social, political, and economic structures (Alexander 1975, 1993; Connah 1991, 2001; Lovejoy 1974, 1984). Production and control of the salt trade are well-known to have contributed to the power and rise of states in Ghana, Mali, and Sudan over the last 1,000 years (Good 1972; Insoll and Shaw 1997). In the Sahel, historical research on the salt trade at Ijil demonstrates that trade extended from northwestern Mauritania to Sudan. This trade facilitated the economic growth and political strength of the complex ancient societies of the Sahara by connecting communities and bringing in commodities that would have been unobtainable without the common demand for salt (McDougall 1990).

Because archaeological research on salt trade and exchange in Africa is limited, most studies have relied on historical and ethnographic written records prior to the nineteenth century. One well-documented African salt trade route is the great Saharan salt caravan route in use from the thirteenth to the nineteenth centuries and possibly earlier (Denton 1984; Lovejoy 1986; McDougall 1990). Stretching about 720 km in length, this was Africa's longest salt caravan route (Carpenter 1956; Lovejoy 1986). Rock salt was transported inland as well as on the Niger River. The route started at the town of Taoudeni in northern Mali, where the salt swamp was located. It traversed at least two crossroads, with a second salt route starting at Idjil in Mauritania. The price of salt from the two sources differed based on variations in their chemical compositions and the distance traveled for the trade. Because of the length of the journey and lack of water along the route, trade was often risky and was organized only twice a year. In the 1900s, caravan members were mainly Kel Arauan kin (Tuareg) joined by other Saharan mobile pastoralists along the route from Gao to Timbuktu (Lovejoy 1986). In the Sahara, people used salt for several purposes—most notably, from the thirteenth century onward, to acquire enslaved people to meet the increasing labor demand for agricultural production.

Timbuktu was the preferred large distribution center for the Saharan salt route due to its proximity to the Niger River. A large portion of Timbuktu's wealth came from the salt trade, and historians argue that the great Saharan salt route played a major role in establishing the city (Ross 2010). The salt source at Taoudeni was also a source of contention and war in North Africa among the Timbuktu chiefs, Moroccans, and Moors (Bovill 1970; Denton 1984, 81).

John Alexander's (1975, 1993) seminal work on the salt industry of West Africa provides a good example of the organization of the salt trade into three distinct phases: before ca. 400 CE, ca. 400–1800 CE, and 1800–today. We do not have archaeological data from West Africa's salt industry around 400 CE to help highlight the connections among its salt-producing areas, trade routes, settlements, and burial cemeteries. Nevertheless, Alexander suggested that the organization of the salt trade around 400 CE would have been limited to short- and medium-range radii in the absence of camel transport. It would also have been unlikely that the desert salt sources were exploited at that time.

Instead, traders would have transported salt from both the savanna and forest zones. Between ca. 400 and 1800 CE, however, with the introduction of the camel from the Arabian Peninsula and the mobile pastoral way of life, the radius of salt trade would have expanded to communities in the Sahel and Sahara—including the rock salt resources of Mauritania, northern Mali, southern Algeria (Amadror), and Niger (Bilma, Dirkou Djaba, and Teggidda-n-Tesemt) (Alexander 1993; Bernus and Bernus 1972; Gouletquer 1975). During this period, the salt trade could have extended as far as 1,500 km in area. Coastal salt exploitation and trade also started around the sixteenth century but were limited to a 500-km radius (Alexander 1993; Daaku 2018).

A dramatic change in the West African salt trade happened after 1800 CE. The introduction of cheaply produced European salt and increased ease of communication between the coast and the inland led to a considerable decrease in salt prices. The inland rock salt continued to be used in small quantities but was much more expensive than the coastal salt and was bought only by those who could afford it. By the 1950s, inland salt was considered a luxury reserved for medicinal or ritual purposes, likely marking the decline of the trans-Saharan and trans-Sahelian salt trading networks (Alexander 1993; Newbury 2018).

Salt Sources and Production Technology

Salt mining and production, if carried out on a large scale, require a considerable amount of labor and social and political organization (Alexander 1975, 1982, 1993). In Africa, people have used a variety of salt sources, ranging from pure salt (NaCl, or sodium chloride) to sodium sulfate, potassium carbonate, and potassium sulfate (Alexander 1975). Ethnographic and historical sources also show that in equatorial West Africa, near Lake Chad, people have figured out a way to extract salt from certain plant species such as *Pistia stratiotes* (H. Barth 1896; Riehm 1961). Salt makers collect these plants and burn them en masse: the ash is either used as a condiment or boiled to make crystal salt (Lovejoy 1986; Parsons 2001; Riehm 1961). This practice of mining salt from plants also exists in other parts of the world, including New Guinea, Brazil, and the southwestern United States.

In sub-Saharan Africa, the collection of naturally formed crystals around salt lakes is the most common method of acquiring salt. People handpick these salt crystals and dehydrate them in the sun (Fawcett 1973; Morgan 1974; Parsons 2001). During the dry season, thick scales of salt form on the surface of salt lakes and sink to the bottom. Harvesters dig this salt out from the lake bottom by hand and transport it to shore using rafts (Fawcett 1973; Parsons 2001; Rivallain 1977).

On the southern margins of the Sahara, harvesters dig artificial wells around 5 m wide to access natural underground saltwater and wait for salt crystals to form (Lovejoy 1986). A typical harvest area is 20–30 by 20–30 m. Residents of Niger at Kawar still practice this method of salt acquisition (Vikør 1982). In both West and East Africa, people collect salt near springs and from coastal lagoons (Alexander 1993; I. Sutton 1981; J. Sutton 1983).

In West Africa and parts of East Africa, people boil brine and salty earth, using ceramic pots to leach out the salt and remove impurities (Connah, Kamuhangire, and Piper 1990; Fagan and Yellen 1968; Lovejoy 1986). An archaeological study of a salt-making site at Ivuna, Tanzania (Fagan and Yellen 1968) and Kibiro, Uganda (Connah 1991) shows that people used this technology as far back as the Iron Age. In humid sub-Saharan areas where salt precipitation is limited, miners form salt gardens in large vessels for evaporating spring and lake waters to maximize crystallization. Archaeologists recovered a large quantity of broken pottery from the site Kibiro, a salt-processing site dating to 700–800 BP (Connah 1991), indicating that people there produced a great deal of salt using the leaching and boiling process. We have documented ethnographic examples of this type of mining in places like Nigeria. In East Africa, the Great Lakes region is well-known for salt production using solar evaporation techniques involving pans or pounds near the lakes (Barrett-Gaines 2004). The Katwe salt industry of East Africa, for example, was founded in this area. Several agro-pastoral groups from surrounding towns and villages traveled to this area in the nineteenth and twentieth centuries to trade salt for cereals, cloth, and other precious goods (Barrett-Gaines 2004).

Salt Transport

In Africa, salt transportation seems to have varied between long- and short-distance travel (Lovejoy 1974, 1984; Parsons 2001). Traders relied on camels, donkeys, and boats for long-distance travel and on human porters for short-distance travel. The Azalai caravan from Bilma to Agades in West Africa is a good example of inland transport (Alexander 1993), and Dahomey is a good example of water transport (Rivallain 1977). Salt was usually transported as blocks or cones (Parsons 2001) and was only minimally wrapped for long-distance transport. For short-distance transport, perishable materials made of leaves, bark, or skin were preferred (Parsons 2001). We have not recorded the use of ceramic vessels to transport salt in Africa; however, their use to dry, mold, or process salt is widespread (Connah, Kamuhangire, and Piper 1990; Lovejoy 1986). Salt trading was a scheduled activity during the dry season in most parts of Africa to protect the salt from rain and other environmental factors, including humidity. I revisit this topic in chapter 5 when I discuss salt transport using the example of the caravanners on the Afar salt route.

CARAVAN ANTHROPOLOGY

Caravan trade requires considerable organizational skills, stamina, social networking, resources, and human capital (Lydon 2008). Caravans and caravan trains were a common economic and ritual activity globally in the past (Biginagwa 2012; Christie and Haour 2018; Clarkson et al. 2017; Förster and Riemer 2013; Kuznar 1993; Nielsen 2000, 2001; Ross 2010; Valenzuela et al. 2018).

Though in danger of extinction, pack-based caravans still exist in some parts of the world (see Vilá 2018; chapter 5, this volume). The nature and beginnings of caravan organizations were not uniform; they varied from place to place and can be further divided into Old World and New World systems (Clarkson 2019; Clarkson et al. 2017). Caravan systems might have started for several reasons; climate change is one major factor proposed by anthropologists and archaeologists. Aridification of the geophysical environment, especially in the mid-Holocene, resulted in a scarcity of resources and separation of ecosystems with complementary resources (Capriles and Tripcevich 2016; Rosen 2016). For example, the aridification of the green Sahara in North Africa around 5000 BP might have pushed some mobile pastoralists to organize seasonal caravans to provide badly needed resources from the forest margins and the Sahel to people living in arid areas. Other reasons proposed include the development of mining and metallurgy, increased demand for luxury and exotic commodities by the elite and non-elite, and the demand for food items such as livestock, grains, and pulses (Clarkson et al. 2017). However diverse their origins, certain aspects of caravan systems—such as their organization—are remarkably similar. The organization of a caravan includes logistics (water and food for drovers and pack animals), the number of pack animals and drovers, ownership of pack animals and resources, the journey, social relations along the route, types of commodities transported, the caravan route itself, rest areas and end points, trading posts and storages, and protection either through armed military or by building walls (Kendall 1997). Another integral part of the caravan route is ritual (Clarkson 2019; Nielsen 2001; Tripcevich 2007; Valenzuela et al. 2018). Rituals are performed at the journey's beginning and end to protect the caravan and commodities en route. Archaeologists have discovered evidence of these rituals at rock art sites along caravan routes in the northernmost region of Chile, South America (Valenzuela et al. 2018).

Having explored why caravan systems might have started, I move to an examination of when they started. Was it a gradual process? While they might have begun with human porters, the domestication of pack animals in the Old and New Worlds certainly led to an increased reliance on caravan systems worldwide (Clarkson 2019; Clarkson et al. 2017; Nielsen 2000; Tripcevich 2007). Ethnographic and archaeological evidence shows that pack animals such as camels, donkeys, mules, horses, and llamas were essential in ancient caravan systems (and continue to be for extant systems). Caravanners also used other non-pack animals such as yaks, goats, and cattle to transport salt and agricultural products on caravan routes (Clarkson et al. 2017). Based on the domestication of donkeys in northeast Africa around 5000 BP (Kimura et al. 2013; Marshall et al. 2007; Rossel et al. 2008; Shackelford, Marshall, and Peters 2013), followed by the domestication of dromedaries around 3000 BP (Almathen et al. 2016; Uerpmann and Uerpmann 2002) in the Arabian Peninsula, we can estimate the range for the beginning of pack-based caravan systems in the Old World to be around 5000 to 4000 BP. In the New World, wild camelids were domesticated into llamas around 7000 to 6000 BP and began to be used as transport animals around 5000 to 4000 BP (Goñalons and Yacobaccio 2006; Núñez, Grosjean, and Cartajena 2010).

Well-known caravans of the ancient world include the New World llama caravans of the Andes, which might have started toward the late Archaic period and the early Formative transition (Goñalons and Yacobaccio 2006; Núñez, Grosjean, and Cartajena 2010; Valenzuela et al. 2018). In the Old World, well-documented caravan routes include the donkey caravans of the ancient Egyptian Abu Ballas Route, which has a calibrated radiocarbon date of 2190 ± 30 BCE (KIA-2068 3–20684) (Förster 2007; Förster and Riemer 2013). In Asia, caravans on the Silk Route dating to ca. 206 BCE–220 CE traveled long and short distances and covered vast terrains using Bactrian camels (*Camelus bactrianus*), horses (*Equus ferus caballus*), donkeys (*Equus asinus*), and mules (*Equus mulus*) (Frachetti et al. 2017; Han et al. 2014; Hansen 2012). In Arabia, caravans on the famous Spice Route dating to 1000 BCE moved goods from Yemen to the Persian Gulf (Fedele 2014; Retsö 1991; Rosen and Saidel 2010; Uerpmann and Uerpmann 2002). Finally, the donkey-based Middle Bronze Age (4000–3700 BP) tin and textile caravans covered varied plains and mountains from Kanesh in central Anatolia to Assur in Mesopotamia and tin sources in Afghanistan (Atici 2014).

Salt caravans were also very popular in many parts of the world. Salt caravans of the ancient trans-Saharan trade in Africa (Carpenter 1956; De Villiers and Hirtle 2007; Lovejoy 1986; McDougall 1990) and Western and central Europe, in places like Austria, Germany, and France, were fully operating in the third millennium BCE right until they were centralized by Roman conquest (Alexander 1982, 1985; F. Barth 1967; Harding 2013). Places like Halle in East Germany were major salt trading intersections in Europe until at least the nineteenth century (F. Barth 1967). Salt was a perfect candidate for caravan systems since it required organized logistics to facilitate its transfer from sources located within short- or long-range radii.

The study of caravans provides unique insights into the trade of consumable goods, ancient and extant economic systems, and interactions between people in different environmental zones. Caravan archaeology also allows us to better understand the role of trade in structuring relationships between different cultural groups and the development of complex social institutions (Clarkson et al. 2017). Multiple ethnographic and archaeological studies of trade and caravans have demonstrated that caravan anthropology allows us to model processes that do not always leave material evidence in the archaeological record. Caravan trade is one of the few areas in which we have performed ethnoarchaeological studies of trade in consumable goods by multiple agents. Caravans are also a good example of Jane I. Guyer's (1997) concept of niche economy, as caravanners were seasonal workers in most parts of the world. When trading halted due to temperature change or over-flooding of trade routes, as in the trans-Saharan region (Lovejoy 1986), caravanners would engage in other economic activities such as farming or pastoralism. Some of the major themes that have emerged from ethnoarchaeological studies of caravan trade have enabled researchers to go beyond strict formalist and substantivist approaches to understand the nuances of trade relationships more fully.

Caravan ethnoarchaeology has identified mechanisms of ancient exchange, trade, and transport, as well as material traces of ancient trade in Egypt and the Andes (Falola 1991; Förster 2007; Roe 2005; Smith 2005; Tripcevich 2007). Archaeologists have also conducted detailed research on the Abu Ballas Caravan Trail, which extended from the Dakhla Oasis in Egypt's Western Desert to the Gilf Kebir plateau in the Libyan Desert and provided evidence of a 400-km-long Old Kingdom caravan route linking the Egyptian state to the Sudanese region (Förster 2007; Förster and Riemer 2013).

Biginagwa's (2012) caravan-based archaeological research at a nineteenth-century site in Tanzania showed that caravans transform the regions they pass through. The fact that we can now distinguish materials associated with caravans and caravan campsites from mobile pastoralist camps in the archaeological record allows us to better isolate and assess their impact. Chapters 6 and 7 elaborate on the transformative effect and archaeology of the Afar caravan route in the Horn of Africa.

3

AKSUMITE POLITICAL ECONOMY

Aksumite kings are said to have achieved their power through Red Sea trade ca. 450 BCE–900 CE. Archaeologists have argued that the interests of a wealthy and powerful Aksumite elite—together with those of the military, high-ranking clergy, and traders—helped shape the Aksumite Empire into one of the great powers of its day (Fattovich 1990, 2008, 2010b; Finneran 2007; Munro-Hay 1991; D. Phillipson 2000b, 2012). In this exploration of ancient trade and the generation of wealth in the northern Horn of Africa, I am interested in whether the focus of the past century's research on elite power has masked other, more diffuse or flatter power structures that might have existed concurrently. Answers to this question are situated in a dynamic social and geographic landscape and are influenced by the history of Aksumite archaeology.

In this chapter, I summarize prior research on the emergence of the Aksumite state, locations of powerful towns in the context of the landscape of the northern highlands, the ancient trade from the capital Aksum to the port of Adulis, and the agriculture and foodways of the Aksumites. Evidence for the organization of ancient trade from Aksum to Adulis reveals the state's role, while recent

https://doi.org/10.5876/9781646424733.c003

research on agriculture and foodways and the trade route to the Red Sea shows more varied power structures operating simultaneously. I complement this picture of ancient Aksumite life with findings from my recent research, which offer a detailed view of the salt trade from the Afar lowlands to the highlands. These ethnographic data and first-ever archaeological excavations of the Afar salt route provide new perspectives on Aksumite wealth generation and society and evidence for contemporaneously functioning hierarchical and heterarchical processes in the Aksumite state. Together, they offer a revised picture of the reach of the Aksumite state, with evidence of non-elite participation in the ancient salt trade and the operation of more diffuse power structures far from the state's dominant trade routes.

THE EMERGENCE OF THE AKSUMITE STATE

The development of the Aksumite state began in the Ethiopian and Eritrean highlands, with social differentiation, urbanization, and trade networks dated to the first millennium BCE (Anfray 1990; Fattovich 2010b; Finneran 2007; Munro-Hay 1993; D. Phillipson 2012; Schmidt and Curtis 2001; Schmidt, Curtis, and Teka 2008). King GDR (ca. 200 CE) may have been the first king of the Aksumite state (D. Phillipson 2012). By the time of his rule in the second century, the Aksumites were trading for exotic goods and exporting their products as far as Yemen in South Arabia. People of the north Ethiopian and Eritrean highlands were in especially close contact with the Sabeans of South Arabia and the Mediterranean region. We can see these influences in Aksumite economic and religious life. Aksumite agricultural systems adopted foreign plants, animals, and farming methods; their religion embraced Judaism and Orthodox Christianity. The Aksumites were also religious and political allies of the Romans and the Byzantine emperors (Munro-Hay 1993). Much of the Aksumite history I have portrayed is drawn from a long history of excavations of cities and monuments. Further evidence comes from Sabean and Ge'ez inscriptions and classical sources, including the *Periplus of the Erythraean Sea* written by an unknown Greek traveler in 60 CE (Casson and MacMullen 2012; Huntingford 1980) and Pliny ca. 77 CE (Carey 2006).

The archaeology indicates that the Aksumite state emerged out of the proto-Aksumite (or Daamat, referred to in inscriptions as D'MT) Kingdom, which flourished in the mid-first millennium BCE (Anfray 1968; Fattovich 1990, 2000; Munro-Hay 1991, 1993; D. Phillipson 1998, 2012; Rossini 1928). While early Aksumite scholars assumed that South Arabian colonizers established the Aksumite polity (Gerlach 2012) and emphasized the role of long-distance trade in the accumulation of wealth, more recent discoveries have documented local developments in the north Ethiopian and Eritrean highlands and drawn attention to agricultural wealth (Curtis 2009; Harrower and D'Andrea 2014; Harrower, McCorriston, and D'Andrea 2010; Schmidt, Curtis, and Teka 2008). This region of the north

TABLE 3.1. Cultural chronology of northern Ethiopia (following Fattovich 2010a, 2010b, and D. Phillipson 2000b, 2012)

	BCE / CE	Fattovich (2010a, 2010b)	D. Phillipson (2000b, 2012)
	1000	Post-Aksumite	
	900		Post-Aksumite
	800		
	700	Late Aksumite	
	600		Late Aksumite
	500	Middle Aksumite	
	400		Classic Aksumite
	300	Classic Aksumite	
	200		Early Aksumite
CE	100	Early Aksumite	
	0		
BCE	100		
	200	Proto-Aksumite	
	300	Late pre-Aksumite	
	400		
	500		
	600	Middle pre-Aksumite	
	700		
	800		
	900	Early pre-Aksumite	
	1000		

Ethiopian and Eritrean highlands has been occupied by Afro-Asiatic–speaking groups for at least 3,000 years. Scholars now think that local indigenous people with strong ties to their first millennium agricultural predecessors were responsible for creating and expanding the Aksumite polity (Curtis 2008).

Chronological divisions proposed by scholars for the pre-Aksumite and Aksumite periods are based primarily on ceramic typologies and radiocarbon dating and vary from scholar to scholar in how they have been used throughout the years (Fattovich 2010b; Gaudiello and Yule 2017; Harrower et al. 2020; Michels 2005; D. Phillipson 2012; Woldekiros and D'Andrea 2017) (table 3.1). The dates for these periods are continually revised through the ongoing excavation of new archaeological sites, the discovery of new artifacts, and the analysis of radiocarbon dating results. In this book, I rely on my own archaeological work, historical texts, and recent excavations. I follow a chronology where the pre-Aksumite period dates from 800 to 450 BCE, the Aksumite period from 450 BCE to 900 CE,

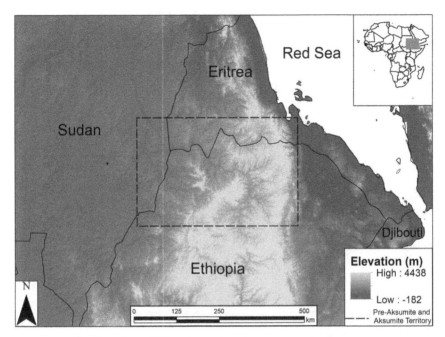

FIGURE 3.1. *Pre-Aksumite and Aksumite territory*

and the post-Aksumite from 900 to 1450 CE. Cultural phases are based on burials, changes in architectural style, stelae, ceramics, and inscriptions. Absolute dates are based on radiocarbon dating and numismatic studies.

Pre-Aksumite and Aksumite society developed in the dramatic landscape of the highlands of present-day northern Ethiopia and Eritrea (figure 3.1). Ranging from 2,000 to 4,400 m above sea level, these highlands are made up of mountains, passes, escarpments, and high plateaus. Cool and well-watered, they support grasslands and forests, with plateaus that have been intensively farmed since the Aksumite period. The Great Rift Valley and the spectacular gorges of the Blue Nile and Tekeze Rivers bisect the mountain massifs. To reach the highlands from the coastal plains near the Aksumite port of Adulis or the salt source in the Afar Depression required following paths as much as 3,000 m up a steep escarpment. The natural border created by the mountain massif in the north was also a cultural boundary between the Aksumites and surrounding peoples. Over time, the political border gradually extended beyond this massif, as far as Yemen in the sixth century CE.

SETTLEMENTS AND TOWNS

The location and development of towns and trade routes reveal much about the political organization of the ancient Aksumites, accumulation of wealth, and distribution of power. Major Aksumite towns appear to be strategically located on

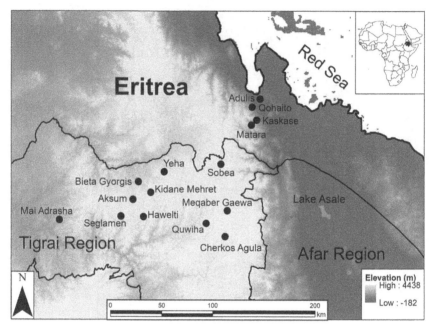

FIGURE 3.2. *Significant Aksumite towns and cities*

routes that were advantageous for trade and on passes leading to the northern Red Sea coast, where trading vessels could carry commodities to South Arabia and the Indian Ocean world as well as to the eastern Mediterranean and the Nile Valley. Although several sites have been identified and studied in the north Ethiopian and Eritrean highlands, nine significant Aksumite towns provide key archaeological information on the organization of towns and cities along trade routes during the pre-Aksumite and Aksumite periods. They include Aksum, Yeha, Adulis, Matara, and Wukro (figure 3.2). The city of Aksum has enjoyed more archaeological investigation than any of the other towns or cities dating to the Aksumite period (Finneran 2007). The city of Aksum was the most important Aksumite capital city during the height of Aksumite rule in the sixth century CE. Major Aksumite international trading outlets included the port of Adulis and the town of Matara, strategically located in the northern highlands en route from Aksum to the coast (Curtis 2008; Munro-Hay 1991). We know much less about the southward reach of Aksumite power or inland trade routes compared to the plethora of information we have about its northward, eastward, and westward trading interactions.

Very few historical texts mention the city Aksum and its origin. Historical documents such as the *Maṣḥafa aksūm* (Amharic) or *Liber Axumae* (Latin) and the hagiography *Gadle Marqorewos* (Amharic) mention the city by a different name and talk about its founders (Selassie 1972). The *Maṣḥafa aksūm*, a collocation of

Geez (ancient Ethiopian script) documents found at the Cathedral of St. Mary of Aksum, detail the history of Ethiopia. The oldest one dates to the period of King Zar'a Ya'qob (1434–1468 CE), and the latter one dates to the late seventeenth century. In this manuscript, Itiyopis, son of Kush, is named as the founder of the city (Munro-Hay 1991). The hagiography *Gadle Marqorewos*, in contrast, states that the city was originally named Atsaba at a place called Mazaber. The founders named in this hagiography are Kings Abreha and Atsbeha—names often used interchangeably to refer to King Ezana (Selassie 1972). Sergew Hable Sellassie (1972) suggested that the name Aksum is a combination of two languages: *ak*, the Cushite term for water, and *shum*, the Semitic term for chief, meaning "chief of the water" (Tamrat 1988, 8)—possibly related to the location of Aksum city next to an important water source. The combination of two languages from two different cultural groups could indicate the presence of a segmentary state (as discussed in chapter 2, this volume) or a sub-state (Finneran 2007). Despite the diversity of kings' names accredited with the foundation of the city Aksum, it is clear that Aksum served as a political and religious capital of the Aksumites for more than 1,000 years.

Archaeology shows that the city itself started at the summit of the hill of Bieta Giyorgis and eventually moved west to the floodplain as the population increased and trade between the Aksumites and the Red Sea region strengthened (Bard et al. 1997). The town was large with diffuse spatial organization, including areas devoted to elite structures, buildings for domestic or industrial occupation, a major church, elite burial grounds, and reservoirs (Finneran 2007; D. Phillipson 1998, 120). The cities of Aksum and Yeha both show that urban planning during the Aksumite period involved separating space into ideological, secular, residential, mortuary complex, and agricultural zones (Finneran 2007). The mortuary complex of the ruling elite was usually the focal point of the town. Aksum's layout shows ranking in buildings. The elite or suburban buildings had private courtyards and walled areas and were located in the western part of the city. To the east, on the slopes of Bieta Giyorgis, and to the north of Aksum, in the areas of Kidane Mehret, were much smaller, poorer structures that archaeologists believe belonged to individuals of a lower social status (Bard et al. 1997; Michels 2005; D. Phillipson 2012, 125). The D site at Kidane Mehret, for example—a series of stone-wall settlements—is considered to have been occupied by low-status farmers who provisioned the city for a long period of time (Cain 2000). I return to the architecture of the non-elite in the Evidence for Heterarchy section later in this chapter.

Archaeological work at the city Aksum, as at other Aksumite and pre-Aksumite sites, has focused on monuments and elite architecture. One well-studied aspect of the city Aksum is the funerary complex. Here we find one of the most remarkable architectural marvels of the Aksumite period. Most of the funerary complexes studied belong to the elite and show a gradual evolution of style from an earlier platform type of burial found at the summit of the hills of Bieta Giyorgis to a more elaborate one found in the valley. For example, the early funerary complexes found at Bieta Giyorgis were considered elite architecture but were not as grand as the later Aksumite kings' burials and monuments. Later elite burials were marked by larger and more elaborate stelae. Some of these stelae have false doors and windows meant to mimic multi-story buildings. More than 100 of these well-dressed stelae have been found to date. There are many funerary complexes in the city itself, but the well-studied ones are those found on an artificial terrace at a focal point at Aksum. Archaeologists have argued that these stelae were built for the royal family. The largest of these stelae weigh between 160 and 520 tons and measure between 20.6 and 33 m (D. Phillipson 2012). Stela 1, the most massive of them all at 33 m in length and 520 tons, was designed to represent thirteen stories. It is the largest single block of stone that humans have ever attempted to stand upright. While it is no longer upright—scholars believe it fell during the initial attempt to raise it—the others are still standing.

Beneath these stelae are underground subterranean tombs with elaborate masonry work. The tomb construction work ranged from elegant stone construction to fired brick walls and roofs made with massive hewn granite slabs (D. Phillipson 2012). After the Aksumites converted to Christianity in the fourth century CE, these tombs appear to have been constructed with a superstructure rather than stelae. The superstructures that replaced the stelae were church chapels (I discuss the significance of these buildings in the Symbols of Power section later in this chapter). The tombs have side chambers and central passageways. On one side of the chambers are multiple sarcophagi, probably for the remains of kings and queens, and on the other side are burial goods. Although looters plundered most of these chambers in antiquity, enough have been recovered to show that elite goods were buried on one side of the chamber, including pottery and items such as cloth, glass, and carved ivory that had been decorated with gold.

While non-elite burials at Aksum have not been well-studied, a cemetery in the southwest outskirts of Aksum with more than 600 stelae shows a large middle-class community residing in the city during the Aksumite period. This area is often referred to as the Gudit Stelae field. The stelae are not tall compared to elite stelae; they range between 1 m and 3 m. Some of them have elaborate masonry work, while some are rough stones. There has been limited excavation at Gudit Stelae field. Less monumental features of the town, including markets, are not well-known. Craft production areas, however, have been discovered at Aksum. Production of stone tools, iron objects, glasses, beads, and masonry work by specialists is well established in the Aksumite period and well reflected in the artifacts discovered at Aksum. Aksum continued to be an important location even after the fall of the Aksumite state. In medieval times, it was a coronation city and a religious center, and it is still a religious center today.

The second most important Aksumite town was the well-known international trading port town of Adulis. Both Adulis and Aksum were vital trading centers for the Aksumite polity from the first millennium BCE onward (see figure 3.2). The port of Adulis lies on the Gulf of Zula, a narrow bay that stretches about 40 km north-south and occupies a junction point between the Danakil Depression and the Red Sea (Beyin 2011a). It has an altitudinal range of −8 m to 80 m above sea level. Today, the temperature varies from 20°C–35°C (68°F–95°F) from December to February to 40°C–50°C (104°F–122°F) from June to September, with annual precipitation of about 200 mm (Peacock and Blue 2007). Several archaeological sites are found in the area covering the Buri-Zula plain in present-day Eritrea (Beyin 2011a). Archaeologists have discovered sites dating from the Middle Stone Age (ca. 125,000 BP) to the early and mid-Holocene (8000–5000 BP) in this important ecological zone where the highland escarpments to the west, the Danakil Depression to the south, and the coastal plains intersect (Beyin 2011a, 2011b, 2013; Peacock and Blue 2007).

Despite its fame in antiquity, the origin and structure of the city of Adulis are still not well-studied archaeologically. Unlike other Aksumite and pre-Aksumite cities, no standing architectural features have been found, but ruins and debris of ancient buildings and architecture abound. Several ancient texts mention the city itself, including Pliny's *Natural History* around 70 CE (NH VI, 34) (Huntingford 1989) and the *Periplus of the Erythraean Sea* in the first century CE (Casson and MacMullen 2012; Huntingford 1980). Both texts mention Adulis as a trading city connected to the highlands in the west. According to the *Periplus*, it took travelers eight days to get to Aksum from Adulis. Based on the description provided in the *Periplus*, Lionel Casson (1989) suggested that trade in Adulis was probably controlled and patrolled by the ruler. Adulis was also very well-known during the Roman period, as seen in Pliny's and Claudius Ptolemy's work (Stevenson 1932). Ptolemy's *Geography* (IV, 7, 8) clearly distinguishes the people living on the eastern coast of the Red Sea and the Indian Ocean by name. For example, he mentions by name and distinguishes the Aduliate and the Barbaria, as well as the people living in the East African interior (Stevenson 1932). It is possible, however, that Adulis started functioning as a trading port before the time of the *Periplus* or the Roman period. Stuart C. Munro-Hay (1991), for one, has argued that trade might have started with the kingdom of South Arabia from the port of Adulis, dating back to the time of the D'MT Kingdom during the first millennium BCE. An even earlier date has been suggested based on evidence for the trade expedition to the land of Punt commissioned by Queen Hatshepsut of New Kingdom Egypt in the fifteenth century BCE (Doresse 1959; Kitchen 1971, 1993). Scholars still dispute the assumption that Hatshepsut's expedition was bound for the port of Adulis, mainly because the exact location of the land of Punt is still unclear (it may have included the entire Horn of Africa and part of Sudan).

Although it is unclear whether trade at Adulis was organized by Aksum or independently or when Adulis was incorporated into the Aksumite kingdom, it is clear that Aksum and Adulis had a dialectical relationship: each depended on the other for wealth and power (Casson and MacMullen 2012; Peacock and Blue 2007). From the *Periplus* and the archaeological record, we know that Aksum was asserting its influence on Adulis by the mid-first century CE. Aksumite texts also document that the market at the port of Adulis was so crucial to the polity that King Zoskales (ca. 100 CE) appointed governors to control its trading activities and assigned military forces to police the trade route from Aksum to Adulis. Interference with caravans traveling these routes was dealt with harshly by the Aksumite state. King Ezana, for example, punished people who tried to loot caravans with captivity, slavery, or execution (Munro-Hay 1991).

It is also possible that Adulis city and the surrounding areas existed as a segmentary state prior to being incorporated into the Aksumite Empire and might have continued to be an independent polity even after absorption by the Aksumite. We have clear evidence that Aksum could not have achieved its great power over the region and the southern Red Sea area without the city and port of Adulis. No matter the relationship between Aksum and of Adulis, it was clear that by the fourth and fifth centuries, the port city of Adulis was an important docking point for ships coming from Egypt, India, Ceylon, and the Arabian Peninsula (Kirwan 1972). I elaborate on how the Aksumites organized trade in the Long-Distance Trade section later in this chapter.

Matara was another important town along the northern highland Aksumite trade route dating to pre-Aksumite and Aksumite times. Where Aksum is known for large, elite buildings and burial structures, excavations of Matara have revealed smaller, rectilinear stone buildings in a tightly packed neighborhood belonging to different classes of people (D. Phillipson 2012). Here, building structures of varying sizes and artifacts belonging to the middle class have been well-preserved (Anfray 1966; D. Phillipson 1998). As in other Aksumite urban sites, the elite and palace quarter was separated from the rest of the town (Anfray 1966; Finneran 2007). Archaeologists no longer believe that Matara was merely an outpost on the trade route from Adulis to Aksum. Archaeological evidence now suggests that imported goods were not only traded but also consumed at Matara, indicating that it was a thriving city in its own right (D. Phillipson 1998).

Yeha is located about 50 km northeast of Aksum and is known chiefly for its pre-Aksumite architecture dating to the first millennium BCE. Situated in the northern region of Tigray along the well-established trade route leading to Adulis, Yeha served as both a hub for ceremonial activities and a melting pot of diverse cultures in an urban setting. The sacral building ruin that still stands today dates to 800 BCE and is one of the oldest buildings in sub-Saharan Africa. Inscriptions indicative of belief systems related to the Sabean pantheon have also been recovered here (Munro-Hay 1991; Wolf and Nowotnick 2010). Yeha is of considerable importance to our understanding of the formation of urban centers and polities in this area of the world, as it represents the earliest archaeological and historical evidence for social complexity in sub-Saharan Africa (Fattovich 2009; Harrower et al. 2019).

Despite Yeha's historical and archaeological significance, there have been very few archaeological investigations in and around the city until fairly recently (Gerlach 2012; Harrower et al. 2020). Archaeological study at Yeha in the past 100 years has focused mostly on the high-status and ceremonial area, which included the Great Temple, the palace at Grat Be'al Gebri, and the cemetery at Daro Mikael (Fattovich 2009; Finneran 2007). The standing wall of the Great Temple at Yeha is 18.5 m long, 15 m wide, and 13 m high. The entrance to the temple was on the west end; inside, there would have been four pillars that divided the different functions of the temple (Finneran 2007). Archaeological investigations at the site of the Great Temple have revealed that the towering temple that currently stands on the grounds superseded an earlier, smaller temple that occupied the same location (Fattovich 2009). There are also indications that the temple was used later in the Christian phase.

South of the Great Temple building at the cemetery complex of Daro Mikael are tombs that represent some of the most compelling evidence for the presence of a well-established polity during the D'MT kingdom. These tombs "take the form of catacombs built into the rock beneath square access shafts" (Finneran 2007, 124). Based on the architecture and the wealth of grave goods found inside the burials, Rodolfo Fattovich (1990) proposed that this cemetery was reserved for royal and elite individuals. The grave goods included various types of ceramics, bronze and iron objects, and incense burners.

The palace complex of Grat Be'al Gebri, found 200 m from the Great Temple, was also constructed and used during two different periods/phases (Anfray 1972). In the first phase, the building included "a stepped podium and a porch with pillars" (Fattovich 2009, 278). A fire destroyed it, and it was reconstructed between 400 and 150 BCE, in a new and distinctive architectural style that included shaped friezes not seen before (Fattovich 2009; Finneran 2007). The palace building, still extant, includes a long wall that runs north-south with a flight of ten stairs, marked with three standing megalithic pillars. The architectural style that developed in Yeha, especially the shaped friezes found in the Great Temple and at Grat Be'al Gebri, became integral to later Aksumite architecture. The dominating presence of these monumental features on the landscape was the main reason early archaeologists assumed that Yeha served only as a religious center during the pre-Aksumite/D'MT kingdom. The recent discovery and excavation of sites like Beta Samati have overturned these assumptions (Harrower et al. 2020).

A contemporaneous, pre-Aksumite sacral temple has also recently been discovered 80 km southeast of Yeha in the town of Wukro (Wolf and Nowotnick 2010). The discovery of pre-Aksumite and Aksumite sites at Wukro is significant because it provides evidence that the Aksumite polity extended farther south than previously thought. Importantly, Wukro is also located at a major intersection of the long-distance trade route that runs north-south and the present-day local salt trade route that runs east-west.

Research at Yeha in the past few decades has focused more on finding connections between the pre-Aksumite/D'MT kingdom and South Arabia than on searching for an endogenous origin of this polity (see Anfray 1972; Gerlach 2012). This focus was motivated mainly by the presence of Sabean/South Arabian inscriptions at some pre-Aksumite sites. There has also been less focus on understanding non-elite contexts and daily life at Yeha. Joseph W. Michels (2005), however, based on his survey of the region between Aksum and Yeha (ca. 714-km² area), proposed that Yeha is not limited to this ceremonial center and that the city or settlement associated with this ceremonial area lies 1 km away at Enda Gully.

Recent archaeological research has also just revealed that Yeha was not abandoned during the Aksumite period as previously assumed but continued to be a vibrant city. Central Tigray, where Yeha is located, continued to thrive past the pre-Aksumite period and up to the late Aksumite period (Harrower et al. 2020). The discovery of the site Beta Samati 6.6 km northeast of Yeha, for example, clearly showed the presence of an urban center that served as a significant administrative center and trading post during the mid-Aksumite period (Harrower et al. 2020). The site Beta Samati is a good indication that the area in and around Yeha contributed to the emergence of Aksum (52 km to the east) as an influential city.

AKSUMITE SOCIAL AND POLITICAL ORGANIZATION

Hierarchy and social complexity are dominant themes in discussions of Aksumite social and political organization. Within a "pyramid" system of social stratification (Kobishchanov 1966; Littmann 1907; Munro-Hay 1991; D. Phillipson 2012; Selassie 1972), the Aksumite king was at the apex, followed by administrative and military positions held by the king's immediate family. Below these positions were posts held by district governors, who were chiefs or sub-kings of the provinces (Munro-Hay 1991; D. Phillipson 1998, 2012). Evidence for this social form comes from archaeological findings of palaces, elite tomb architecture, and elaborate stelae found in the towns discussed above (as well as others not mentioned). Placement of the title "King of Aksum" before "King of kings" in addition to the territories kings claimed on inscriptions, coins, and listings found in Aksum support the assertion that the Aksumite monarch was a supreme king (D. Phillipson 1998, 2012, 71). Pre-Christian Aksumite kings Kaleb and Ezana claimed divine descent from Mahrem, associated with Ares, the Greek god of war (Munro-Hay 1991, 150). In the fourth century, King Ezana was converted to Christianity by Frumentius, a Syrian of Tyre and the first bishop of Aksum (Munro-Hay 1991; Seland 2014). The rulers who succeeded Ezana used the title "servant of Christ" instead of "son of Mahre." The supremacy of Aksumite kings is also evidenced by the use of the title *negus* or *nagashi*, equivalent to "king." Inscriptions of various Aksumite rulers show that their titles included the personal name, *Ella* name, *Bisi* name, a real or divine affiliation, several epithets, and a listing of territories (Munro-Hay 1991, 159). Scholars use these mentions of territories—including those in Africa, Ethiopia, and South Arabia—in rulers' titles as indications of the extent of the Aksumite polity.

The way Aksumite power succession worked is still unclear. However, a few primary and secondary Aksumite documents indicate hereditary succession. Succession could have passed from father to son, from father to grandson, or from brother to brother. A primary Aksumite document mentions the succession of King Kaleb by his son Wa'zeba (530–575 CE) (Budge 1970; Munro-Hay 1991; D. Phillipson 2012; Rossini and Guidi 1907). Based on evidence from Aksumite coins and sparse inscriptions, some scholars believe the practice of dual kingship may also have existed during the Aksumite period. These scholars suggest that at least six kings, including Kings Wa'zeba and Ousanas, exercised dual kingship (Drewes 1962; Littmann 1907). It has also been argued that a matrilineal clan system influenced military organization and resulted in Aksumite rulers taking their mothers' family name (Kobishchanov 1966; Munro-Hay 1991).

Indirect archaeological evidence, such as flourishing Aksumite towns and urban centers and strong long-distance trade, indicates the stable and long-term succession of power during the Aksumite period. Security does not seem to have been an issue in the heartland of the Aksumite polity. Scholars argue that the absence of walled towns and cities and the length of the long-distance trade routes indicate that the Aksumites were confident in their ability to protect themselves (Munro-Hay 1991). Recent research has also identified elite farming communities, such as the one found at Mezber, which—though far from Aksumite towns—were not fortified (D'Andrea et al. 2008).

SYMBOLS OF POWER

Aksumite architecture provides essential information about the demand for building materials and the relationships among different elements of society. Elite buildings of the Aksumite period can be divided into two categories: villas and domestic structures (Anfray 1974; Fattovich and Bard 2001; D. Phillipson 1998,

2012). Villas ranged in size from large to small. Large villas included buildings designated as palaces and usually consisted of a complex with a large building at the center and several structures around the outside. The central building was typically the largest and had broad steps on three or four sides and projections on the four corners for possible towers (Littmann 1907; D. Phillipson 2012). The largest existing building of this type is Aksum's Ta'akha Maryam, which originally covered more than a hectare. A similar structure, called Dungur, is also found in Aksum and may have initially been a four-story building. Villas for the elite, which were smaller than palaces but had similar architecture, have been discovered at Matara and Kidane Mehret (Phillipson, Phillips, and Tarekegn 2000).

Stone thrones are another distinctive feature of Aksumite political authority and have been found mostly in and around Aksum and Matara (Anfray 1966; D. Phillipson 2012, 132). Historical texts cite the use of cathedral (ecclesiastical) thrones by kings, bishops, and judges during religious ceremonies. It is unclear exactly how roadside thrones were used (136).

One notable difference between elite and non-elite structures during the Aksumite period is the presence or absence of wood (D. Phillipson 1998). Wood was used to support and reinforce wall structures from the inside and the outside. However, during the Aksumite period, research suggests that wood was scarce. As a result, wood became a luxury item that the elite used for extravagant displays (Lyons 2007). Churches also used wood for reinforcing stone-wall structures, particularly those built after the Aksumite conversion to Christianity (Buxton 1947, 1967, 1971; Machado, Peréz-González, and Benito 1998; Munro-Hay 2002; D. Phillipson 1998). Diane E. Lyons (2007) argues that control of wood by the secular elite and religious institutions during the Christian period signifies the institutional control of resources at that time.

In addition to the architecture and style of residential buildings and palace structures, commemoration stelae were among the most important symbols of power for the Aksumites. These mega-stelae, carved to mimic multi-story buildings of wood and stone and placed on top of multi-chamber tombs, signified the burial place of a king. They may also have been intended to exert the ruling elite's power over the landscape for eternity. The size of these stelae and the human energy cost of making and moving them clearly indicate that they were displays of power (the 520-ton monolith mentioned earlier in the chapter is one of these). These stelae also symbolically mark the difference between the pre-Christian- and Christian-phase Aksumite rulers.

Traditional and archaeological accounts indicate that the elite were the first among the Aksumites to embrace Christianity (Aquilea and Rufinus 1997). This may have remained the elite's religion for some time before it became widespread. The immediate impact of this conversion is evident in the altered perception of space and symbology (Finneran 2007). The elite reflected their new cosmological belief on monuments, artifacts, and coins minted in their name. Aksumite kings stopped using stelae. The sign of the cross on coins—used for both regional and long-distance trade—portrayed Aksum as a Christian kingdom internationally as well as locally. King MHDYS's coin states in Ge'ez "by this sign (the cross) you will conquer" (182). Later in the sixth century, Aksumite kings took names mentioned in the Old Testament. The Aksumites took further action by building churches on top of pre-Christian temples (Finneran 2007). Even the Great Temple of Yeha was later used as a Christian church. I return to the significance of Christianity in our understanding of political organization in the next section.

HIERARCHY AND ANCIENT AKSUMITE CHURCHES

In ancient Aksum, religion also exerted influence on power structures. The state used ideology to maintain power in rural areas and at the fringes of the kingdom (D. Phillipson 2012). Pre-Aksumite religion was characterized by a polytheistic belief system that resembled ancient South Arabian religion (D. Phillipson 2012). Deities were represented by crescent-and-disc and bull symbols found on temples at Yeha and Wukro. This ancient religion flourished until the mid-fourth century CE, when the Aksumites officially replaced it with Christianity. Unlike most contemporaneous ancient states, Christianity was introduced to the Aksumites from the top down (Selassie 1972) when King Ezana was converted (Finneran 2007; Munro-Hay 1991; Taddesse 1968). As a result, the church had a parallel political structure with, and sometimes served as an arm of, the state, especially in regions distant from the seats of Aksumite power.

Aksumite church structures have been discovered in urban settings in Aksum, Matara, Adulis, Yeha, the Hawzen plain, Haiki Mesihal, and Eritrea (see figures 3.1 and 3.2). In these ancient cities, churches were centrally located, finely made, and often constructed on sites of ancient non-Christian temples. These churches also have similar features to elite buildings. In rural landscapes, the connection between church and state is evident in the strategic location and construction of churches and monasteries. Country churches and monasteries were often built in inaccessible places on the tops of cliffs to distance religious spaces from the public and symbolically dominate the landscape (Di Salvo and Gossage 2017; Finneran 2007). Sometimes they were stone-hewn and more formally constructed than churches in towns; at other times they were less formal. Today, some of these churches are still functional, while others are in ruins.

During the sixth century, especially during the reign of King Kaleb, there was an explosion of Christian churches on the Tigray Plateau. New churches included the Cathedral of Tsion Maryam in Aksum (constructed around the fourth century CE), the sixth-century monastery Debre Damo in northern Tigray (90 km from Aksum), and Enda Maryam at Asmara (D. Phillipson 2009b, 2012). Sixth- and seventh-century Aksumite churches have been studied at

Bieta Giyorgis, Mahraf, and Yeha (D. Phillipson 2009a, 2012). The style of these churches had ties to elite architecture and varied from stone to rock-hewn buildings. They usually had "stepped-back walls, basilican in form," and a central nave with aisles on each side (Di Salvo and Gossage 2017; D. Phillipson 2012, 127). A few Aksumite churches were domed. On occasion, the Aksumites also used marble screens, brick, and wood. They carved stone with symbolic figures, including crosses, animals (for example, ibex), and geometric designs. The contrast between elite urban houses of worship and the monastic tradition or non-elite churches in rural areas is marked. In some cases, churches were situated not in inaccessible places or towns but on trade routes. During the medieval period, churches were collection points for state taxes on trading caravans; however, little is known about how they served the state in remote trading areas during the Aksumite period.

EVIDENCE FOR HETERARCHY

Information about the structure of the Aksumite polity comes from irregular intervals of time, and it is clear that the Aksumite administration did not remain static (Munro-Hay 1991). Political structures may have shifted after the conversion of Aksumite kings to Christianity, as evidenced by the abandonment of their claim to divinity and assertion that they were sons of the God Maharem. There are also indications that despite the tendency to focus on kings, they did not always occupy the positions of greatest power. Aksumite writings document situations in which military generals took kingly positions without the king's consent. Abreha (525–547 CE) was King Kaleb's general in Yemen but deposed the viceroy King Sumyaf "Ashwa," who was appointed by Kaleb and took a kingly position in the sixth century (Littmann 1907; Taddesse 1968). Abreha's move was not approved by Kaleb, who sent Aksumite soldiers to Yemen to fight against him. This attempt failed because the second wave of viceroys joined Abreha (Kobishchanov 1966; Littmann 1907; Taddesse 1968). The event shows that some non-royals took ruling positions during the Aksumite period. However, there is very little information regarding the influence or power of nobles, traders, or other actors in settings outside of Aksum or in international trade.

Citing the hierarchical clustering of pre-Aksumite and Aksumite settlements along the trade route from Aksum to Adulis in the northern highlands, scholars have argued that a single political center (Yeha or Aksum) controlled the other towns and polities (Finneran 2007; cf. Curtis 2009; Curtis 2008). Recent research by Michael J. Harrower and A. Catherine D'Andrea (2014) on the highland area encompassing the main luxury-good trade route between the important cities of Aksum and Yeha and between Aksum and the key Red Sea port of Adulis (dating to 800 BCE–700 CE) has suggested a more heterarchical settlement pattern extending from the pre-Aksumite through the post-Aksumite periods. They proposed that this settlement pattern suggests that political control of these towns was nonhierarchical, with each settlement or town playing a significant role in local politics (Harrower and D'Andrea 2014). Still, further exploration of variability outside the ancient urban areas and through time is needed to better assess power dynamics in ancient pre-Aksumite and Aksumite societies.

OTHER DIMENSIONS OF SOCIETY

A prosperous Aksumite middle class and craft and technical specialists are well represented in the archaeological record by elaborate elite architecture. Examples of this architecture, which varies in size and sophistication, can be observed at Aksum, Adulis, and Matara (Finneran 2007; Munro-Hay 1991; D. Phillipson 1998, 55). These structures would have necessitated the mobilization of specialists and large labor forces as well as building materials and luxury goods (D. Phillipson 1998). David W. Phillipson (1998) also demonstrates the presence of established specialist groups at Aksum and other sites by the third century through local pottery production, metalwork, and carpentry. Fine carpentry was central to Aksumite architecture and was used to create elaborate furnishings, such as those preserved at the Debre Damo monastery and in royal tombs. There is also abundant evidence for iron production and specialized metalwork at ancient Aksum.

At the Gudit Stelae field in Aksum, large quantities of obsidian "Gaudit" scrapers and backed microliths suggest use by specialized leatherworkers (Phillipson, Phillips, and Tarekegn 2000) to produce leather for export. Despite the prevalence of iron and other metal, Aksumites continued to use stone tools, and obsidian was a significant component of the economy (Connah 1987; Munro-Hay 1991; Pankhurst 1961). Scrapers made from obsidian and other raw materials, including chert and siltstone, are found in large numbers at Aksumite sites (Phillipson, Phillips, and Tarekegn 2000). Obsidian does not occur naturally in the Ethiopian highlands; although we believe it came from the Afar region, little is known about how this essential commodity was obtained.

Although monumental sites and Aksumite texts mainly provide information about the elite and the relatively prosperous, there is some information about other members of society. Non-elite areas of Aksumite towns are little studied, but some examples of non-elite buildings have been found at Bieta Giyorgis and several other sites in and around Aksum, Matara, and the highlands of eastern Tigray. Non-elite residences were usually small rooms constructed of rough stone walls with mud and stone filling. They were typically one-story buildings with wooden windows and doors. The roofs of non-elite houses were mostly flat and made from thatch, mud, and stone. Non-elite Aksumite houses in urban and peri-urban settings were built close together and were separated by narrow stone-paved streets or arranged to circle a courtyard (Phillipson 1998, 2012).

Aksumite texts mention the acquisition of a large number of enslaved people as a result of expansion into neighboring districts in Sasu and Beja (McCrindle 1897; Sadr 1991). Historically, the Beja lived in southern Sudan. Four inscriptions of King Ezana—RIE 185, 185bis, 270, and 270bis—on two trilingual slabs (Phillipson 2012) discuss how the Aksumites conquered the pastoral Beja west of the highlands. The Aksumites enslaved Beja people and resettled them at a place called Matlia in the heart of Aksumite territory, together with their herds of cattle, sheep, goats, and pack animals (Munro-Hay 1991; Phillipson 1998). The texts also mention other people the Aksumites conquered, including the kingdoms of GDT [Agwezat?], GBZ [Gbaz], HMS, SMN [Samen], and WYLQ (Littmann 1907; Phillipson 2012). Interestingly, inscription RIE 188 also mentions a people called the Afan who interfered with the Aksumite trade route. George Wynn Brereton Huntingford (1989) proposed that Afan might refer to Awan, related to the Aua/Aue mentioned by Cosmas Indicopleustes and Nonnosus (cited in Wolska-Conus 1962). I argue in this book that the Afan might refer to the Afar mobile pastoralists in the Danakil Desert salt source area.

AGRICULTURE, EXCHANGE, AND AKSUMITE WEALTH

The location of the Aksumite Empire on the well-watered and fertile highlands provided diverse resources for agricultural and pastoralist lifestyles (D'Andrea et al. 1999; Phillipson 1998). Earlier Aksumite scholars emphasized the significance of long-distance trade to the wealth development of this complex and highly stratified kingdom (Chittick 1974; Henze 2000). However, more recent scholarship has come to view locally based agriculture as the Aksumites' basis for wealth, subsistence, and social diversity (50 BCE–900 CE) (D'Andrea 2008; Harrower, McCorriston, and D'Andrea 2010; D. Phillipson 1998). Despite growing information on the Aksumites' subsistence basis, little is known about the organization of local and regional trade, the extent of households' self-sufficiency, or the state's role in redistributing food or controlling subsistence trade.

The larger economic landscape of northern Ethiopia and Eritrea was characterized by a mosaic of economic strategies within very short distances. Today, in the arid lowlands of both Ethiopia and Eritrea, the economy is based predominantly on pastoralism. The highlands, however, continue to be occupied by agro-pastoralists. These systems are complementary in many ways, leading to exchange and trade. D. Phillipson (2012) emphasizes the significance of cattle to the Aksumite economy (see also Cain 2000). Cattle are the dominant domestic fauna found at Aksumite and pre-Aksumite sites in the highlands. Zooarchaeological studies demonstrate that cattle, sheep, and goats were used by mobile pastoralists, settled farmers, and urban dwellers alike (Cain 2000; Chaix 2013; Mitchell 2005). Aksumite agricultural cultivation included a mix of African and Asian plants and animals. Both West Asian domesticates—including wheat, barley, flax, and lentils—and African domesticates, such as *te'f* and sorghum, were utilized in the Horn of Africa by the early to mid-first millennium BCE (Bard et al. 1997; Beldados and Costantini 2011; D'Andrea, Schmidt, and Curtis 2008; Phillipson, Phillips, and Tarekegn 2000; Schmidt, Curtis, and Teka 2008). Cereals were significant crops, and *te'f*, wheat, and barley came from both elite and non-elite sites (D'Andrea 2008).

Aksumite highland farmers relied on rain-fed agriculture and trade. The dam at Qohaito provides evidence that they also used irrigation (Littmann 1907, 70–73). Further evidence from the Aksumite basin (in Aksum) shows that the Aksumites relied on water conservation strategies (Munro-Hay 1991). Today, farming in the high plateau is characterized by seasonal tasks (McCann 1995). In Aksumite times, just as today, farmers would have been busy plowing, planting, and harvesting between September and February. They would have had slower times during the dry season in April and May and during the summer season in June, July, and August. Heavy rain falls during the summer season. In Aksumite times, highland farmers would have stayed home during the summer rainy season and worked for the emperor as laborers or in other state-sanctioned jobs and participated in the salt caravan trade during the winter and spring seasons. The past several thousand years have seen climatic fluctuations, but major patterns were established by ca. 3000 BP (Bard et al. 2000; Marshall, Grillo, and Arco 2011). Just as today, Aksumite farmers would have expected periodic crop failure due to drought or disease. It is likely that instituting ways to mitigate famine was critical to managing internal politics, acquiring prestige, and reducing the risk of food insecurity. Ezana's inscription, which mentions food rationing, demonstrates the state's role in food storage (Bernand, Drewes, and Schneider 1991; Littmann 1907). This inscription also refers to commercial/entrepreneurial-based and redistributive modes of goods transfer.

Foodways distinctive of the Aksumite elite and highland farmers included the production of bread and beer. Food types consumed during the Aksumite period, including flour, bread, and beer (Munro-Hay 1991, 169), are mentioned explicitly in the Safra inscription. Recovery of bread-making ovens and griddles at Aksum sites shows the importance of cereal crops as staple foods and components of the local economy (Lyons and D'Andrea 2003; Wilding 1989). Evidence for special foods, like grapes used for winemaking, was found only in elite contexts (D'Andrea and Haile 2002; D'Andrea et al. 1999; Lyons and D'Andrea 2003; D. Phillipson 1998, 2000b). The extent to which elite and non-elite households drew on local and regional trade for domestic products or were largely self-sufficient is still debated (Cain 2000; D. Phillipson 1998).

Long-Distance Trade

While cattle may have contributed substantially to early Aksumite wealth, the primary focus of most studies has been the role of long-distance trade in luxury commodities in establishing elite power in the Aksumite state (Fattovich 1977; Henze 2000; Munro-Hay 1991; D. Phillipson 1998). Ever since the translation of the *Periplus of the Erythraean Sea* (600 CE) (Huntingford 1980) and Roberto Paribeni's excavation at the Aksumite Red Sea port Adulis in 1906, the primary focus of studies of Aksumite trade has been luxury goods used by the elite (Kobishchanov 1979; Munro-Hay 1991). Historical records and numismatic studies indicate that long-distance trade was part of a market-based exchange system.

Using Aksum as a central point, major long-distance trade routes during the pre-Aksumite and Aksumite periods seem to have been oriented east-west and north-south. The north-south, Aksum-Adulis land route also stretched to the south in Sasu (cf. Gurage region of present-day Ethiopia). The route from Aksum to Adulis stretched 160 km and was about a fifteen-day walk (Kobishchanov 1979; Munro-Hay 1991). The route stopped at major Aksumite towns found along the modern Kohaito plateau (Bent 1893; Harrower and D'Andrea 2014; Wenig 2006). The route would have passed through Aksumite towns such as Kohaito, Tokonda, Kaskase, Matara, and Gulo-Makeda (Harrower and D'Andrea 2014; Huntingford 1989). These towns were not only the most practical routes to follow in terms of altitude and precipitation, but they would have also offered security and provided a good opportunity for traders to acquire agricultural products for trade (Harrower and D'Andrea 2014). The key marine route from Adulis accessed the Mediterranean trade network through the Red Sea—just as modern container ships do—and moved south to the Indian Ocean and the shores of India. The east-west overland trade route included a caravan route that began at Aksum and followed the Tekeze and Atbara Rivers west through the highlands. These rivers connect with the Nile River in Sudan and allowed the ancient trade route ultimately to link with routes moving up the Nile to Egypt. According to Cosmas and Procopius, this route from Aksum to modern-day Khartoum took about thirty days (Kobishchanov 1979; Wolska-Conus 1962).

Aksumite long-distance routes spanned from Nubia (in present northern Sudan) to the Gulf of Aden in the Red Sea. These routes facilitated the transport of goods from Egypt, Rome, the Byzantian Empire, India, South Arabia, and Nubia. Artifacts from this trade have been found at sites along the routes, including Adulis, Matara, Yeha, Debre Damo, Aksum, and the area near the Tekeze River (Fattovich 1977; Kobishchanov 1979; D. Phillipson 1998). The most detailed account of Aksumite imports and exports comes from Pliny (ca. 65 CE) (Carey 2006) and the *Periplus of the Erythraean Sea* (600 CE) (Casson and MacMullen 2012; Huntingford 1980). These historical sources list precious and exotic goods exported by the Aksumites, including gold, emeralds, obsidian, ebony, ivory and other wild animal products, aromatic substances, and enslaved people. Even though we have to be cautious about interpreting ancient texts, they provide a perspective of travelers and traders and can be a useful resource for studying ancient commerce (D. Phillipson 2012).

Unlike the exported goods, most imports were luxury finished products, including metals, glass, fine ceramics, fabrics, wine, sugarcane, olive oil, myrrh, incense, and spices. A substantial number of the imported goods came from the Roman Empire (the Mediterranean), India, Egypt, and Nubia. Archaeological evidence for this includes large quantities of Indian/Kushana (220 CE) coins found at the monastery Debre Damo in Ethiopia and Roman coins and Antonine jewelry (96–192 CE) found at the highland city Matara. A few Himyarite coins from Yemen were also recovered at Aksum (Munro-Hay 1991). Further evidence of elite Aksumite imports includes Merotic metal bowls at the site Addi Gelamo and large numbers of Mediterranean amphorae and Egyptian and Nubian pottery (especially bowls and platters) found at Aksum. Glass and ceramic vessels of Byzantine and Roman origin were also present at Yeha, Aksum, Matara, and Tio.

Despite the long-standing assumption that this trade was the source of elite wealth, investigation of its mechanisms has not progressed beyond a discussion of military security on the Adulis route. We still know little about the markets, intermediaries, and range of participants in trading activities. Did organized groups travel to obtain raw materials, or did entrepreneurial individuals or groups innovate themselves? More investigation is needed to understand the role of smaller-scale processes in Aksumite trading systems.

Local Trade

The organization of local trade in consumable goods is especially interesting because it involves multiple agents participating in flatter power relations. Local trade brought together communities and institutions through a common demand for necessary commodities. The salt trade is one area where we see communities from different ecological zones coming together due to the dietary demand of both the elite and non-elite.

Archaeological evidence for Aksumite local trade is very scarce. Ceramic data indicate some form of local trade network. Rodolfo Fattovich (2009, 285) identifies Aksumite exchange networks through common ceramic traditions, particularly black-topped polished ware and red-orange coarse ware found in towns and districts like Matara on the Adulis trade route, as well as Yeha closer to Aksum, and Keskese, Gulo-Makeda, Yeha, Hawlti, and Kidane Mehret in northeastern Tigray (see figure 3.2). Fattovich (2009) proposes that these common ceramic types, which started to appear around the middle of the first millennium BCE, developed either through intense interaction surrounding trade and exchange or through social networks and technology transfer facilitated by marriage. There is no well-documented evidence for either of these mechanisms;

nevertheless, Fattovich's is the only archaeological work that addresses the issue of local exchange in the north Ethiopian highlands in antiquity.

Although historical evidence of Aksumite local trade is also scarce, we get a glimpse of it through Pliny (Carey 2006), the *Periplus of the Erythraean Sea* (Casson and MacMullen 2012; Huntingford 1980), and the writings of Cosmas Indicopleustes in the sixth century CE (Wolska-Conus 1962). Historical accounts also mention regional trade with the Beja, from whom the Aksumites acquired emeralds they used mainly for international trade (Sadr 1991).

Cosmas wrote of the Aksumite trading relationship with regions in the south Ethiopian highlands. He did not accompany Aksumite traders to these regions but interviewed them on their way to towns. Therefore, as with all historical sources, Cosmas's report should be interpreted with caution. From his descriptions, we learn that the king regularly sent his agents south to a place called Sasu to trade for gold. The person responsible for organizing the trade caravan was usually the governor of the district through which it would pass. In addition to the king's agents, individual traders also formed part of the caravan party. Cosmas gives detailed accounts of the number of people involved, suggesting about 500 participants on overland caravans from Aksum to Sasu (Kobishchanov 1979).

Research by Aksumite scholars substantiates that the Aksumites valued gold and went to great lengths to acquire it. The search for gold—along with agricultural land and ivory—was one of the main reasons the Aksumites and medieval Ethiopians expanded into the north Ethiopian highlands. According to Munro-Hay (1989), gold was mined in the Aksumite territory and exchanged with neighboring territories as far as Sudan. Ancient gold mines have been discovered in the Eritrean highlands and Ethiopia. In the south, most gold was acquired through panning or from riverbeds rather than mining (Munro-Hay 1991, 171).

Cosmas suggests that the Aksumites traded with the Sasu for gold in exchange for salt, iron, and cattle (the three major commodities mentioned in his account). The journey to Sasu was reported to take about six months. Cosmas describes the southern Ethiopian gold trade as a "silent" trade since neither party spoke the other's language, and they lacked qualified interpreters:

[The Aksumites] deliver bulls, salt, iron, and pieces of meat. Then the natives arrive, bringing with them gold in the form of pea-sized nuggets called *tankharas*, and place one, two, or more of them near a piece of meat or near salt or iron which they wish to acquire and go off some distance. The owner of the meat then arrives and takes the gold if he is satisfied with the price offered for the goods. After this the native who had made the offer draws near and carries off the meat, salt, or iron. If the owner of the goods is not satisfied with the amount of gold offered for his goods then he does not touch the gold and the native who had walked a little way off seeing that his gold is not taken either adds a few more pieces or takes his gold and leaves. (Kobishchanov 1979, 178)

We do have evidence to corroborate Cosmas's account. We know from the archaeological record that the Aksumites valued cattle and that they could have functioned as a major trade commodity. Gold—which he suggests was the Aksumites' primary trade acquisition from the Sasu—has been recovered from Aksumite sites in the form of coins and other objects. Unfortunately, there has never been any study of the source of Aksumite gold, and there has been no excavation in the Sasu/Gurage region for artifacts from the north. Salt—another of the trade commodities Cosmas mentioned—is difficult to detect in the archaeological record because it is perishable, although it can be studied through landscape data.

To date, there has been no exhaustive discussion of Aksumite resource-bearing areas, which makes this research more challenging. The lists of goods given by Pliny (Carey 2006) and the *Periplus of the Erythraean Sea* (Casson and MacMullen 2012; Huntingford 1980) suggest that some goods came from the immediate vicinity of the Aksumite territory, while others came from the far south. Due to the location of the Aksumite state in the Ethiopian highlands, adjacent to the Danakil Desert's salt lakes, one could reasonably hypothesize that the Aksumites extracted most of their salt from the Danakil. Cosmas Indicopleustes mentions both the Aksumites' use of Danakil salt for themselves and their export of Danakil salt to the Sasu region (Wolska-Conus 1962). Textual evidence from medieval times also refers to the mining and trading of block salt from the Danakil to regional markets (Beckingham and Huntingford 1962; Huntingford 1980). No known source mentions the import of salt to the Aksumite state (Kobishchanov 1979). As a result, we can infer that the Aksumites were exporting salt in bulk to other parts of Africa and possibly South Arabia.

In summary, it is clear that Aksumite society was highly diversified and oriented to both local production and long-distance trade. While we lack definitive evidence, it can be argued that separate infrastructures may have existed for long-distance and local trade.

Archaeological and textual evidence on architecture, the location of towns and religious temples, as well as imported and exported goods found on ancient trade routes stretching from Aksum to Adulis indicate the extent and power of the state on the economic and sociopolitical aspect of life during the pre-Aksumite and Aksumite periods. Evidence from non-luxury agricultural products and foodways provides a clearer view of non-elite participants in the ancient economy and a more varied and horizontal distribution of power among different elite and non-elite individuals and groups. The locations of towns, major trade routes, and religious centers were advantages for wealth generation for elite, middle-class, and non-elite individuals alike. Religious temples and complexes served as institutional node points for traders.

The modern Afar salt trade route provides unique proxy data for understanding the ancient salt trade and its role in power relations. I use the information from ethnoarchaeology not as a direct analogy to the past but to examine the changing pattern of human behavior in this niche economy through time. Archaeological evidence from the Afar salt route, in contrast, speaks not only to the existence of multiple thriving heterarchies in Aksumite times but also to the nature of their relationship to Aksumite rulers, even on the fringes of the kingdom.

4

THE HISTORICAL, PHYSICAL, AND CULTURAL
LANDSCAPES OF THE AFAR SALT TRADE

When I undertook fieldwork between 2009 and 2012, I did not assume that the
nature and parameters of salt production and trade had remained constant
throughout history. Indeed, political institutions, labor organization, ideolo-
gies, market systems, land tenure systems, and environmental conditions have
all shifted since the pre-Aksumite period. I was aware that I needed to account
for these changes. At the same time, certain aspects of the traditional salt industry have remained consistent since the Aksumite and medieval periods: the use
of donkeys, mules, and camels; block salt mining technology; the landscape;
the climate; and the location of rivers and mountain passes. These unchanging
aspects of the industry allowed me to create ethnographic analogies that I use
as comparative models (rather than as literal representations of the past) (following Stahl 2001). A study of contemporary practices in modern salt production
and trade along the Afar route, approached relationally (*sensu* Wylie 2002), helps
refine which questions about the distant past I pursue. With such queries in
mind, I examine the *source-side* (ethnographic) data and the *subject-side* (archaeological) data separately, looking for similar and dissimilar patterns. I expand on

https://doi.org/10.5876/9781646424733.c004

the analogies by examining additional sources, such as historical documents and inscriptions.

For example, to understand the ancient salt trade and its role in the Aksumite economy, it is useful to explore the modern locations of salt resources, the scale and intensity of production, the locations of processing areas (i.e., whether they are near salt sources or in central urban or rural towns), the categories of participants (both elite and non-elite), the relationships among participants, and the relationships between the state and salt producers and traders. This information about the contemporary salt trade may indicate areas for further archaeological inquiry into the Aksumite salt trade, such as how people shared resources and negotiated social relationships. This further inquiry could deepen our understanding of the Aksumite state's growth, reach, and sustainable income sources, including alliances the Aksumites established with local and long-distance trading partners to acquire state goods.

This chapter, divided into three parts, provides historical, environmental, and cultural contexts surrounding the ancient Afar salt route and serves as a backdrop for the ethnoarchaeological research presented in chapter 5. These sections depict the physical and social landscapes the Afar trade route traverses and proceed to a discussion of how trade is organized today versus during the Aksumite period.

In section one, I provide a broad overview of Ethiopia's history and culture and examine the country's cultural development through the lens of historical and archaeological evidence. This examination covers the longest period of history in the Horn of Africa, beginning with the origin of humans and ending with early and late state-level societies.

The second section describes northern Ethiopia's unique environment, which includes cool, steep highland plateaus and precipitous mountains, as well as adjacent dry lowlands that dip below sea level. Here, I highlight Lake Asale (Lake Karum) and its significance as a major source of salt in the region.

The region's contemporary salt traders, the Afar and the Tigray, are introduced in the final section, where I discuss their social and political organization, subsistence methods, and settlement patterns.

HISTORICAL BACKGROUND OF ETHIOPIA

The term *Ethiopia* is of Greek origin and is believed to have first appeared during the Aksumite period. Its earliest known use is in a trilingual inscription of King Ezana, which dates to ca. 330–356 CE. Following the translation of the Bible into Ge'ez, the term continued to be formally used in some circles. A literary account from 700 years ago, the *Kebra Nagast* ("Glory of Kings"), also uses the term. The *Kebra Nagast* discusses the history of Ethiopian kings and Ethiopians' religious beliefs, and it has played a significant role in the writing of Ethiopian history. For a very long time, Ethiopia and Ethiopians have been referred to as Abyssinia and Abyssinians by the rest of the world. For centuries, however, Ethiopians and Eritreans have referred to themselves informally as Habasha, and they continue to do so today (Zewde 2002).

The Prehistory of Ethiopia

To truly understand Ethiopia's history, we must begin with its prehistory. In this chapter, *prehistory* refers to the time period between the first hominids and the Late Upper Paleolithic. With its abundance of fossil and material preservation, Ethiopia lays claim to one of the world's longest histories; a chronological study of the country would be incomplete without including early humans and their diverse environmental niches. The earliest entry in this historical record dates to ca. 3.5 million years ago based on archaeological evidence of the first hominid stone tool. Ethiopia is even more famous for being the home of the earliest fossilized hominids. The discoveries of the ca. 3.2-million-year-old *Australopithecus afarensis* (Denqenash in Amharic) by Donald Johanson in Hadar in 1974 (Johanson and Wong 2010) and of the ca. 3.3-million-year-old *Selam* by Zeresenay Alemseged (Alemseged et al. 2006) and his team in Dikika in 2000 have increased the magnitude of Ethiopia's long historical record. Other sites such as Kibbish in southwestern Ethiopia's Omo River Valley have yielded 195,000-year-old fossils.

Ethiopia is believed to be a cradle of *Homo sapiens*. While the discovery of *Australopithecus afarensis* cemented the country's national and international reputation as the home of early humans, it is not Ethiopia's earliest fossilized hominid. *Ardipithicus ramidus* (Ardi), discovered in Ethiopia's Afar Depression, is believed to have lived between 5.8 million and 4.4 million years ago (Haile-Selassie 2001; White, Suwa, and Asfaw 1994).

In retrospect, non-fossil discoveries in Ethiopia spanning the Late Pliocene to the Late Pleistocene have uncovered a wealth of information about the emergence of modernity or modern human behavior. These data were gathered primarily from the diverse stone tool industries that developed in East Africa and the Horn of Africa over this lengthy period. Archaeologists have classified the numerous types of stone tools discovered from this period into distinct phases and typologies. The terminology used to refer to the tools varies according to the expertise of the scholar as well as the region. Ethiopia and Eritrea are known to have developed the following range of stone technologies: chopper tools (Mode 1 or Early Stone Age); Acheulean (hand ax) tools (Mode 2 or Early Stone Age); prepared-core technology, bifacial, and Levallois points (Mode 3 or Middle Stone Age); a blade industry (Mode 4 or Middle Stone Age and Later Stone Age); and microlithic industries (Mode 5 or Later Stone Age) (see Finneran 2007). These technologies that hominids evolved often depended on the types of sites they inhabited, which were heavily influenced by resource availability and a favorable climate. Early humans preferred savanna-like habitats that offered diverse animal and plant food webs and predator protection. Archaeologists have discovered sites utilizing Mode 1 technology in a few locations throughout northeast Ethiopia, the Afar Depression, and southwest Ethiopia's Omo region. Mode 1 tools were primarily made of cherts, basalts, trachytes, and quartz and are frequently associated with the fauna people hunted and butchered (Asfaw et al. 1991; Chavaillon and Piperno 2004; Domínguez-Rodrigo et al. 2005; Finneran 2007; Stout et al. 2005).

Mode 2 stone tools have been discovered in Ethiopia's southwestern Rift Valley and at a few sites in the north and to the west of the highlands. Diverse techniques for preparing flakes and widespread use of obsidian are associated with Mode 2 technology (Asfaw et al. 1992; Finneran 2007; D. Phillipson 2005; Todd, Glantz, and Kappelman 2002). The fauna found associated with Mode 2 technology indicated that during this period, it appears that small-mammal hunting was an important activity for people.

Distinct Mode 3 tools are associated with the Middle-Late Pleistocene. Ethiopian sites with Mode 3 stone tools are uncommon. Most Mode 3 industries that are found are concentrated in the Rift Valley region (Clark et al. 1984; Shea et al. 2002; Yellen et al. 2005), with a few exceptions in the southern and northern highlands (Brandt, Manzo, and Perlingieri 2008; Finneran and Phillips 2003; Leakey 1943; L. Phillipson 2000).

The Mode 4 and 5 industries, which developed during the Pleistocene-Holocene transition period, are the most recent in this prehistoric time line. Paleoenvironmental evidence shows an increase in the diversity of both technology and human-occupied sites during this period. One reason for this is that the terminal Pleistocene's African warm and humid phase granted humans access to newly hospitable ecozones (Kuper and Kröpelin 2006). This event resulted in the occupation of previously uninhabitable areas and consequent regional technological diversity. The Ethiopian highlands, which were cold and arid during the Pleistocene, were one of these places.

We locate industries in Modes 4 and 5 throughout Ethiopia's lowland and highland regions (Brandt 1986; Clark and Prince 1978; Dombrowski 1970; Gutherz et al. 2015). These modes appeared during Africa's wet and humid terminal Pleistocene stage (Tierney and deMenocal 2013) and persisted until the late Holocene. In the northern highlands, Mode 5 industries have been discovered in association with rock art sites (Negash 1997). Along with ceramic technology, Mode 5 stone tools have also been discovered in northern Ethiopia (Finneran 2007). While the raw materials used in these tools were incredibly diverse and varied according to their function, selection shifted toward sedimentary rocks during this time period.

While this Mode 1–5 categorization is commonly used along with a few other classification systems, Niall Finneran (2007) contends that these typologies do not effectively portray the diversity of Ethiopia's stone tool industry. Ethiopia may benefit from a regional approach rather than a large-scale analysis that characterizes the country as a whole or treats Ethiopia in conjunction with other East African sites.

Stone tool technology is necessary not only for understanding the Horn's prehistory; it persisted into the Aksumite period (L. Phillipson 2000). Scrapers are abundant in pre-Aksumite and Aksumite environments and are frequently associated with the large-scale hide work prevalent during this era.

Early to Late Holocene

The preceding section covers nearly 3 million years of cultural evolution solely through an examination of stone tools. As we jump ahead 6,000 years, we find a relative explosion of new technology and cultural innovation. By the Middle to late Holocene, the Horn of Africa had developed new tool industries and economic systems such as herding and agriculture.

Throughout the Holocene, Ethiopia's lowland and highland populations relied on domestic animals and plants to supplement their incomes and provide for their families. This agricultural complex was created by a mixture of African and Asian plants and animals. The animal economy also included integrated African and Asian species. The mechanism and routes through which these different African and Asian domesticates were introduced to the Horn of Africa are highly complex. The best studied are the North African route from the Nile Valley and the Red Sea route to the Horn of Africa from Arabia. During this period, we see the domestication of indigenous African plants, including *enset* (*Ensete edule* Bruce ex Horan.) (Hildebrand 2007) in southwest Ethiopia, *khat* (*Catha edulis* Forsk) in the eastern region, and *te'f* (*Eragrostis te'f* [Zucc.] Trotter), *noog* (*Guizotia abyssinica* [L.f.] Cass.), and finger millet (*Eleusine coracana* Gaertn) in the northern and eastern highlands (Barnett 1999; D'Andrea 2008; D'Andrea et al. 2011; Lyons and D'Andrea 2003). Imported grains such as free-threshing wheat (*T. durum/aestivum*), barley (*Hordeum vulgare* L.), and emmer (*Triticum turgidum* L. ssp. *dicoccum* [Schrank] Thell) and pulses such as lentils (*Lens culinaris* Medik.) and flax (*Linum usitatissimum* L.) were used in the northern Ethiopian and Eritrean highlands as early as 6000 BP (D'Andrea and Haile 2002; D'Andrea et al. 2008, 2018).

Cattle were introduced into the southern lowlands and northern highlands between 3900 and 3400 BP. Around 3500 BP, sheep and goats were introduced into the northern highlands, and chickens followed around 2800 BP (Lesur et al. 2014; Marshall and Hildebrand 2002; Negash and Marshall 2021; Woldekiros and D'Andrea 2017). Ox-plow technology had been developed in the northern highlands by 3500 BC and was used to revolutionize agriculture in Ethiopia and Eritrea (McCann 1995). However, despite the gradual adoption of northern highland ox-plow farming technology in the Southern Hemisphere beginning around the sixteenth century, hoe-digging culture continued to thrive in the south and southwest.

These collective technological, cultural, and economic developments laid a strong foundation for the powerful empires and state-level societies that arose over the following 3,000 years. Because of the favorable wet and humid climate of the Holocene, highland plateaus more than 2,000 m above sea level became habitable. In these north Ethiopian and Eritrean highlands, the D'MT or pre-Aksumite kingdom developed between 800 and 400 BCE and was followed by the Aksumite Empire, which flourished between 450 and 900 BCE (Finneran 2007; D. Phillipson 2012).

Ethiopia's post-Aksumite history is one of its most intriguing. From its inception ca. 900 CE, post-Aksumite Ethiopia was shaped by a constant flux of cultural diversity. This period is encapsulated by competing kingdoms differentiated primarily by religious beliefs: Christianity and Judaism in the north, Islam in the east, and polytheism in the south (Selassie 1972; Taddesse 1968). I return to the subject of religion later in this chapter.

Two sociopolitical developments occurred in the northern latitudes between 960 and 1270 CE: the transfer of power from the Semitic Aksumite to the Cushitic Agaw and the transfer of power from the northern to the central highlands (Taddesse 1968). Historically, this period from the end of the Aksumite phase to 1270 CE was referred to as "the dark age" by historians due to a scarcity of historical and archaeological resources (Selassie 1972). In any case, the term is being phased out due to the fact that ongoing archaeological and cultural resources continue to provide evidence for this so-called dark age (Finneran 2007).

Historians classify Ethiopia into medieval and post-medieval periods following the collapse of the Aksumite state. At the end of the ninth century, a powerful Christian kingdom known as the Zagwe dynasty (960–1270 CE) emerged in the north-central highlands south of Aksum (Selassie 1972; Taddesse 1968). The Zagwe dynasty was founded by the Agaw, who were speakers of Cushitic, one of Ethiopia's oldest languages. Although archaeological evidence for this period is scant, the monuments constructed and the ideology developed during this period are unparalleled in Ethiopia and have left an indelible mark on the landscape. Lalibela's rock-cut churches, approximately eleven of which were constructed during the Zagwe dynasty, are regarded as a monumental feat of ancient humanity (Di Salvo 2016). These monolithic churches are a UNESCO World Heritage Site.

Although the exact dates of the Zagwe dynasty are unknown, local historical documents such as *Gadla Yemrehane Krestos* (Selassie 1972) place it between 960 and 1270 CE. The *Gadla* ("lives" in Amharic) enumerates the kings who ruled this dynasty. For this period, at least three different versions of the list of kings exist: short, long, and longer (see Sellassie 1972, 240, for all versions). Mera Tekla Haymanot, who is frequently credited with initiating the dynasty, was succeeded by Tetewudem, Girma Seyoum, Yemrehane Krestos, Harbe, Lalibela, Ne'akuto Le'ab, and Yitbarek. The legendary monolithic churches bear the name Lalibela in honor of the ruler. In antiquity, the legitimacy of the Zagwe dynasty was contested; in response, legends and biblical origin stories were used to reinforce the authority of the dynasty and its kings. The biblical story of Queen Sheba and Israel's King Solomon is frequently intertwined with this dynasty. In addition, historical documents detail power struggles within the royal family, demonstrating that succession to power within the ruling elite was not always peaceful (Selassie 1972). For instance, King Lalibela lived in exile as a fugitive during his brother's reign and prior to his coronation (Taddesse 1968). Despite such rare exceptions, power generally transferred from father to son and from son to grandson.

At the end of the Zagwe dynasty, we get a clear picture of the various types of segmentary states that developed and coexisted in medieval Ethiopia between 1270 and 1527 CE. These disparate states conveniently reflected religious divisions.

The Zagwe dynasty was succeeded in the north by a powerful Christian kingdom known as the Solomonic dynasty that ruled from 1270 to 1527 CE (Taddesse 1968). The Solomonic dynasty rivaled the Aksumite state in terms of political and economic might; according to some scholars, it may even have been more powerful (Taddesse 1968). The Solomonic dynasty was established by the ruler Yekunno-Amlak after he overthrew the Zagwe dynasty around 1270 CE. Historians believe Yekunno-Amlak came from a segmented state created by a Showan-Amhara lineage in the north-central highlands (Selassie 1972). He was succeeded by even more powerful rulers such as Amda-Tseyon (1314–1344 CE) and Zar'a Ya'qob (1434–1468 CE). As was the case with the Zagwe kings, the rulers of the Solomonic dynasty legitimized their rule by referencing Old Testament Judaism in the Bible, specifically the story of King Solomon of Israel and Queen Sheba. In addition, they legitimized their power by claiming descent from the pre-Zagwe Semitic rulers of the northern highlands.

As with their Aksumite forebears, Yekunno-Amlak and his successors gained power and prestige through their involvement in local and long-distance trade networks. Their economic goal was audacious and mirrored their military goal: to control the country's domestic and international trade networks, which began at the port of Zeila at the confluence of the Red Sea and the Gulf of Aden. Zeila, east of the Gulf of Aden, was as critical to the Solomonic dynasty's long-distance trade network as Adulis was to the Aksumites. The port of Zeila was connected to global trade networks and received goods from both the Indian and Red Seas (Pankhurst 1961). The port of Zeila also connected the Solomonic dynasty's local trade networks to the global trade network.

However, the kings of the Solomonic dynasty were not alone; during this period, a number of well-established dynasties emerged in the southern highlands and eastern lowlands of the Horn of Africa. To the east, the Ifat dynasty had established an Islamic state by the end of the thirteenth century. Walsma is widely believed to have been the state's first monarch (Taddesse 1968). He coexisted with the Solomonic dynasty's Yekunno-Amlak. Archaeological ruins associated with the Islamic Ifat dynasty were recently discovered in the Showa plateau near Nora, confirming the dynasty's date and the plateau's flourishing Islamic towns—which included multiple mosques, caravanserai, marketplaces, and residential sections (Fauvelle-Aymar et al. 2006; Pradines 2017). Apart from the Showa plateau, a network of well-established Islamic segmentary city-states and commercial communities extended from the coast of Zeila to Ethiopia's central highlands. To the south lay Damot, a great and powerful state (Bouanga 2014; Dunnavant 2017). Though little explored archaeologically, it is believed that the Damot kingdom was founded prior to the thirteenth century (Dunnavant 2017). Historical sources describe the Damot kingdom as a polytheistic state that posed a significant threat to the Solomonic dynasty in the north-central highlands. For instance, the Arab historian Ibn Khaldun (1332–1405 CE) mentions a power struggle between these two states in the late thirteenth century at the opposite end of the Ethiopian highlands (Taddesse 1968). The Christian highlands' relationship with the string of segmented Islamic republics in the southeastern and eastern lowlands was not always amicable. Control of caravan and trade routes was a major point of contention.

By the end of the fifteenth century, the eastern lowlands' Muslim, nomadic Afar, and Somali pastoralists had staged a massive revolt against the Solomonic dynasty rulers. Ahmad Ibn Ibrahim, also known as Ahmad Gragn, is credited with disrupting the medieval highland Christian empire and assassinating the Ifat dynasty's monarch (Hailu and Jemere 2017). Gragn founded these Islamic segmentary republics around 1529 CE and was also known as a prominent Muslim leader of the kingdom of Adal. Sufficient information about the Adal sultanate is preserved in the city Harar and other sites in the Horn. (The city Harar is discussed further in the Islam section later in this chapter.)

For at least four decades, Gragn is said to have wreaked havoc in the Ethiopian highlands (Taddesse 1968). Gragn and his followers were defeated in 1543 at the Battle of Wayna Daga by a combined Ethiopian and Portuguese army. Around 400 Portuguese soldiers under the leadership of Christopher da Gama arrived in Ethiopia in response to an invitation from Ethiopian emperor Lebna-Dengel (1508–1540 CE) (Zewde 2002). Lebna-Dengel died in 1540, just prior to the arrival of the Portuguese. Ahmad Gragn was assassinated at the Battle of Wayna Daga, forcing some Adal remnants to retreat to Harar and others to their respective regions. According to scholars, the Afar pastoralists who were once a part of

Gragn's sultanate may have returned to Afar at the end of the sixteenth century to establish their own sultanate/state, providing them with their own lineage and protection from population movement from the south, from the Oromo states (Getachew 2001; Hailu and Jemere 2017; Trimingham 2013).

Although the origins of the Aussa sultanate are still unknown, historians have argued that it was a relic of the kingdom of Adal. Aussa is a strategic location in the Afar region, and Imam Mohammed Jasa was crowned sultan following the establishment of the sultanate in 1577. Imam Mohammed Jasa is believed to have been a relative of Gragn, which bolstered his claim to political leadership. The Aussa sultanate was long-lived, enduring from 1577 to 1975 despite internal rivalries and external threats from forces such as the Oromo movement and Yemen's Imams (Trimingham 2013). Due to the Afar Desert's proximity to Yemen, ca. 35 km away, it was easy for Yemen's Imams to prey on the sultanate's internal political division (Abir 1968; Hailu and Jemere 2017; Yimam 1994). During stable periods, power was passed from father to son. This pattern persisted until the time of Sultan Mohammed Hanfare "Illalta" (1861–1898) (Hailu and Jemere 2017). Sultan Mohammed Hanfare chose to transfer power to his nephew over his son because he believed his nephew was the most qualified candidate for the sultanate (Hailu and Jemere 2017). This was the only time in the sultanate's history when a son failed to inherit power from his father. Overall, these leaders were extremely powerful (Getachew 2001; Hailu and Jemere 2017). Their dominance, coupled with the sultanate's strategic location in the Afar triangle, proximity to a salt source, and the ability to exploit it through caravan trade and livestock keeping, allowed the Aussa sultanate to prosper and flourish in the Horn of Africa for centuries.

Following the end of the conflict between Christian highland agriculturalists and Muslim lowland mobile pastoralists, the country remained politically and economically unstable for an extended period. Until the time of Fasiladas (ca. 1632–1667 CE), the highland city-states reverted to movable cities that strategically migrated around highland communities (Zewde 2002). Fasiladas succeeded his father, Emperor Susneyos (1607–1632 CE), who faced rebellion from his populace over his contentious ideological endeavor to convert the country to Catholicism, which he accomplished through the initiation of Jesuit missionaries brought by the Portuguese. Fasiladas then established Gondar as the capital of the Christian highland state. Gondar developed into a significant urban center in the seventeenth century. A new architectural style was adopted, and the castles and churches built in and around Gondar at this time became hallmarks of the era.

In the second half of the nineteenth century, a new era of Ethiopian history, dubbed Zamana Masafent (Era of Princes), was ushered in by an influx of contending segmentary kingdoms. These segmentary kingdoms destabilized the country, eroding the authority of the Gondarian rulers to the point where they became symbolic. The Era of Princes is defined by strong local leaders/princes of segmentary states vying for power with other northern regional lords. There was competition not only between monarchs from different segmentary states but also within the Gondarian royal family. Leaders from disparate locales such as Gondar, Tigrai, Wallo, and Gojjam all sought to become the head of a centralized power structure (Abir 1968).

While northern politics remained unstable, a new polity was established in the central highlands of the Showa region. The Showan rulers avoided the northern conflict, preoccupied with establishing their own power. Their new polity surpassed the northern states embroiled in royal feuds in terms of political and economic strength (Abir 1968; Zewde 2002). Again, the new Showa rulers claimed descent from the Solomonic dynasty upon ascending to the throne. This assertion provided them with the necessary legitimacy and support they needed to secure political control.

During this time, the regional states in the south were not involved in the political and economic conflict raging in the northern polities. Socioeconomic and political structures in southern Ethiopia varied considerably during this period, ranging from strong segmental states ruled by kings to heterarchical/cooperative societies ruled by clan leaders. Among the southern segmentary states were the kingdoms of Kafa, Gamo, Walayta, and Janjaro (Zewde 2002). These southern states originated in the fourteenth century (Dunnavant 2017) but peaked in power around the turn of the eighteenth century. Agriculture, mobile pastoralism, and foraging were all integral parts of their socioeconomic system. Their diet consisted of year-round plants such as *ensat* (*Ensete ventricosum*, "false banana") and yams. They also raised cattle, sheep, and goats and supplemented their meat consumption with wild antelopes (Hildebrand 2007; Lesur et al. 2014). The northern highlands' agriculture, in contrast, was based on cereals and pulses.

We also witness the emergence of Oromo states in the south and north of the kingdom of Kafa at the end of the eighteenth century (Zewde 2002). Through regional trade, southern states and Oromo states developed a strong economic relationship. Between southern states, the primary economic commodities traded were enslaved people, coffee, honey, and ivory (Abir 1992).

Despite the fact that Ethiopia's socioeconomic and political landscape remained highly heterogeneous until the second half of the nineteenth century, divided—for lack of a better term—into a north-south and east-west dichotomy, it was united by an intricate network of trade routes. Historians have identified two distinct segments of commercial networks. The first is defined by a web of regional trade networks that ran north-south through towns, regions, and states. The second is defined by long-distance trade networks that linked local trade routes to the rest of the world by way of the Red Sea coast, the Gulf of

Aden through the Somali ports of Zeila and Berbera, and the Nile Valley (to Egypt and Sudan). Salt and enslaved people were the two primary commodities that connected these local and long-distance trade networks from the end of the Aksumite phase until the nineteenth century. From the Danakil Depression, the most valuable salt was transported in all directions. Despite the fact that trade networks had connected the various branches of segmentary states for centuries, it was not until the second half of the nineteenth century that all the distinct segmentary states and polities were unified under one state. Sahla-Sellase (1813–1847 CE) initiated this process, which was completed by Menelik II, laying the groundwork for the modern state of Ethiopia.

Language

Ethiopia is home to a diverse range of ethnic groups divided primarily by language. Eighty-six languages are spoken in Ethiopia today, which are classified into four linguistic groups: Cushitic, Semitic, Omotic, and Nilo-Saharan (Ehret and Posnansky 1982; Ferguson 1970). The first three groups are included in the Afro-Asiatic language phylum. Nilo-Saharan and the Afro-Asiatic languages are unrelated to one another. Agaw and Beja, spoken in the northern highlands, are the oldest and most important Cushitic languages (Zewde 2002). The Beja often maintain a nomadic pastoral way of life, and they live only in Sudan at this time. The Oromo are the largest of the Cushitic-speaking groups in Ethiopia; they are concentrated in the country's southern and central regions. All of the Cushitic language groups are still spoken in Ethiopia today. Some of these speakers include the eponymous Afar, Saho, Hadiya, Kambata, Gedeo, and Konso peoples. With the exception of the Afar, who inhabit the eastern lowland desert, all of the Cushitic language speakers live in southern and southwestern Ethiopia (Ehret and Posnansky 1982; Zewde 2002). On both sides of the Omo River in southwestern Ethiopia are people who speak Omotic as a first language.

The second largest group consists of people who speak Semitic languages. They include Amharic speakers in northern and central Ethiopia, Tegregna speakers in Eritrea and Tegray, Gurage speakers in south-central Ethiopia, and Harari speakers in the east. The Tigre language is another Semitic language that is only spoken in Eritrea. Ge'ez is a Semitic language dating back thousands of years that is now spoken exclusively by members of the Ethiopian Orthodox Church. The languages of Amharic, Tegregna, and Tigre are all descended from the Ge'ez language. It is believed that Ge'ez originated during the Aksumite period. Nilo-Saharan speakers can still be found in the western part of Ethiopia, near the border with Sudan. Sudanese speakers of Nilo-Saharan languages are also widely distributed throughout the country. The Gumuz, Barta, Koma, Majangir, Anuak, and Nuer peoples of Ethiopia are among those who speak Nilo-Saharan languages.

Religion

In the northern highlands and low deserts, religion is an important determinant of identity. This region is dominated by three major religious traditions: Christianity (Ethiopian Orthodox), Judaism, and Islam. All three religions have a long history in Ethiopia, and their origins are well documented. During the Aksumite period, around 360 CE, Christianity spread rapidly. The history of Christianity during the Aksumite period is discussed in detail in chapter 3.

JUDAISM

Judaism is thought to have arrived in Ethiopia and Eritrea prior to Christianity and Islam. The process by which it was introduced to Ethiopia remains a mystery. Except for Rebecca A. Klein's (2007) work on the seventeenth- and eighteenth-century Beta Israel of Gondar, there has been no archaeological investigation of sites associated with Judaism in Ethiopia. Since the beginning of the twenty-first century, however, there has been a great deal of ethnohistorical analysis of the identity of the Beta Israel, or Ethiopian Jewish community. Numerous local sources in the form of myth, legend, and history speak to the origin and identity of Beta Israel (Abbink 1990; Pankhurst 1998). Both Ethiopian Orthodox Christians and the Beta Israel themselves have created origin myths and histories about the Beta Israel. The Ethiopian Orthodox Christians' origin story about the Beta Israel is mostly supported by historical documents such as the *Kebre Negest* ("Glory of the Kings"), whereas the Beta Israels' version is supported by oral histories. Regardless, it is clear that the Beta Israel are Agaw people—speakers of one of the oldest extant languages in Ethiopia.

There are at least two hypotheses about when Judaism arrived in Ethiopia. One proposes that the Beta Israel are descended from immigrant Judaic Israeli people who were absorbed into the Agaw community prior to the Aksumite period. The second hypothesis is that the Ethiopian Agaw were converted by outsiders who came to Ethiopia for various reasons. According to the first hypothesis, the Beta Israel of Ethiopia are thought to be direct descendants of an "ancient Judaic, Israelite community" (Abbink 1990, 403) that migrated to Ethiopia from either South Arabia or Egypt. Some scholars believe these immigrants were descended from Israelites prior to the exile. Others argue that the Beta Israel are an Israelite community who fled Israel to escape persecution, first during the Assyrian siege of Jerusalem between the eighth and seventh centuries BCE and then during the Babylonian invasion of Judah between the sixth and fifth centuries BCE. Ethiopian traditional sources, in contrast, argue that the Israelites came to Ethiopia with Menelik I, who was legendarily the son of King Solomon and Queen Sheba.

The spread of Islam to Ethiopia began early due to the proximity of the Horn of Africa to the Red Sea and Arabia, the birthplace of Islam (Selassie 1972; Trimingham 2013). Archaeological evidence from Islamic sites in Ethiopia and Eritrea is sparse, but numerous historical sources are available that point to the uniqueness and magnitude of Islam in the Horn. Historical records indicate that Islam arrived in the Horn of Africa in the Aksumite era somewhere between 615 and 628 CE (Insoll 2003; Selassie 1972). Arab writers such as al-Masudi, Ibn Ishaq, and al-Tabari cite early Arab sources that say Muslim refugees, escaping religious persecution from the Quraysh, traveled to Ethiopia at this time and sought refuge with the Aksumite king Nagashi, who was a Christian. According to these reports, Muhammad sent his followers to Ethiopia because he knew Ethiopians who lived in Mecca and respected the fact that the Aksumite king was a religious and just ruler. Evidence from these sources indicates that the Prophet's nurse, Baraka Umm Ayman, was Ethiopian (Insoll 2003). As far as is known, his grandfather traveled to Ethiopia numerous times to conduct trade and business (Pankhurst 1998). The descendants of the Prophet who migrated to Ethiopia to escape persecution arrived in two successive migrations (Pankhurst 1998). The Prophet's daughter and her husband, along with their disciples, were among the first wave of Muslim immigrants to arrive in Ethiopia (Selassie 1972). The second wave of arrivals was larger than the first (Ahmed 1992; Insoll 2003). According to historical records, the Aksumite king gave the Muslim refugees shelter in Negash. The town Negash is located in northern Ethiopia's Tigray region; it is home to one of Africa's oldest mosques and a cemetery dating to the seventh century. Commemorative stelae on these burials, inscribed in Arabic, describe the town's first Muslim immigrants (Henze 2000).

While the relationship between Islam and Christian Ethiopia was sporadic following the collapse of the Aksumite Empire, trade between the Horn of Africa and the Muslim world never ceased (even when relationships were strained because of disputed rights to trade routes). Commodities such as ivory, gold, enslaved people, animal skin, and salt were exported from the interior; exotic items such as glazed pottery, glass, and cloth were imported (Insoll 2003). This commerce was instrumental in the spread of Islam throughout Ethiopia and Eritrea (Insoll 2003).

The most direct evidence of Islam's introduction to the Horn of Africa comes from the Dahlak islands in the Gulf of Massawa, which are located off the coast of modern-day Eritrea. By the early eighth century, Islam had established itself as the dominant religion in the Dahlak islands (Insoll 2003). By the tenth century, Aksumite sites at Dahlak had been replaced by Islamic-occupied sites, which included cemeteries, settlements, and cisterns (Insoll 1997, 2003; Oman 1974). Around 200 Arabic inscriptions discovered on funerary tombstones dating from

911 to 1539 CE provided critical information about the Dahlak sultanate (Insoll 2003; Oman 1974). Together with the texts, the archaeological remains clearly indicate a powerful sultanate with extensive trading relations along the Red Sea and in the Indian Ocean world. Dahlak islands is a critical site in the discussion of Islam's emergence as a significant religion in the Horn of Africa. Today, the Dahlak islands are inhabited by various ethnic groups, the majority of which are Dahlakin and Afar.

While Islam initially found its foothold at coastal sites, it expanded inland between the tenth and fourteenth centuries. By the eleventh century, it is clear that Islamic towns and settlements were thriving throughout the interior and farther south in the Ethiopian highlands. Quiha, in Ethiopia's Tigray highlands, is another significant archaeological site where basalt stelae bearing commemorative Arabic inscriptions have been discovered (Anfray 1990). Unlike the Arabic inscriptions discovered at Negash and Dahlak, the inscriptions at Quiha most likely commemorated indigenous converts rather than immigrants or traders (M. Schneider 1967), indicating that Islam was well established in the interior between the late eleventh and twelfth centuries.

Islamic sites have also been discovered farther south, beginning in the highlands and progressing eastward into Afar, with a concentration of sites in central Ethiopia near and around the modern-day town Shoa-Robit (Fauvelle-Aymar et al. 2006; Pradines 2017; Tilahun 1990). The Shoa-Robit region is considered to be the heart of the Islamic Ifat dynasty, which ruled from the port of Zeila to the coast of modern-day Somalia between the thirteenth and early fifteenth centuries. The sultanate of Ifat was an amalgamation of various ethnic groups linked by a series of trade networks. Ifat dynasty sites from this Shoa-Robit region have documented large and small stone-wall mosques as well as cemeteries and stelae with Arabic inscriptions (Tilahun 1990). Other Arabic inscriptions and Islam-related features were discovered at sites farther south near Lake Zuwai, Bate, and Heyssa (Huntingford 1955; M. Schneider 1970). The locations of the engraved stelae and commemoration were extremely varied. Several were directly related to the caravan trade, while others were for converts and missionaries on the ground (Huntingford 1955; Insoll 2003).

Harar, in eastern Ethiopia, is another significant center with evidence of Islamic expansion in the interior of the country beginning in the late eleventh century. Harar served as the sultanate of Adal's political capital (more on the sultanate of Adal in The Afar Region section later in this chapter). Adal coexisted with the Ifat dynasty until the dynasty absorbed it in the late fourteenth century (Hiskett 1994; Insoll 2003). Harar's history is rich and fascinating due to the town's continued use as a center for Islam and scholarship to the present day (Insoll 2003). Harar maintained extensive contacts both within Africa and beyond. There is still debate over the precise date of Islam's establishment in the vicinity of Harar. Recent archaeological discoveries at the Harlaa site near Harar indicate that the area was an important urban center in the Horn of Africa as early as the sixth century (Insoll 2017, 2021). The presence of both locally minted and imported coins dating from the twelfth to the eighteenth centuries (Pankhurst 1982) bolsters the argument that Harar was part of an important trade network that connected the Horn of Africa to Islam by way of the eastern Horn port of Zeila. Radiocarbon dating from the Harlaa site indicates the presence of a pre-Islamic settlement that was eventually superseded by Islamic settlements beginning in the late eleventh century (Insoll 2017). This date is consistent with historical evidence and texts.

Harar is a walled city; Nur ibn Mujahid constructed the wall to protect the city from Oromo incursions in the mid-sixteenth century (Ahmed 1990; Insoll 2003). The walls are made of granite and sandstone and the mortar of coarse clay (Ahmed 1990; Hecht 1982; Wilding 1976). Harar's five entrances symbolize the Five Pillars of Islam (Ahmed 1990; Insoll 2003). Within the fortifications, the city is subdivided into five quarters or neighborhoods named after Muslim shrines or historic trees (Hecht 1982). These neighborhoods represented the communities and social identities of those who lived in them.

Numerous historical and archaeological data support the significance of Harar as a religious center from the late eleventh century through the eighteenth century and beyond. Harar is referred to as the "shining city" due to a local legend that claims the Prophet Muhammad looked down on the earth one evening and saw a shining spot, which the Harari believe is their beloved city (Foucher 1994). Harar is also known as the "city of saints" because of its many dedicated shrines. There are over 150 shrines dedicated to saints in and around the city (Foucher 1994; Insoll 2003).

As participants in this Islamization process, which began in the seventh century and continued until the late thirteenth century, the Afar mobile pastoralists helped ensure that Islam became the dominant religion of the Afar—their Somali neighbors to the east—and eventually of the entire region. The preexisting Cushitic religion was incorporated into the Afars' Islamic tradition—an admixture that has flourished to the present day (Insoll 2003; Lewis 1965). This distinctive Islamic tradition is reflected in the Afars' burial practices and material culture, both of which are unique to the region.

These distinct burial practices are exemplified by the northern Afar in particular, who place burials in the middle of stone circles or cairns. By contrast, burial practices of the southern Afar, who live near Awash, include headstones, footstones, and walled burials (Insoll 2003, 76). Goitom Weldehaweriat (2016) recently discovered one such site at Ab'ala, where rock circle burials and burial tumuli were densely concentrated, with a high degree of diversity and intensity. Located in the transition zone between the highlands and lowlands, these monuments at Ab'ala can be seen from all directions (Weldehaweriat 2016). While they have not been radiocarbon dated, the monuments are believed to date to the late Holocene.

These burial/ceremonial sites are still in use by Muslim Afar pastoralists who live in the surrounding area. Ethnohistorical accounts from the community reveal that the tumuli zone is regarded as a sacred landscape of social memory where ritual ceremonies are held in remembrance of ancestors who have passed away. Contemporary Ab'ala Muslims create non-religious, spiritual, and symbolic connections among ritual performances, monuments, and the landscape in which the monuments are situated (Weldehaweriat 2016).

The burial practices of the southern Afar, who live near Awash, differ from those of the northern Afar in that the southern Afar burial includes head and footstones as well as walled burials, whereas the northern Afar burial does not (Insoll 2003, 76).

The modern-day Afar still practice Islam, which was introduced to the region more than 1,000 years ago, in the ninth century or earlier (Getachew 2001). The majority of the Afar belong to the Qadiriyya order and practice Islamic law (*Shariyya* or Sharia) side by side with African customary concepts and practices (Getachew 2001; Trimingham 2013).

PHYSICAL GEOGRAPHY AND ENVIRONMENTAL CONTEXT

Contemporary Ethiopia extends over a landmass of approximately 1.1 km^2 and is the second most populous country in Africa (after Nigeria). Ethiopia is situated in the Horn of Africa and is bordered by Eritrea to the north, Djibouti to the east, Kenya and Somalia to the south, and Sudan to the west. Its capital is Addis Ababa (figure 4.1). Because of its proximity to the equator, Ethiopia represents a diverse range of environments and landscapes. The Ethiopian highlands cover much of the country's northern and central regions. These highlands are divided by the Ethiopian Rift Valley into two distinct regions: the northwestern and southeastern portions. The Rift Valley itself extends all the way to Kenya and Tanzania. The highest peaks have cool climates, with the mean minimum temperature during the coldest season reaching 6°C (43°F). Mount Ras Dashen, located in the northern part of the country, is the highest point, at ca. 4,550 m above sea level; the lowest point is 1,500 m above sea level. Surrounding the highlands are lowlands, which dip to ca. 155 m below sea level in the Afar Depression to the east.

The Afar Region
Structural Setting of the Afar Depression

Located in the Danakil Depression, which is below sea level and forms a part of the Ethiopian Rift Valley, the Afar salt pan is one of the world's largest salt flats

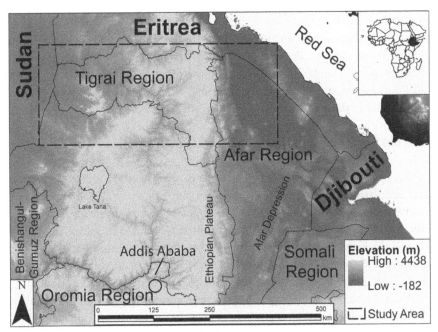

FIGURE 4.1. *Map of Ethiopian plateau and Afar Depression*

(figure 4.1). The Danakil Depression lies at the intersection of the Ethiopian Rift Valley, the Red Sea Rift, and the Gulf of Aden Rifts—which join in the Afar region to form the Afar Triangle (Mohr 1974, 51). It is estimated that salt covers approximately 1,200 km² of the Danakil Depression. These salt plains, known as the Dallol, are composed of salt- and gypsum-based marine sediments that formed when this region was part of the Red Sea. There are two major salt lakes in the Dallol salt plains: Lake Afrera and Lake Asale. Lake Asale is twice as salty as Lake Afrera (EGS 1973, 195) and is a major salt source today. It is reached by way of the Dallol plain, which measures ca. 40 km × 10 km and is located 125 m below sea level.

Afar's northern region is characterized by dry evergreen forests as well as montane evergreen shrubs and scrubs such as *Acacia etbaica*, *Tarchonanthus camphoraths*, and *Cordia purpurea*, among other species (Liao, Ruelle, and Kassam 2016).

Lake Asale (Lake Karum)

Today, the Arho caravanners mine rock salt from the salt crystals found in the area surrounding Lake Asale. Arho is the indigenous name for the caravan's participants from highland villages and the Afar lowlands. Lake Asale contains sodium chloride, or salt, as well as varying amounts of calcium, magnesium, and potassium. It receives water from runoff from the highlands, as well as from nearby hot springs and springs beneath the lake. Due to the high evaporation rate in the area, the lake receives less water than it loses to evaporation (Kürsten 1975). The Afar lakes have a salinity of up to 4.5 times that of seawater. Evaporation, the closed nature of these lake basins without outlets, and the enrichment of the water with soluble ions other than those found in seawater all contribute to the salinity (UN 1973, 179). The source rocks, soil, rainfall, evaporation, residence time of the water, and geothermal heat all contribute to the lake water's geochemistry (UN 1973, 179).

The upper layers of Lake Asale are saline earthy material composed of white clay and gypsum, while the lower layers are pure salt that gradually crystallizes, thickens, and purifies. The lake becomes bright white and appears frozen during the final stage of this process. The salt crust is typically 0.5 m thick, but it can reach a thickness of up to 10 m at times. The caravanners mine salt blocks with an average thickness of 5 cm. This preferred thickness is the result of a strategy of acquiring only bright white, hard salt (US Technical Project in Ethiopia 1945, 3). Around Lake Asale, the vegetation is sparse, consisting primarily of tamarisks, thorn bushes, sedge grass (an excellent source of food for camels), and palm trees.

From current perspectives, the economic potential of Afar salt deposits for development is very high. The reason salt exploitation here has remained one of the largest pack-based trades in the world is because of the difficulty of engineering and maintaining roads or rail systems in this extreme environment. Due to the dramatic escarpment between the Afar and the Ethiopian highlands and the difficulty of the uphill terrain in the mountains, exploitation of the Afar salt deposit to meet large-scale demand has only been possible with pack animal transport (donkeys or camels). Large-scale transport systems are planned for the near future but did not exist at the time I studied the Afar salt trail.

North Ethiopian Highlands

The north Ethiopian highlands are composed of distinct blocks of varying altitudes characterized by massive plateaus and steep escarpments (Behrens 1971, 86). The relief of the highlands—that is, their extreme difference in elevation and slope—has a significant impact on settlement patterns, resource accessibility, communication, agriculture, and other cultural patterns. A sizable portion of the area is located at elevations of up to 2,000 m above sea level. Without access to pack animals, communication and land transport are extremely costly due to the high altitude, steep escarpments, and extreme local relief.

Due to the large disparities in relief over short distances, climate, vegetation, and soil are highly variable. Ethiopians traditionally divided their country into five major climatic zones: *wirch* (alpine zones), *dega* (temperate zones), *weina dega* (subtropical zones), *kola* (tropical zones), and *bereha* (desert zones) (Behrens

1971, 86; Zewde 2002). These Ethiopian classifications of climatic and ecological zones are usually used to describe regional agricultural and vegetation zones, which are linked to different human activities and subsistence.

HUMAN AND ECONOMIC GEOGRAPHY

A thorough understanding of the economic, social, ritual, and political structures of those who participated in the Afar salt route, as well as their interactions with their neighbors, is essential to comprehend the operation of the salt trade. Therefore, in this section I introduce the people of Tigray and Afar, who have been mining, transporting, and trading salt for more than a thousand years. Due to the scarcity of research on the Afar, I also draw on ethnohistorical literature and my own ethnographic data.

North Ethiopian Highlands

In the north Ethiopian highlands, identity is fluid and determined by language, subsistence, and religion. While Cushitic languages are the most ancient and diverse, Semitic languages—the other major subgroup in the Afro-Asiatic language family—are predominant in northern Ethiopia's highlands, where highland caravanners originate. It is believed that these Semitic languages have dominated the highlands since the Aksumite period (D. Phillipson 1998).

Social and Political Organization

The social and political organization of participants on the Afar Salt Caravan Route has a significant influence on their behavior in the salt trade. The Afar and Tigray represent two distinct socioeconomic groups. These divisions date back to ancient times and continue to exist within the community. Both the Tigray and the Afar are patrilineal, claiming descent from up to seven generations of ancestors. The Tigray elite frequently emphasize their ties to the Solomonic dynasty's ruling elite (1270–1974 CE) (Zewde 2002). In the highlands, women are typically responsible for household chores while men work in the fields. Women do, however, assist in harvesting, grinding grain, and milking cows. Today, women do not work in caravans, but they may have done so in the past.

Very few ethnographic studies have been conducted in the northern Ethiopian highlands, but the available information indicates that household units are non-kin and are organized around individuals (Bauer 1975, 1977; Lyons 2007). Tigray households employ non-kin labor to demonstrate their self-sufficiency and autonomy within the village. Certain non-elite householders have the potential to rise to prominence in their village as a result of their wealth accumulation (Apaak 2008). Non-kin, disadvantaged households in the village frequently seek assistance from these individuals, which they compensate for by working for influential men or remaining loyal to them (Lyons 2007, 185).

Participants in the Afar salt trade are likely to be non-elite members of villages with a local tradition of seasonal salt trade. Most caravanners do not own pack animals but rent them from wealthy farmers. Further, they do not employ drovers; they do the work themselves. In the village/town, those who lack the means to hire labor during times of emergency typically belong to communal associations called *edir* and *mahabar*. These associations are made up of members from diverse villages, families, and church parishes (Lyons 2007, 186; Pankhurst 1990, 190). *Senbete* is the name of the church association, and its members assist one another during funerals and memorial services (Bauer 1975, 1977). In addition, neighbors are a significant source of labor. Through daily coffee and beer ceremonies held in the courtyards of houses, old and new neighbors form bonds (Bauer 1975; D'Andrea and Haile 2002; Lyons 2007).

Until the 1970s, political organization in the Tigray highlands was based on a hierarchy of power. Social classes that existed included the monarchy, the clergy, the nobility, and the peasants (Lyons 2007; Pankhurst 1990, 18). The emperor owned all the land and only gave rewards to those who were loyal to him and his policies. He also bestowed land and titles on warriors as a reward. These bequests were referred to as land grants, or *gults* (Pankhurst 1990). *Gult* holders were responsible for collecting tribute and surplus labor from local farmers, raising armies, administering the countryside, and sending supplies to the capital (Crummey 2000; Lyons 2007; Pankhurst 1990; Zewde 2002). Only a few noble families held the authority to distribute land to their followers. The *Chika shum* was the lowest administrative position (Pankhurst 1990) in charge of a parish. These agents had the authority to assign land, collect taxes, and resolve disputes with the help of three village elders. Access to *gult* holders' labor, tribute, and provisions is important in understanding elite roles in the past salt trade.

Rural villagers who were not members of the elite held land through a system known as *rest* and landshare (Bauer 1975; Nadel 1946). *Rest* land was inherited from ancestors through blood ties. Each generation divided the land equally among their children; as a result, *rest* landholdings tended to decrease in size over generations. Villagers were allocated landshare through a lottery system, as opposed to the traditional method of redistribution (Bauer 1977; Crummey 2000). The tax and *rest* systems were changed between 1941 and 1966 by Emperor Haile Selassie, who mandated direct tax payment to the emperor and terminated the *rest* system. People in the Tigray highlands resisted the new laws and continued to practice the *rest* system until the 1970s (Crummey 2000; Zewde 2002). When the *Derg* socialist government came to power in 1974, it abolished the *rest* system and redistributed land in the highlands based on marital status and the number of children living in a household, among other factors (Lyons 2007). Ethiopia's current Federal Democratic Republic government continues to adhere to the *Derg* policy of land ownership, which stipulates that all land belongs to the state and should be developed. This policy affects who participates in the salt trade and who benefits from it: people from lower socioeconomic classes are more likely to take part in the route, while those from higher socioeconomic classes may provide support or profit from its distribution. An understanding of highland social and political organization sheds light on the significance of the local salt trade in the broader political economy and also on the diverse participants.

Socioeconomic Organization

Agriculture remains the primary economic activity in northern Ethiopia's highlands today. The primary source of food and income for households is grain cultivation, specifically wheat, barley, sorghum, maize, and *te'f*. Most villagers farm with non-mechanized, ox-drawn plows and rely on seasonal rain for agriculture. Emmer wheat (D'Andrea and Haile 2002) and Ethiopian domesticates such as *te'f* (D'Andrea 2008; D'Andrea et al. 1999; Harlan 1969; Simoons 1983) are the major cereal crops. In the highlands, farmers grow non-cereal crops such as the banana-like *enset*, the oil seed *noog*, and the stimulants *chat* and coffee (Hildebrand 2007). *Enset* and coffee were introduced to the north from Ethiopia's southern highland.

Settlement and Houses

Another significant aspect of regional identity is architecture. Household architecture is inextricably linked to the three identifiers mentioned previously: religion, language, and subsistence. The architecture along the salt route reflects the route's long history of participation in the trade. Researchers have observed similarities in architecture and material culture between the Aksumites and present-day Tigray, which they attribute to a common ancestor (Lyons 2007; Michels 2005; D. Phillipson 1998). While houses in contemporary northern Ethiopian urban areas indicate social status and wealth, just as they did during the Aksumite period, architecture in rural areas is more pragmatic. This non-elite (*vernacular*) architecture is typical of Tigray highland farmers and caravanners (Apaak 2008). The housing structures are referred to as *hidamos* in Tigray. *Hidamos* are circular or rectangular and are typically mud-mortared stone with flat earthen roofs (Lyons 2007). They can last between 100 and 120 years, depending on the conditions (figure 4.2). Clement Abas Apaak (2008) and Diane E. Lyons (2007) describe them as constructed in rectilinear compounds surrounded by stone walls, with kitchens built separately from the main living quarters and more than one *hidamo* per compound. Apaak (2008) found that *hidamos* in salt caravanner compounds are typically larger than those in non-caravanner compounds. However, a significant amount of variation exists in *hidamo* construction throughout the Tigray region. Room sizes as well as floor plans differ from one location to the next, so size and construction may reflect regional variation rather than the national standard. In

FIGURE 4.2. Hidamo-*style house in Agula. Photo by Helina S. Woldekiros.*

contrast to the houses built by their pastoralist neighbors, highlander houses are typically constructed by men, though women oversee the majority of interior maintenance throughout the year.

In highland villages and towns, residents prefer to build their own houses rather than hire contract labor, as this demonstrates their ability to work hard. Although the state owns all the farmland, people own their homes. Until the 1970s, land was purchased and sold on an ongoing basis. Currently, land can only be leased or rented from the government and cannot be passed down through family. Houses, however, can be inherited. As a result, highlanders consider building a home a necessity. In some communities, the practice of newlyweds living with their parents until they construct their own homes (figure 4.2) is acceptable (Lyons 2007, 185). Some salt traders use the money earned from the salt trade to purchase materials for house construction. The caravanners are often distinguished from their neighbors by the size of their houses and the number of compounds they have (Apaak 2008).

The locations of a family's settlement and farmland are entirely distinct from one another. Houses are constructed on the crests of hills or mountains overlooking grazing land and farmland, while farmland is usually situated on floodplains, in valleys, and on the sides of mountains.

The Afar Region

People from the lowland Afar region are pastoralists and caravanners who inhabit a well-defined area known as Cafar-burro, or Afar land (Getachew 2001). The Afar region's inhabitants speak Lowland East Cushitic, a language related to Somali and Oromo (Ehret and Posnansky 1982). Archaeologists believe the earliest pastoralists in the African Rift Valley, such as those who lived around 1500 BCE at the site Besaka in the south Ethiopian Rift, spoke Cushitic languages (Ambrose 1984; Brandt 1982).

Social and Political Organization

Afar land is located in northeastern Ethiopia and shares international borders with Djibouti, Eritrea, and Somalia, as well as regional borders with Oromiya, Amhara, Tigray, and Somali (Getachew 2001). Compared to the patterned permanent settlements of the Tigray, the Afar live a more nomadic way of life. Contact between the Afar and their neighbors is driven primarily by trade and marriage. There have been both peaceful and violent aspects to these relationships throughout history.

Afar peoples have been able to maintain a distinct, autonomous cultural identity despite contact with neighboring regions and a series of governing bodies, from the central administration of Ethiopia from the time of Menelik II to Haile Selassie, the *Derg*, and the country's current government (all of which have been / are based in the Aussa region in the south of the Afar Depression). As in the Sahel, it has been common in this region for kings to function side by side with more segmentary groups in adjacent territories (McIntosh 1999; Southall 1999). The Afar functioned in parallel to highland kings and politics until 1974 and in many ways relate similarly to the modern state. The central advantage of these horizontal relationships and interactions among settled and mobile peoples is integrating and spreading knowledge about technological, ecological, religious, and political issues across vast areas (McIntosh 1999; Stahl 1994, 1999).

The modern Aussa continue to recognize the hereditary sultan Ali Mirah Hanfere (Getachew 2001). The Aussa people are one of two major social groups into which contemporary Afar peoples are divided. The other group is the Badhu, who live in the Afar Depression in central and northern Afar. The Badhu do not recognize the Aussa sultan (Getachew 2001). The Aussa and Badhu have significant differences in their economies, political leadership, marriage organization, and practice of female circumcision (Getachew 2001, 36). The Badhu are organized horizontally through clans and lineages and are pastoralists who also engage in the salt trade (Getachew 2001). The Aussa of the south are less involved than the Badhu in the salt trade. Aussa families are sedentary agropastoralists who rely heavily on local and international trade, agriculture, and pastoralism for economic survival (Chedeville 1966; Getachew 2001).

Afar society is divided into four major social units and two major clan confederations. The four social units are the family (*burra*), the extended family (*dahla*), the lineage (*gulubldahla*), and the clan (*kedo*). Social networks among families and between groups provide support after adversity, such as a drought or a war. They are maintained through the exchange of livestock, milk, meat, and labor as well as small-scale trade (Getachew 2001). The Adohimarra and Asahimarra are the two major clan confederations (Getachew 2001; Savard 1966; D. Schneider 1979). The Afar are patrilineal, with all four major social units claiming descent from the male line. Most people claim ancestral ties spanning four to six generations.

In the Afar lowlands, there is a strong interrelationship among shared territory, traditional authority, and kinship. This complex web of relationships affects the way people view resources, the salt flats, and the salt trade. Unlike their highland counterparts, the Afar have historically not owned or claimed land as a household unit but rather as a lineage within an extended family. Clan land is subdivided using natural boundaries such as grazing land, water, mineral deposits, and burial and ritual sites (Chedeville 1966; Getachew 2001; D. Schneider 1979). Clan members are expected to migrate within these boundaries, and they also have the right to rent or lease land for a limited time to non-clan members and clients. The land may be compensated in cash, material, or labor.

Afar leadership is based on the authority of elders, a group of lineage spokesmen (called *daar-idomla*) and clan heads (called *kedo-abba*) (De Blois 1984). Their primary responsibilities include managing resources and resolving disputes between clans or over territories. The institution Finaa/Fimaa is in charge of enforcing clan and lineage agreements, and individuals who violate those agreements are subjected to punishment. This institution is made up of young, capable men, with a few older men thrown in for good measure (Chedeville 1966; Guedda 1989; Lewis 1965).

Socioeconomic Organization

Livestock ownership and the pastoral lifestyle figure largely in the Afar economy and identity. Afar people today are either pastoralists or agro-pastoralists. Herding is often combined with small-scale cotton and *chat* cultivation, particularly in river floodplains. Agricultural cultivation is difficult and relatively new in this arid region. Despite the difficulty, Afar families rely heavily on agricultural products. They have also come to rely on luxury goods such as cloth and modern medicine.

The Afar who live near the salt trail are predominantly mobile pastoralists who keep multi-purpose stock: camels, sheep, goats, and cattle that provide milk and meat. Livestock also allow the Afar to manage risk during droughts and to strengthen social networks, as animals are an important part of social contracts. In addition, milk- and meat-giving animals such as cows and goats are kept for trade and exchange. Camels are the most valued animals, as they provide milk and carry heavy loads for the Afar during journeys between camps. Because of the lack of water and grazing resources, pastoralists manage their herds through short- and long-distance mobility. Herds are divided into home-base lactating stock (*homa*) and satellite camp stocks (*magida*) (Getachew 2001). Pack animals such as camels and donkeys are always kept with the home-based lactating stock so they can be used to transport milk and other trade commodities to nearby markets.

Current research at Aba'ala Woreda—a district located in the Afar region's salt trading zone—indicates that some northern Afar pastoralists, like their southern neighbors, are transitioning to semi-pastoralism (Zerihun 2015). The Afar at Aba'ala Woreda are incorporating plant agriculture into their economy, albeit on a small scale. Like their other economic activities, this agriculture is performed seasonally rather than year-round. According to Degsew Zerihun (2015), these pastoralists are planting crops that are typically found in the highlands, such as barley (*Hordeum vulgare*), wheat (*Triticum aestivum* L.), finger millet (*Eleusine coracana*), te'f (*Eragrostis te'f*), and chickpeas (*Cicer arietinum*). Zerihun (2015) observed that while highland plants are new to the area, the Afar are well versed in using wild plants found in their environments, including edible and medicinal species such as *Acacia etbaica* Schweinf and Gara, or *Dobera glabra* (Forssk.) Poir.

The Afar peoples' mobility, pack animal husbandry, and proximity to the salt flats render them uniquely suited to the salt trade. For many Afar households and communities, salt continues to be a stable and profitable source of income.

Settlements and Houses

Afar settlements are mobile; their locations are determined by dry-season and wet-season pastures as well as clan and lineage affiliation. Daily life is divided among local grazing areas (*gawra*), the main household unit (*homa*), the extended family unit (*dahla*), the clan settlement (*kedo*), and the land beyond (*bahri*), where the trade route falls. Figure 4.3 shows a traditional Afar settlement that was reproduced following Kassa Negussie Getachew (2001). A male household head, his wife or co-wives, and their children occupy a nuclear home base (*burra*). This unit also includes herds of cattle, camels, sheep, and goats, which belong exclusively to the nuclear household. The extended family household (*dahla*) includes five to sixteen huts and the family's herd. Both the nuclear and extended family units have two settlements: the home base (*homa*) and the dry- and wet-season camps (*magida*).

The distinctive house structures of Afar participants on the salt route are influenced by functional and cultural factors and can be distinguished from those of highland farmers in the area. The settlement structure is broadly comparable to that of other contemporaneous East African mobile pastoralists (Grillo 2012; P. Spencer 1965). Wooden fences surround settlements to keep predators out and

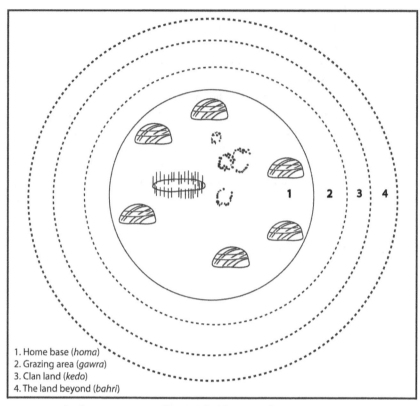

1. Home base (*homa*)
2. Grazing area (*gawra*)
3. Clan land (*kedo*)
4. The land beyond (*bahri*)

FIGURE 4.3. *Settlement structure of the mobile Afar pastoralists*

denote residential space. Huts/tents are located within circular fenced enclosures, and pens for small stock and large herds are located in the enclosures' centers (figure 4.3). Each nuclear family unit is connected to a larger family unit, the *dahlu*, who prefer to live in close proximity to one another and participate collectively in rituals, ceremonies, and herd management.

Houses are built in the main settlement/home base (*homa*). The Afar word for a traditional house is *senan'ar*. These houses are usually built by women, using very simple materials. The Afar must be able to move easily during migration season; as a result, they use materials that can be loaded onto a camel or a donkey. Typically, Afar women create a dome-like shape by bending acacia wood frames for the hut's walls (figure 4.4), then they use rope to connect the bark. They place one strong wood pole in the middle of the wooden frames, then cover the outside with a *selane*, a mat made of grass or leather. A similar mat is used to cover the floor (figure 4.5). Sometimes, women encircle the base of the hut with stones to anchor it against the wind. The diameter of the huts I

FIGURE 4.4. Settlement and houses of pastoral mobile Afar near Melabdi. Photo by Helina S. Woldekiros.

FIGURE 4.5. Inside structure of a mobile Afar house near Melabdi. Photo by Helina S. Woldekiros.

FIGURE 4.6. *Houses in settled Afar towns. Photo by Helina S. Woldekiros.*

measured during my fieldwork varied from 3 m to 5 m, and the wooden pole measured about 2 m.

Some Afar people are now constructing permanent structures in towns near truck routes and market centers that are distinct from traditional Afar homes in their architectural design (figure 4.6). Afar people have told me that they typically hire their highland neighbors to build the new houses because they are not familiar with the construction of these types of structures. The permanent houses are built of wood and mud or dung mortar, depending on the region. They are rectangular, and their stone foundations are similar to those of highland houses in appearance. The Danakil Depression's high temperature necessitates ventilation, which open spaces in the walls provide in abundance. Despite this, most Afar people prefer to sleep outside in the fresh air rather than in their homes.

The second type of Afar settlement is found in towns and is called a *ketema/ katma*. These settlements are made up of permanent houses and are inhabited by other cultural groups besides the Afar. Traditionally, these settlements are associated with market centers, trading hubs, and new opportunities. Most salt warehouses and markets are located in *ketemas/katmas*, marking one of the many nodes of salt distribution. Not all Afar favor these settlements; some people I spoke with think outsiders might corrupt the culture and obtain access to resources that are exclusive to the Afar.

To comprehend the role of the Afar salt trade in the Aksumite state's socioeconomic and political organization, we must do two things. First, we must place the salt trade within a broader context of economic strategies that have been employed over time in the northern Horn of Africa in response to environmental and cultural realities. Second, we must look for its connections to the state apparatus. In this chapter, I have demonstrated that seasonal farming in the highlands and mobile pastoralism in the low deserts were the most important economic strategies for the past 4,000 years in the Horn of Africa. Long- and short-distance trading, as well as skilled labor activities, supplemented these economic strategies. The salt trade was an economic niche that farmers and pastoralists exploited for a portion of the year. Throughout history, trade routes were managed by a variety of agents—including local princes, Muslim merchants, and prominent towns, in addition to the state. The state's economic policy was very similar to its political policy during the Aksumite and medieval periods, which included control and expansion of trade routes.

The steep highlands of northern Ethiopia and Eritrea and the adjacent scorching hot deserts provided an early trading opportunity for salt and obsidian. In northern Ethiopia, crops are abundant enough to trade, but land travel to more distant markets is extremely difficult without pack animals. In the Danakil Desert, mineral resources such as salt and obsidian are abundant, but plant life is deficient. Even a very early state such as Aksum could not have ignored the opportunity to exploit an abundant, essential, and profitable resource like the salt flats.

5

THE ETHNOARCHAEOLOGY OF SALT
PRODUCTION AND TRADE

In 2012, I followed the Afar salt caravan trail for six months over the pack-based trade route and the trails I could access by road, conducting research through participant observation. I rented five camels on a lowland portion of the trail and traveled with four Arho (caravanners) and three Addis Ababa University students, joining a group of drovers in a gargantuan daily caravan of up to 1,000 people and 6,000 animals that camped en masse nightly. Each of my camels carried 72 l of water. I also brought tents, sleeping bags, kitchen utensils, pasta, flour, sugar, tea, and canned food. The data I discuss here are drawn from the fieldwork and interviews (table 5.1) I conducted during this journey, as well as my extended studies in Ethiopia between 2009 and 2012.

Pack-based caravans of camels, donkeys, and mules still move most of the salt that supplies Ethiopia today, traveling along a 72-km portion of the Afar salt route. This is one of the largest functional pack routes in the world. Roads and paths in the highlands connect to the pack-based route, and most caravanners actually travel between 132 km and 220 km before they reach the salt source. These caravanners work and interact with salt miners, brokers, warehouse

https://doi.org/10.5876/9781646424733.c005

TABLE 5.1. Summary of caravanners interviewed from Tigray and Afar regions

Origin (towns) of Participants	Group	No. of Members			
		Humans	Camels	Donkeys	Mules
Agula	1	6	23	7	6
	2	8	21	9	–
	3	5	10	12	–
	4	8	35	–	–
	5	4	19	–	–
	6	2	–	7	–
Gejit	7	3	–	19	1
	8	2	–	20	–
	9	4	–	19	–
	10	6	27	–	–
Raya	11	5	–	20	–
	12	5	39	–	–
	13	4	21	–	–
	14	8	42	–	–
	15	3	10	6	–
	16	6	19	–	–
	17	6	34	–	–
Samre	18	4	13	6	1
	19	2	8	–	–
	20	3	–	18	–
	21	3	–	11	–
	22	4	–	14	–
Wekro	23	10	22	–	–
Quwiha	24	6	–	27	3
Aduka	1	4	20	–	–
Berhaile	2	4	24	–	–
Afar	3	4	30	–	–
Afar	4	1	11	1	
Afar	5	3	21	–	–
Afar	6	4	5	–	–
Afar	7	5	33	–	–
Allah ale	8	3	18	–	–
Dalul	9	4	11	–	–
Degad	10	5	33	–	–
Lela Ala	11	4	17	–	–
Grand total	366	154	566	196	11

owners, shop owners, government tax collectors, and residents of settlements along the route to procure, transport, and distribute salt to consumers.

This chapter explores the organization of contemporary salt production and trade on the Afar salt trail and discusses the ethnoarchaeological techniques I used to conduct regional research on the modern-day caravan route. It identifies state and local participants and social networks involved in moving perishable goods along the Afar trade route from the highlands to the lowland salt flats of the Danakil Depression and examines the sequences of salt production and distribution. It also discusses the role of the salt caravan trade and other niche economies in diverse resource acquisition as it considers overarching frameworks for the subsistence choices made by the Tigray and Afar peoples along the salt route. Insights gained here are used to model the organization of Aksumite trade routes and to recognize ancient caravan sites.

SOCIAL CONTEXT

Salt is distributed in modern-day northeastern Ethiopia through a variety of both formal and informal trade and exchange networks. The Afar salt trade route encompasses many participants, with salt producers and caravanners serving as the initial link in the chain. The caravanners transport salt along the portion of the route that modern trucks cannot cover. Caravanners deliver the salt to warehouses positioned at various points along the route. Urban salt merchants dispatch trucks to collect the salt and deliver it to the nearest large city and from these cities to locations farther south and throughout Ethiopia.

The social framework in which salt traders operate is determined largely by their geographic origins, the division of labor within those areas, and the people directly involved in salt distribution. Contemporary traders come from certain places in the north Ethiopian highlands and lowlands referred to as trade corridors. Highland traders come from a region known as Enderta, located in south-central Tigray. Most of the highlands' population is situated in Enderta. Its cities and villages are positioned near the border with the lowlands, making it a convenient location for travelers. Lowland traders from the Afar region are drawn mainly from the districts of Dalul, Allah ale, and Aduka, among other places.

SALT ROUTES

During the course of my ethnoarchaeological work, I determined that today, highlanders take three major routes to the lowlands: the Desi'a route (route 1), the Usot route (route 2), and the Shiket route (route 3), which were mapped for the first time during this fieldwork (figure 5.1, table 5.2). As shown on the map in figure 5.1, these routes are defined largely by the availability of passes through the desiccated highlands down the 3,000-m escarpment to the lowlands. The Usot route is traveled by only a few caravanners, usually from the Atsbi

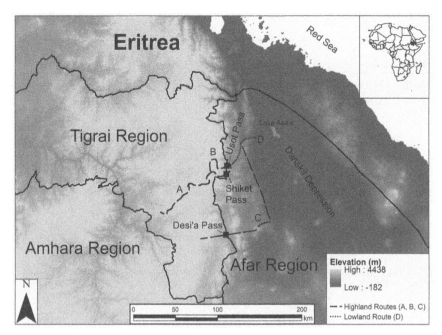

FIGURE 5.1. *Map showing the three major Afar caravan routes: the Usot, the Desi'a, and the Shiket*

Wonberta district in eastern Tigray. The Usot route in the lowlands goes through the towns Dalgena, Korha, Darguni, Berhaile, Melabdi, Asabolo (Sabba), and Hamed Ela before ending at the salt flat (Reged).

The Desi'a route is the most traveled of the three, connecting the northern and southern routes. Caravanners from the towns Mekelle, Semere, Quhia, Raya Azebo, Gijet, and Temben follow this route, which crosses the lowlands through Desi'a, Korha, Darguni, Berhaile, Melabdi, Asabolo (Sabba), and Hamed Ela before ending at the salt flat. The route is used primarily by caravanners based in Tigray's central and southern provinces.

The third option is the Shiket route, which traverses the lowlands over a pass located in Shiket. This pass can be used if there was rain during the rainy season and when pasture is available, although it is normally too hot for travelers leaving the highlands to use it in the summertime. The terrain, however, is flat, making it particularly conducive to camel caravans. Shiket is located 28 km south of Desi'a and, at the height of 1,350 m above sea level, is the highest point in the area.

The lowland section of the journey, which I walked on foot with caravanners, began at Berhaile, which also serves as the starting point for the route's Afar section. Caravans from both the highlands and the lowlands make their way to this Afar village before continuing to the salt flat.

TABLE 5.2. Travel to the salt flat from the highland and lowland towns one way, distance traveled and days

Region	Zone	Woreda (District)	Towns	Distance to the Salt Flat (km)	Days
Tigray	Central Tigray	Degua Temben	Hagere Selam	135	9
	Eastern Tigray	Atsbi Wonberta	Agula	92	8
			Wekro	86	7
			Desi'a	74	7
			Usot	64	7
		Kilte Awlalo	Haiki Meshail	78	7
	Southern Tigray	Mekelle	Mekelle	112	8
	Enderta		Qwiha	110	8
		Hintalo Wajrat	Gijet	152	10
		Seharti Samre	Samre	152	10
		Rya Azebo	Mehoni	162	10
Afar	Zone two	Dalul	Aduka	20	2
		Ab Ala	Ab Ala	40	3
		Megale	Lile	27	3
		Berhaile	Berhaile	44	4
			Melabdi	24	2
			Asa Bolo (Sabba)	14	1
			Hamd Ela	7	1
		Koneba	Koneba	44	4

Once it reaches the highlands, salt from the Afar lowlands is redistributed over a north-south highway/trade route that runs along the edge of the eastern highland escarpment. Historical texts mention this highway as having been used by Aksumites engaged in extensive trade with South Arabia and Asia through the port of Adulis (Fattovich 2012; Kobishchanov 1979; Sernicola and Phillipson 2011). This well-known route also connected the Aksumite trade network inland to the north, toward Sudan and Egypt (Kobishchanov 1979). From this highway, the Aksumites subsequently distributed salt to towns and cities in the highlands, to Sudan, and—possibly—across the Red Sea to Yemen.

PARTICIPANTS ON THE AFAR TRADE ROUTE: SALT DISTRIBUTION

Today, the distribution of salt in northern Ethiopia is a collaborative effort by various stakeholders from both the highlands and the lowlands. The stakeholders I observed between 2009 and 2012 included caravanners, warehouse owners, brokers, and the markets themselves. Caravanners from each village were supposed to supply salt for their own houses and the rest of the village. They also supplied salt warehouse owners and brokers, who then distributed the salt to distributors and store owners in major towns and metropolitan marketplaces, such as Mekelle in the north of the country. From these towns and marketplaces, salt was transported to locations farther south and throughout Ethiopia. In the sections that follow, I describe the function of each party in the organization of the salt trade, as well the *chaînes opératoires* (sequences of operations) that are involved in the salt production and distribution process as salt is moved from the lowlands to the higher elevations.

Pack caravan transportation has proven to be the most effective means of delivering salt from the northern Danakil Desert, primarily because of the parched nature of the highland landscape and the intense heat of the Danakil, which makes road construction and transit extremely difficult. Today, a large portion of the route is covered by roads, which are used by both trucks and pack animals.

Walking the Danakil salt road alongside caravanners allowed me to discover more about the individuals who comprised the caravans, their preparation for the journey, and where and how they camped along the road, among other things. Individuals, families, and the government all factor into this logistical process, as do brokers and the market system as a whole.

Caravan Members

Caravanners are the most emblematic participants in the Afar salt trade. They come from the Tigray, Raya, and Afar regions of northern Ethiopia, where they live in towns and villages. All of them are men. To become a caravanner (Arho), one must be related to at least one other person who was also a caravanner at some point in their lives; thus, the occupation is passed down from father to son, son-in-law, or grandchild from generation to generation. The majority of caravanners are middle-aged, but their ages range from approximately fifteen to sixty-five; some are older than sixty-five, but none are younger than fifteen. The task is difficult, requiring self-discipline and strong personal character; at four to six weeks per trip, it necessitates a significant amount of time away from immediate family and friends. Caravanning is a well-respected career. Caravanners are revered in their home villages, where people recognize the enormous physical and emotional strength required to traverse such a long and demanding path.

A diverse range of cultural and geographical backgrounds is represented among caravanners, but they are all subsistence farmers or herders who begin their journey in their home villages and do not live in towns. Highland caravanners are smallholder agriculturalists, while Afar caravanners from the lowlands are pastoralists who move about from place to place. Participants from both regions are skilled linguists fluent in at least three Ethiopian languages, including

Afar, Amharic, and Tigrinya. The caravanners from the highlands speak a Semitic language and are mostly Christian, whereas the caravanners from Afar speak a Cushitic language and are predominantly Muslim. These variations result from the region's long history as well as the interactions between terrain and subsistence techniques. In addition to sharing the part-time nature of the salt trail work, the two groups also work the trail during the same time of year—from the end of the long rainy season until Ethiopian New Year in September.

The smallest social units on the caravan road are the groups of drovers, which consist of seven to fifteen persons who share companionship, labor, and logistical resources with one another and with the caravan. There is no single group leader; instead, multiple people take turns leading and guiding the pack caravan. Each caravan member also takes turns preparing food and loading and unloading at each campsite and terminus—which includes salt warehouses, markets, and the salt flat—as well as at each campsite and end point. End points are predetermined; as a result, they restrict the options available to caravanners when planning their journey. Itineraries are influenced by environmental factors as well as other economic methods they employ. The main factor is the logistical requirement of the trail (location of water and food).

Most highland caravanners go to the salt flat with donkeys. A few villagers take donkeys, mules, and camels. All of the Afar travel to the salt flat with camels. The number of animals per caravan group varies according to the number of members and their prosperity. On the caravan trip I accompanied, the number of donkeys and camels run by an individual drover ranged from three to twelve, with an average of five. The number of pack animals per caravan group varied from five to thirty-nine (see table 5.1).

Surprisingly, none of the people I spoke with owned their pack animals. Purchasing and maintaining pack animals is a costly endeavor for both agropastoralists and pastoralists and necessitates more money than caravanners have. Rather, the animals were rented or lent on occasion. They paid the rent with the proceeds from the sale of salt blocks at the end of the journey. Caravan drovers shared profits equally with pack animal owners, who were typically much wealthier. As a result, the maximum number of pack animals a caravanner can bring on a trip is determined by their ability to pay the animal owner.

Neighbors, village members, brothers, cousins, and distant relatives may rent pack animals to caravan drovers. They are, however, usually people the caravanner knows personally. Overall, the salt trade is more profitable for pack animal owners than for caravan drivers. First and foremost, the drovers must cover all logistical expenses, including food for themselves and the animals. The journey is also difficult and exhausting, and the drovers must financially compensate the pack animal owner if one of the animals dies on the trip. In such cases, the owner is informed of the death of a mule or a donkey by a caravan

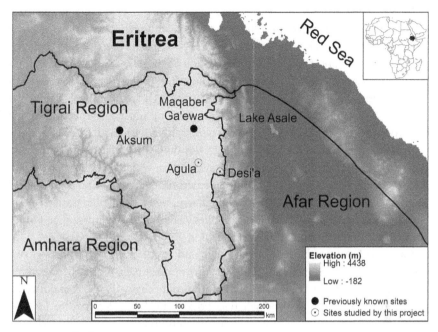

FIGURE 5.2. *Study area*

member cutting the tail off the carcass and transporting it back to the highlands as proof of loss.

The journey from the highlands to the salt flat takes longer than the one from the lowlands to the salt flats. Tigray farmers traveling from highland villages and towns—such as Samra, Haiqi Meshal, Qwiha, Gijet, Mehoni (Raya), Agula, Wekro, and Hagere Selam—take an average of two weeks to get to Berhaile, the first major Afar town. From there to the salt flats, they travel an additional three to four days. From interviews, I learned that many highland caravanners make at least eight trips a year from their village to the salt flat—roughly one trip per month during the dry season. However, while they are on the salt route, most caravanners make two trips from the salt flat to Berhaile—the Afar town with warehouses from which trucks transport salt back to the highlands.

The Afar pastoralists have shorter distances to cover over flatter, hotter land-scapes. They travel three to four days from their pastoral villages in the lowlands (Dalul, Allah ale, or Aduka) to the salt flats and Berhaile. The Afar caravanners make at least three trips per month, or twenty-four to thirty-eight trips annually. Most caravanners told me they had only started unloading at Berhaile in the 1990s; prior to that time, they went all the way (162 km) to Mekelle, the capital of the Tigray region (see figure 5.2).

In part because of the vast variances in the distance traveled and also because of the profound differences in culture and socioeconomic organization that exist between highland and Afar caravanners, the two groups prepare for their journeys in vastly different ways. The organization of the Afar trade route is unique and requires a specialized logistical arrangement. It is necessary to pre-plan provisions along the trade route, since it passes through two completely different landscapes: highlands and low desert. This planning must account for the journey from the caravanners' hometowns to the salt flats and back. A caravanner's logistics plan depends on where they live relative to the trade route. To provide sustenance for both humans and pack animals, caravanners and other traders have developed a system that is based on environmental conditions and is likely as old as the salt trade itself. Other factors that influence meal preparation on the path include the availability of food supplies, the pace of the journey, and one's own identity, politics, and social relationships, among other things.

Caravans from northern Ethiopia's highland and Afar regions transport supplies for the journey, including food for drovers and pack animals. The items caravanners transport are determined by the route they take. The majority of caravanners who travel to the salt flats do so with loads designed to last the entire round trip rather than with items or commodities to trade in exchange for salt. Their cargo includes a variety of commodities such as food, containers, cooking equipment, and personal belongings for drovers and pack animals (see appendix A).

Highland salt caravanners must also bring hay for their pack animals. Unlike camels, donkeys and mules are unable to graze on trees or consume low-lying vegetation. Highland caravanners typically allow their camels to graze, but they must calculate how much hay will be required for their donkeys and mules for the one-way trip to the salt flat. On the way to the salt flat, each animal usually carries its own hay. The lowland territory provides all the supplies for lowland caravanners. Highland caravanners, however, rely on lowland pastoralists for provisions on their way home. On the return journey—or in the event that a repeat trip between the salt flat to Afar town (where they unload salt to warehouses) is necessary—caravanners must buy hay from Afar pastoralist villages. In fact, only a few settlements along the route fit this description, and in my research, I found only two that did. Some caravanners bring extra hay from the highlands and leave it with the women who sell water containers, intending to pick it up on their way back to their homes. On their journey back from the salt flats, donkeys and mules are typically forced to go without nourishment for at least one day. Water is essential for both drovers and pack animals and is transported using *sar* (water containers) obtained at Berhaile.

The salt caravanners procure at the salt flat is cut into blocks for transportation and distribution. Each block of salt from the Afar Salt Lake is standardized

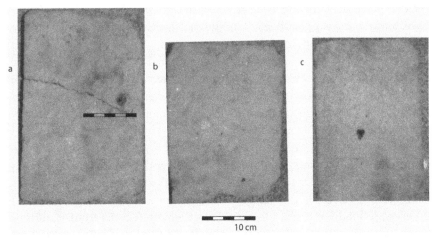

10 cm

FIGURE 5.3. *Three types of salt blocks: a* = gole'o, *b* = gerawayni, *c* = ankarabe. *Photo by Helina S. Woldekiros.*

into different weights and sizes. I measured the three standard sizes of salt blocks processed at the salt source, called *gole'o*, *gerawayni*, and *ankarabe* (figure 5.3, appendix B). Their sizes ultimately change after they arrive at secondary warehouses in the highlands. Here, they are shaped into another standard block, called an *amole*. *Amole* are further divided in half or crushed to a coarse salt or a fine grain in towns and villages before being sold in shops. Standardization of salt blocks has a long history in the region, and blocks have been used as currency. A variety of standard sizes were recorded in the early twentieth century. For example, the Italian geographical mission reported its observation of three different standard salt blocks that were traded and consumed in the early twentieth century: an *amole*, which was a bar used as money; an *abroita*, which was twice the size of an *amole* and was used as money and for consumption; and a *ganfur*, which was three times the size of an *amole* and was used only for food (Pankhurst 1968; Tancredi 1903). In the 1930s, Raimondo Franchetti (1935) also reported that salt from the Danakil was initially cut into a large block that was later divided into eight *amoles*. Standardized measurement of salt blocks from the Danakil prior to the early twentieth century is scarce.

Caravanners attach these salt blocks to the pack animals' saddles using leather, fiber, or plastic ropes. As the salt is not packed in containers, caravanners rely on sturdy packsaddles brought from home to protect the animals' backs. Pack padding is applied in layers and is standardized for the different animal species. These pack pads are important because without them, the salt will damage the animals' skin as it melts from their sweat. These pack pads are also used by pack drovers for sleeping at overnight camps. Hay and water are also placed on the animal.

Personal possessions are usually easily visible and are tied to wooden hooks (*anabu, koree, koyeta*) using a rope, whereas foodstuffs are generally put in a synthetic sack.

Departure places for caravans include residential settlements, short- and long-term camping grounds, and the salt flat itself. The majority of long-term campsites are used for overnight stays, and they serve as a resting location for caravanners traveling to and from the salt flats after a long day on the road. Long-term campsites are found at roughly 20-km intervals along the route; however, they are not equally spaced.

Campsites for long-term use in the highlands are typically placed adjacent to or outside small farming communities; in the low deserts, they are generally located next to or outside small permanent pastoralist communities. For drovers, being close to villages is advantageous, since it allows them to access water and, if necessary, food. Aside from that, campsites provide security from assaults by carnivorous animals (mostly jackals) and raids by adjacent ethnic groups (however irregular). Such campsites are large because they may be occupied at night by as many as 700 to 1,000 caravanners and 6,000 animals. The number of drovers and pack animals given here is based on my estimation from scanning the campgrounds at night, previous studies, and information from tax collectors (Apaak 2008; Pankhurst 1961; Wilson 1976). Given that most of the salt for northern Ethiopia is derived from the salt flats and is accessible by caravan only, the large numbers at these campsites are not surprising.

Brokers

Salt brokers connect caravanners with warehouse owners in bigger markets and towns and are also important participants in the salt trade. Although there are several salt warehouses and markets along the trade route, caravanners prefer to sell the vast majority of their load through brokers. As part-time salt traders, caravanners do not have the time or the resources to sell salt directly in the market or to network with warehouses or individual shop owners and merchants. As a result, it is worthwhile for them to hire brokers to act as facilitators.

Brokers are not wealthier than warehouse owners, but they are much higher up the economic ladder than caravanners or salt miners. Brokers are a diverse group that can be found in Berhaile, the first Afar town on the route. Some work as small-scale brokers, negotiating on caravanners' behalf or connecting caravanners with primary warehouse owners. Others are large-scale brokers who rent trucks to major warehouse owners in highland towns and cities. Salt merchants also travel from Tigray and Afar. During my fieldwork, I interviewed brokers in warehouses, markets, and coffee shops, speaking to nine in total: five from Tigray and four from Afar.

Brokers facilitate the distribution of salt in two ways. First, they directly connect salt caravanners with salt warehouse owners, allowing caravanners

TABLE 5.3. Summary of salt price in 2010

Salt Type	Salt Flat	Berhaile	Mekelle	Hometowns
Size	Ethiopian Birr	Ethiopian Birr	Ethiopian Birr	
Gole'o	2.5	10.5	19	18
Gerawayni	1.0	8.0	14	12
Ankarabe	0.65	5.0	0	0

to offload their salt at the warehouses. Second, they rent trucks that transport salt from lowland towns to larger warehouses in the highlands (although some warehouse owners send their own trucks to brokers in the lowlands). In highland Ethiopia, the use of brokers has a long history. Aksumite kings (ca. 600 CE) used to send their brokers, accompanied by warriors, to regions far beyond the Aksumite territory to acquire resources such as gold, iron, and exotic animals (Kobishchanov 1979).

Caravanners benefit from using brokers to sell salt because they are guaranteed immediate cash payment for their load. They also get a chance to make at least two trips from the salt flat to the first salt warehouse in Berhaile before returning home. The disadvantage is that caravanners receive very little money from brokers compared to the profit they would gain if they sold their salt directly in the market. The price of rock salt increases considerably with distance from the salt flat, with the cost of small bars (*gole'o*) increasing fourfold at Berhaile, 60 km from the salt flat, and eight times at Mekelle, 160 km away (table 5.3). These figures reveal a considerable difference in the price of salt once it leaves the salt flat, becoming six to twelve times more expensive in the highlands. Participants in Mekelle, the main highland town, discussed with me the fuel and labor costs associated with transporting salt from Berhaile to Mekelle. The caravanners are aware of this price differential, and some caravanners take the salt all the way to their hometowns with their animals and get the same price as the people who own trucks.

The price of salt today is determined by warehouse owners and brokers, since caravanners do not market directly. Because salt increases in price as it moves farther away from its source, it is more profitable for caravanners to deliver salt to larger towns and markets themselves; however, it takes longer to get to these places with their loads, and it might take weeks or months to sell their supply. The guarantee of immediate cash from warehouse owners and brokers for their entire load is immensely attractive.

Market System

While caravanners' participation in the salt trade did not extend beyond short- and medium-range trade routes during my fieldwork, it may have done so

2,000 years ago, during the Aksumite period. Today, salt distribution involves several stages and phases, including market-based distribution. While the initial phase begins with salt caravanners, the broader market system involves a web of participants—including brokers, wholesale distributors or warehouse owners, shop owners, the state, residents of settlements, salt miners, and salt cutters. The Afar trade route is linked to several highland market towns that distribute salt. From these regional markets, the salt's farther destinations—and its prices—are subject to socioeconomic and political influences.

In the eighteenth, nineteenth, and twentieth centuries, the salt market was well established in the Ethiopian highlands and extended beyond the eastern escarpment. During the nineteenth and early twentieth centuries, the main route for salt transport was Asmara (Eritrea), Mekelle (Ethiopia), and Dassie (Ethiopia) (Gebrelibanos 2009). Salt was distributed throughout the region and beyond from a series of markets located in towns along this major highway. Hentalo, Samra, Saqota, and Balassa were among the towns used as distribution hubs. The market centers in these towns effectively linked the salt distribution towns on the eastern escarpment to another important route to the northwest—the Basso-Gondar-Adwa-Massaw route. Naturally, markets in towns closer to the trade route and the salt source had a competitive advantage over markets farther away. Samra, for example, benefited from its location at a crossroads between key capital towns in the western, northern, and eastern regions and what was the major salt trade route from the sixteenth century until the end of the nineteenth century (Gebrelibanos 2009). Samra was a prominent salt market until the emerging city Mekelle surpassed it at the end of the nineteenth century. Tsegaye Berhe Gebrelibanos (2009) contends that the salt trade not only provided state revenue in the nineteenth and early twentieth centuries but also played a significant role in urbanizing towns along the trade route. As a result of a competitive salt market, new towns emerge while others decline. The development of Mekelle is inextricably linked to the salt market.

In the eighteenth, nineteenth, and twentieth centuries, foreign travelers remarked on the amount of salt that circulated in the major salt markets of the Ethiopian and Eritrean highlands. The amount reported appears to vary greatly. Werber Munzinger (1868, 1869), a Swiss administrator and explorer, for example, estimated that 30 million *amole* were moved annually in the early nineteenth century. The Egyptian governor of Massawa, Arakel Bey, reported in 1875 that 31.2 million *amoles* were traded each year (Douin [1869–1873] 1933; Pankhurst 1968). A few years later, the Italian geographical mission reported an annual output of 11.5 million *amole* (Tancredi 1903). This variation could be due to a number of factors, including the fact that these early travelers did not actually visit the salt source in Danakil. Annual quotas may also have varied as a result of social conflict on the route—some years saw fewer participants because of conflict between Christian and Muslim caravans—or the seasonal nature of the mining. In the 1960s and 1970s, Richard Trevor Wilson (1976) documented the distribution of 36 million *amole* in the market system. Today, the market system moves 70,000 tons of salt, with wholesale distributors/warehouse owners, shops, and the state dominating the volume and scope of salt distribution.

Wholesale Distributors/Warehouse Owners

The second stage of salt distribution begins with caravanners selling their salt to warehouse owners in the Afar and Tigray regions. Warehouse owners are usually wealthier than caravanners and salt miners. Salt miners, however, have the potential to become warehouse owners, whereas that is not an option for caravanners. I interviewed twelve warehouse owners, ranging in age from thirty-four to eighty years: ten in the highlands and two in the lowlands (appendix C).

I divide warehouses into two types: primary and secondary. Caravans returning from the salt flats have direct contact with primary warehouses. Caravanners unload salt at these warehouses before returning to the salt flats for another round or heading home. The majority of primary warehouses are in Berhaile, an Afar town. This, however, has only been the case since the 1990s. Previously, caravans delivered salt directly to the highlands, as far north as Mekelle.

Some caravanners still transport salt to the highlands today, but these are mostly Samra caravanners who prefer to deliver salt to warehouses in their hometowns or sell it themselves at Samra's open-air market. This market has designated areas for salt vendors. Salt is usually piled directly on the ground or delivered to these areas in fiber sacks. Samra is located in the highlands at a major crossroads between the Tigray and Amhara regions, and it was an important salt market town during the sixteenth century, making it a popular destination for salt buyers. Large town markets are usually found within 2–5 km of caravanners' homes.

Secondary warehouses are located in the highlands and are responsible for the regional distribution of salt. Secondary warehouses, unlike primary warehouses, do not have direct contact with caravanners. Rather, salt is supplied to them by brokers or primary warehouses. Trucks, for example, transport salt from Berhaile to secondary warehouses. The secondary warehouse owner reshapes the salt to a smaller *amole* size and distributes it regionally. In contrast, primary warehouse owners do not process salt onsite. They simply collect salt from caravanners and resell it to a broker or a wholesaler.

Both primary and secondary warehouses have permanent structures in specific market areas. The warehouse buildings are either rented or purchased by the owners. As a result, warehouse sizes vary depending on the owner's economic capital. Warehouses are one-room structures that are typically arranged in rows.

Since warehouse owners have to pay to truck salt from the Afar region and process it into bars, they raise the market price for salt from their warehouses accordingly. Price is also affected by when, where, and how salt is distributed. Warehouse owners transport salt over long distances, all the way to Addis Ababa (800 km) and beyond, as well as to major cities and towns in the south, east, and west, including Jimma, Wolega, Arsi, and Gambella (850 km). Salt is also transported all the way to Sudan (1,000 km).

Shop Owners

Shops range from single-room establishments to open-air markets. Shop owners sell a variety of subsistence goods, from grain to household goods, in addition to salt. Shop owners may have an economic status equal to or lower than that of warehouse owners, depending on the size of their shop and the quantity of merchandise they sell. They are usually the last people on the trade node that connects the salt flat to the market and are in charge of distributing salt to customers. Shop owners vary in age, gender, and socioeconomic status; I found more women in this occupation within the salt trade than in other categories. During business hours, I interviewed eighteen shop owners, four of whom were women and fourteen of whom were men. All were from the Tigray region. Shop owners control the price of salt by raising it when salt production at the salt flat is low and lowering it when there is surplus production. In either case, they are in a good position to influence the salt market.

The State

The state also participates in the market system by collecting taxes at three points along the salt route. The first point is Hamed Ela on the journey to the salt flat, where caravanners pay a tax per donkey, mule, and camel to Afar regional or district administrators. Tax is collected at this point, before the salt is acquired, to avoid wearing out the pack animals (they must typically stand in line for at least two hours). Tax is also collected from both warehouse owners and shop owners. All of these taxes are collected and logged by government workers. Today, it can be argued that the salt trade is profitable for the government, which incurs minimal costs in the form of the salaries of the civil servants who collect the taxes.

Residents/Settlements

The Afar salt trade relies heavily on towns, villages, and settlements at strategic points along the trade route, such as mountain passes and watering holes. Both the highland and lowland sections of the route have a settlement hierarchy. Larger settlements are densely populated and have state government representatives, market areas, religious centers, and salt warehouses. Smaller settlements are occupied by small highland farmers and mobile pastoralists. Residents who participate in the trade include town elders, retired caravanners, donkey merchants, vendors (of tea, coffee, soda, water, food, and hay), and town administrators. These settlements make the difficult donkey and camel travel between the highlands and lowlands manageable. The services they provide include logistics, food for drovers and pack animals, and security for caravanners from looters and large carnivores. Village prosperity may come from agriculture or the salt trade and is seasonal. There is also a difference in size and specialization between larger settlements found in high-altitude farming towns and smaller foothill towns located along the salt trade route, where the farming potential is limited.

Salt Miners and Salt Cutters

Salt miners are also essential participants in the Afar salt trade. I interviewed thirteen salt miners: five from the highland Tigray region and eight from the lowland Afar region (appendix C). The role of miners at Lake Asale is clearly defined according to culture and occupational specialization. There are two types of salt mining specialists—the *fokolo* from the highlands and the *hadeli* from the lowlands. The main task of the *fokolo* is to carve out salt slabs, which the *hadeli* cut into different standard sizes. This task is materialized by tools employed, including a *godama* (a metal ax) and a *hodu* (a thick pole) used to mark the ground and lever the slab (figures 5.4 and 5.5). The *fokolo* carve out 1–2 m² of salt at a time, after which the *hadeli* cut and shape the rock salt using *godma*, an ax with a sharp, wide edge (figure 5.6). Both ax heads are made of iron and are locally produced and purchased in the highlands. There is no iron mining or production in the lowlands.

Salt miners work in groups of three or four, consisting of two to three *fokolos* and one *hadeli*. If the group is made up of experienced miners with a large number of clients, the *hadeli* may also have an assistant known as a *kudu*. These are typically young boys ages eleven to fourteen who have the potential to progress to the status of *hadeli* over time.

The *fokolos* I interviewed said that throughout the salt season, they work for two months and then go home to the highlands for a month of rest. This process is called *hidalgo*. During their two-month stay in the lowlands, they rent rooms from Afar pastoralists in Hamed Ela town. The Afar miners live close enough to return home at the end of each workday.

On the salt trail, production and transportation occur in the following order. Miners provide salt bars to their clients on a first-come, first-served basis. Individual caravanners are responsible for loading any salt they purchase. At the salt flat, caravanners pay salt miners according to the number of pack animals loaded. The price paid per pack animal varies based on the size and type of animal. Caravanners pay more for camels and mules than they do for donkeys because the former carry more salt blocks. However, there can be variations within the same species; large camels carry greater loads than small camels do. The same is true for donkeys and

FIGURE 5.4. Godama—*narrow metal ax used for mining salt. Photo by Helina S. Woldekiros.*

FIGURE 5.5. Hodu—*salt mining tool. Photo by Helina S. Woldekiros.*

FIGURE 5.6. Godma—*wide ax used to shape salt. Photo by Helina S. Woldekiros.*

mules. In 2010, caravanners paid the salt miners eleven Ethiopian birr (US $0.57) for one camel, one mule, or two donkeys—or five birr (US $0.26) per donkey. In addition to making these cash payments, the caravanners also provide *birkuta* (bread) and water for the miners. The three or four people in the mining group distribute the cash, bread, and water among themselves.

TAX AND THE PRICE OF SALT

Salt caravanners do not pay for the salt itself, which is free, but rather for the labor of the *fokolos* and *hadeli* who mine and cut it. This arrangement is consistent with the pastoral approach to pastures, wherein grazing land is a free resource shared by the community. As a result, salt in the Danakil is not appropriated by lowlanders. The Afar are proud that the use of a commercially important resource such as salt is consistent with their principle of the use of other natural resources—including water. Caravanners pay the miners, but the miners come from the lowlands and highlands. In the eighteenth and nineteenth centuries, caravanners used to mine salt themselves (Abir 1966; Pearce 1831; Wilson 1976), but the hard work of both mining and transporting salt at the same time is not something their twenty-first-century counterparts are willing to undertake. On the outgoing journey, caravanners also pay a tax per donkey, mule, and camel to Afar regional or district administrators in Hamed Ela.

During the Aksumite and medieval periods, salt may have been taxed as well. Agula, the medieval Tigray city located 80 km southeast of Aksum (the Aksumite capital city) and 45 km north of Mekelle, was one of the most important southerly points on the north-south trading route. The collection of salt taxes at Agula was first mentioned in the sixteenth century during the reign of Emperor Eyasu II (Crawford 1958; Huntingford 1989). Agula was most likely the first major town to receive lowland salt and collect taxes.

However, the tax records of Emperors Amda Seyon (ca. 1314–1344 CE) (British Library, London, OR 481, 124R) and Tewodros II (ca. 1818–1868 CE) provide a good indication of the amount of salt bar collected from salt traders between the fourteenth and nineteenth centuries. According to their records, traders' taxes were collected monthly or per trip (Abir 1966, 1968; Gebrelibanos 2009; Gebre-Meskel 1992; Pankhurst 1961). Amda Seyon's tax records show that the number of *amole* individuals paid to the state ranged from four to forty bars per month or per payment (British Library, London, OR 481, 124R). The state then distributed the salt bars collected from individuals to pay the salaries of state employees such as soldiers and artisans. Today, as in the medieval period, the state collects taxes from each caravan based on the number of animals in the caravan. To pay these taxes, caravans gather outside the town Melabdi, where they count out and deliver their tax in cash to a state representative, who issues a receipt and keeps a log of funds collected. This log is a one-of-a-kind source of information on the magnitude of recent trade. Wilson (1976, 1991) studied these logs and produced a detailed analysis of taxes paid per animal, empirical data on pack animals, and development issues of animals on the trail—all of which agreed with the calculations and observations I made during my fieldwork.

USE OF SALT IN THE HIGHLANDS AND LOWLANDS

In addition to being a significant source of revenue, salt has long been an essential resource for Ethiopia and the Horn of Africa, serving a variety of functions. Today, the salt mined in the Danakil Depression is used as a condiment for human consumption throughout Ethiopia. It has been a key culinary item for centuries and is the main ingredient in the two most important condiments in highland and lowland cuisine: *berbere* (chili pepper) and *shiro* (chickpea powder), consumed daily in both the highlands and the lowlands. To produce 10 kg of *berbere* and 5 kg of *shiro*, at least 1 kg of salt is required. Salt is also used to dry meat, such as in the production of *quanta* (dried beef), a highland delicacy. Most families in rural areas purchase ground salt or rock salt, whereas city dwellers consume ground salt in a variety of grain sizes.

Salt from the Danakil has also long been used as an important source of nutrition for animals, aiding digestion, lactation, and fertility. Herders understand that salt is essential for their livestock and that it increases animal production.

Rock salt is used as a livestock lick and is a highly valued commodity among highland agriculturalists and lowland pastoralists.

Danakil salt has also been used in the processing of hides and the production of dyes. In the Aksumite period, leather production was a significant source of revenue for the people. Thousands of stone scrapers, which were used to prepare hide, have been discovered at Aksumite sites, including the city Aksum (see D. Phillipson 2000b). Even into the nineteenth century, hide manufacture remained a significant source of income for many people. Ethiopia's leather industry is still a significant source of export revenue.

In addition, salt is used ceremonially and medicinally. Highlanders and lowlanders add salt to the wounds of humans and animals. However, salt is not used on large animal wounds, such as those I saw on camels' backs, because it aggravates the pain. Furthermore, there is a fossilized salt source in the Danakil, 1 km from the salt lake, that Afar pastoralists maintain for ritual and medical use. The Afar regard this salt as potent and valuable, and taking any amount requires permission from community leaders. This therapeutic salt is grayish and distinct from the rock salt that caravanners trade.

Historically, until the late eighteenth century, salt served as a form of currency alongside iron, gold, and imported coins. In medieval Ethiopia, blocks of *amole* were used exclusively as a form of currency for trade and exchange (Pankhurst 1961, 1968). Indeed, the use of salt as currency dates back to Aksumite times, as early as 525 CE, according to Cosmas Indicopleustes. The Aksumites, for example, were said to have traded salt for gold and meat with a region in the south known as Sasu (see Kobishchanov 1966; D. Phillipson 2012). Although the use of salt blocks as a major currency item is mentioned as far back as the sixth century, most of the information we have about salt's use as a monetary item comes from travel reports from the eighteenth and nineteenth centuries.

In the eighteenth century, salt was used as money, on its own or in conjunction with monetary currency. For example, salt was used as small change in the Ethiopian economy until the early twentieth century, when Austrian Maria Theresa thalers—a type of silver bullion coin—were in circulation (Gebrelibanos 2009). Because the Maria Theresa thalers were used in specific contexts, salt bars were widely utilized to fill these gaps. Salt bars were particularly popular as a convenient payment method for small and medium-sized transactions, as well as for many transactions in rural areas. Even after the introduction of Ethiopian coin currency, the use of salt bars persisted. For example, in the early twentieth century, Emperor Menelik (1889–1913 CE) issued his own currency. It took some time for his newly minted coins to supplant the preferred *amole* transactions (Pankhurst 1968).

Salt was also seen as a luxury item to be distributed by the elite to allies and visitors (Pankhurst 1961). In the late nineteenth century, the salt tax from the

Danakil mines drew the attention of foreign governments, which attempted to exert influence over the revenue generated (Munzinger 1869). Belgium made such an attempt in the 1830s, followed by Egypt in the 1870s and Italy in the 1890s. These efforts were unsuccessful.

NICHE ECONOMY STRATEGIES AND THE POLITICAL ECONOMY OF CONTEMPORARY NORTHERN ETHIOPIA

The northern Ethiopian environment is extremely unpredictable and requires constant strategizing and specialization changes. The salt trade is one of many economic strategies practiced in northern Ethiopia, and I argue that the modern salt trade is an economic niche for salt caravanners. It is clear that there are multiple stakeholders in the contemporary salt trade and that the benefits gained are different for each stakeholder. Salt miners and caravanners, for instance, participate in the salt trade at a subsistence level. Those who are higher on the economic ladder—including warehouse owners, brokers, and shop owners—profit from the trade. At the top of the economic ladder are those living in urban areas, whose lifestyle is completely different from those in rural areas. In the following sections, I discuss varied economic strategies that convey a broader understanding of the economic context of the salt caravan trade. Urban populations, including government employees and civil servants, are excluded from this discussion (figure 5.7 provides a sketch of the status of salt caravanners in the larger system).

The leading economic strategies practiced by Tigray agriculturalists and Afar pastoralists in northern Ethiopia include highland farming, mobile pastoralism in the lowlands, caravan and other trade, pack animal rental, construction and salt mine labor, redistribution/wholesale of salt and agricultural products, and reciprocity with extended family units and clan in the lowlands.

Highlanders in and around central and southern Tigray prioritize farming activities during the rainy seasons. However, the people I spoke to said the farmland generally supports only the most immediate family/household needs. Farmers in this region supplement their income through the salt trade. They use the cash they obtain to buy staples such as coffee, tea, sugar, chili powder, and *shiro*; electronics such as flashlights, batteries, and radios; and other necessities such as building materials, clothes, and shoes for their families. They are also able to purchase cattle, sheep, goats, and seeds for their farms and pay membership fees to *eqûb, eder, mehaber,* and *senbete* that fulfill community needs.

In Ethiopian culture, in addition to *senbete*, several sorts of traditional social arrangements play an important role in sustaining individuals and communities. One such organization is *eqûb*, a savings and credit association in which members pool their financial resources to fulfill their financial objectives, such as saving for significant expenses or obtaining credit. On the basis of trust and

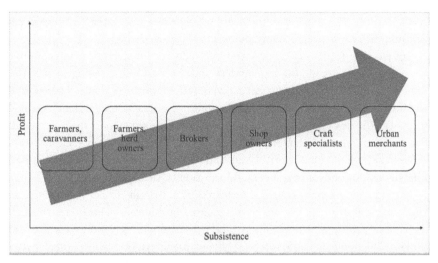

FIGURE 5.7. *Model of the economic ladder in modern-day rural northern Ethiopia*

mutual support, members routinely donate a defined amount of money, and one member receives the entire total each cycle, as selected by a lottery or by consensus. *Eders* are another type of social arrangement that primarily provides informal support and assists the grieving with funeral-related tasks while also being called upon to help with a variety of other social events. *Mehabers* are social or cultural associations that bring individuals together around a shared interest, profession, or social identity—providing a sense of community, belonging, and support for members through activities such as organizing social events, religious celebrations, cultural festivals, and advocacy work.

In the lowlands, pastoralism is the dominant way of life, and the Afar move their herds between dry- and wet-season camps. Afar families diversify their herds by keeping sheep and goats near their settlement for household consumption and cattle and camels for subsistence. Camels are especially vital because they carry household goods during seasonal mobility. Herds are also used to strengthen social ties with clan members and extended family units. Some Afar participate in the salt trade during the dry season to support their family unit, as they often sustain two or more wives and several children. Trade in salt is also important for the Afar because it allows them direct access to cash, which helps them acquire necessary highland agricultural products such as wheat, barley, sorghum, *te'f*, flour, and rice.

Both Tigray and Afar people use wage labor to make ends meet during low-yield seasons in farming or salt trading. Labor can be provided for house construction, mountain terracing, and salt mining. Salt mining is undertaken by both highlanders and lowlanders, but the division of labor is based on skill and specialization. The work is arduous and requires resilient, experienced workers. Salt miners have seasonal clients, but salt is always in demand.

Salt caravan trade and other forms of trade are important niche economic strategies for many Tigray highlanders and the pastoralists living in the Afar region. As an industry, the Afar salt caravan trade is contingent on environmental variables and closely follows the highland farming season and lowland seasonal mobility. The destinations of highland and lowland caravanners include the salt flat, warehouses, and markets. These prescribed destinations give caravanners limited strategies on the caravan trail, and these strategies require careful scheduling to accommodate other highland subsistence strategies.

The highlanders make eight to fourteen trips to the salt flat per year, using donkeys, mules, and camels. Caravanners engage in the salt trade in two ways: through direct access to the market economy and exchange with warehouse owners and brokers. Selling salt in the market and relying on the market price is a much better option for caravanners because the market price is at least three times higher than the price offered by warehouse owners and brokers. However, this option is risky because the markets in the caravanners' towns are very small; it might take them days, weeks, or even months to sell their entire load. In contrast, a transaction with warehouse owners and brokers guarantees immediate cash for the entire load.

Afar lowlanders travel to the salt flat with their close kin and split the profit from the salt trade among them. In the past and similar to the highland caravanners, they would go to Mekelle city in the highland to deliver salt. However, this is no longer possible due to city regulations that prohibit pack animals, and they now conduct most of their transactions in the lowlands.

The Afar are also connected to other market systems in the highlands and neighboring pastoralist regions. They supply markets with animals such as goats and cattle and animal products such as camel milk and animal hides. Their trade schedule is different from that of the highlanders because it is determined by seasonal mobility and the division of labor within the household or extended family unit. For example, men will go to dry-season camps to herd livestock, while women will stay at the home base or go to the market to sell milk and other pastoralist products.

Reciprocity with extended family units is also an important economic strategy for Afar families. To minimize risks associated with the pastoral way of life in this region, a householder may borrow from or lend herds to their extended family unit or clan members. This strategy is usually applied when one needs to bring a new bull into the herd or when there is an emergency. For example, if a household loses all its herds, it is provided with a starter herd. Marriage alliances are also used to keep herds within the family unit.

Camel and donkey rental is another source of income in the Tigray highlands. About 80 percent of the population lives in rural areas and does not have access to modern trucks. Most agricultural products—including crops, animals, and animal products—are transported from rural villages and towns to urban areas and market centers using pack animals. People who rent out their pack animals, including those who have extra pack animals or who are not able to make the trip to the salt flats, are usually wealthier than their neighbors. Renters pay pack animal rent through profit sharing, with the owner entitled to half of the salt or grain sale profit.

A redistribution/wholesale economic strategy is an extension of the caravan trade and is practiced by a few rich individuals who situate themselves in both urban and rural areas. The main stakeholders in this category are warehouse owners, brokers, and shop owners. They depend on salt supplied by both pack caravans and trucks. They must own or rent a space to accumulate and sell salt. People who use this economic strategy do not necessarily need to engage in other activities; they can remain in the salt trade throughout the year using salt they accumulate in their warehouses.

Political Economy and Niche Economies

The range of niche economic strategies rural Ethiopian highlanders and low-landers engage in on a subsistence basis is affected by the region's political economy. Here, I discuss interactions among internal and external variables and their effect on the larger economic system.

Internal Variables

Internal variables such as work ethic and access to resources can influence an individual's success within an economic system. In northern Ethiopia, high-landers and lowlanders practice different primary economic strategies subject to different variables. Internal variables that influence participation in highland farming include the availability of resources such as land and livestock. Farm size, individual strength, entrepreneurship, and social ties to community membership associations also affect highlanders' economic success. In the case of lowland pastoralists, household affiliation with extended family units and access to clan land determine success in the system.

Both highland farmers and lowland pastoralists rely on the salt caravan trade as a niche activity. Participation in the salt trade is affected by factors including herd ownership and the number of donkeys or camels available for salt transport, as well as the availability of pasture to sustain herds en route. The availability of pack animals (either for rent or ownership) creates a significant wealth difference among villagers. The ability to participate in wage labor as a niche strategy is also dependent on internal factors such as health, age, and sex. If people need labor, they can either request help from their social ties or hire laborers. In general, the internal variables that affect people's ability to employ multiple economic strategies are predictable, and Ethiopians have developed ways to deal with them.

External Variables

The success and failure of an individual in the broader economic system are also affected by a range of external variables, including the government and political and environmental conditions. These variables are mostly beyond the control of small-scale highland agriculturalists and lowland pastoralists.

Government influences small farmers and pastoralists in the salt trade through its effect on land ownership, taxes, and market locations. Since the 1990s, the region has seen increasing political stability and population growth. Today, Ethiopia has a population of approximately 95 million, with an annual population growth of 2 percent and a high ratio of young people to older people. More people are living in the highlands than in the lowlands, and the population increase has put pressure on the availability of farmland per household unit. Land is owned by the state; as a result, there is no guarantee of personal expansion unless one can accumulate capital through farming, trading, wage labor, or other avenues. Most caravanners from the highlands would rather farm than engage in the salt trade. However, they told me that even though farming is relatively easier than the salt caravan trade, the harvest yield is not always guaranteed, the yield does not usually do more than feed the household, and crop sales are not profitable. The salt trade is hard work, but they are guaranteed an immediate cash return with each journey.

Nonetheless, the salt trade, for both highland and lowland caravanners, is not as profitable as it once was. One major reason for this is that caravanners are no longer allowed to drive their herds all the way to big highland cities like Mekelle, where demand and prices for salt are high.

Today, tax is collected from salt caravanners by the Afar regional government at the salt flat and from wholesalers by the state in the highlands. Tax changes at tolls might affect the number of herds caravanners take to the salt flat. In addition, a sudden increase in taxes might not be compatible with logistical expenditure. In the Aksumite period, salt taxes might have been collected at several stops.

Additional external variables to consider include political conditions such as war, conflict, and the environment. Conflict affects the availability of labor for farming, herding, salt mining, and trading. Climate conditions can change over time, and seasonal rainfall is unpredictable. There have been years in northern Ethiopia when the rainy season started earlier or later than expected, creating a gap in farming and related activities. In the lowlands, drought is common, with a subsequent reduction in livestock size. The farmers I interviewed during my fieldwork also mentioned that during harvest failure seasons, they were forced farther south—even beyond the capital—to participate in development projects such as mining and road and dam construction to support their families.

Finally, insights I gained from the present-day niche economy in northern Ethiopia helped me understand the motivation and investment required to participate in the Afar salt trade during the Aksumite period. External variables that affect and affected farmers and herders both today and in the eighteenth and nineteenth centuries—such as war, climate change, drought, changes in government policy, and so on—could also have affected Aksumite farmers and pastoralists. Indeed, the collapse of the Aksumite state has been linked to a number of external factors, including regional and global wars, drought, social erosion, and human-caused landscape degradation. Deforestation caused by millennia of cutting down wood for construction, cooking, and mining is seen to have degraded the north Ethiopian and Eritrean highlands during the pre-Aksumite period, exposing the landscape to wind and erosion of fertile soil, which resulted in people moving farther east and south to look for more fertile farmlands and green pastures for their herds (Ruiz-Giralt et al. 2021; Terwilliger et al. 2014). Changes in government policy were also visible in the city of Aksum's decline at the end of the sixth century.

At the end of the Aksumite Empire, the political economy of the Aksumite state was also influenced by events occurring outside Africa. For example, the decline and loss of power of the Roman Empire, Aksum's powerful ally, as a result of the Persians' and later the Arabs' rise to power in the Mediterranean region and the Red Sea area is believed to have weakened the Aksumites' political and economic standing globally as well as locally. The Aksumites eventually lost access to the Red Sea waterway/maritime trade route and hence to the world market and their trading partners (Finneran 2007).

At the conclusion of the Aksumite period, there was also a significant collapse in the internal economy. This is manifested in a decline in the number of big monuments built, a decrease in the size of the population—particularly in the capital cities, such as Aksum—and a decrease in the grade of coinage struck, which is frequently related to inflation (D. Phillipson 2012).

MATERIAL CORRELATES OF THE SALT TRADE

There are at least seven nodes on the Afar Salt Caravan Route where material traces of the salt trade can be identified: 1. caravan campsites, 2. the route, 3. salt warehouses, 4. salt shops, 5. sar makers' residences, 6. tax polls, and 7. the salt flat. Caravan organization in particular leaves a distinctive pattern on the landscape at both regional and local scales.

Understanding ancient caravan activity requires analysis of the material correlates of caravan activity within the larger economic settings of caravan traders. Although the material aspects of salt caravans leave tangible clues in the archaeological record, the social organization of these activities is difficult to glean through the archaeological record alone. To address this issue, I turn to ethnoarchaeology to formulate hypotheses and relational analogies (*sensu* Wylie 1985) for understanding the social and organizational aspects of the Afar salt trade. In the Afar setting, the Afar salt source is located more than 220 km from the ancient Aksumite heartland and requires trekking one of the most rugged terrains on earth with bulky salt to carry. I argue, therefore, that a large caravan party must have been organized from the highlands to acquire Afar salt for the state or the general public.

In contemporary northern Ethiopia, caravans exclusively transport salt, which is only available in the Afar. Everything caravanners carry is intended for the logistical support of the salt enterprise. Modern caravanners on the Afar salt route accumulate material culture on the route and at campsites, rest areas, and the salt flat. However, the scale and redundancy of material accumulation vary between these sites. The highest redundancy and greatest concentration of caravan residue are found at overnight (long-term) campsites—particularly those located in the transition zones between the highlands and the lowlands, due to the high level of traffic in these areas. Such zones are not only mountain passes relied on by pack caravans but are also merging places for caravanners traveling from different highland and lowland villages. Figure 5.1 shows the three major passes identified in this study: Desi'a, Usot, and Shiket. Thousands of caravanners camp at and pass through these areas every year, creating abundant residue on the salt caravan route. Indeed, in my study, I found archaeological sites and artifact scatters at all these places.

Long-term caravan campsites are usually situated on a large area of relatively level ground across a river or near or next to towns or villages. As mentioned earlier, the proximity of long-term campsites to towns and villages offers protection from looters and large carnivores and is logistically ideal. Caravanners, especially those from the highlands, need to replenish their provisions for the long trek to the salt flat and back. They do not camp at the same spot within a particular rest area. Drovers usually look for a relatively clean camping space or accept what is available. Long-term campsites are in the open air, and there is no time for caravanners to erect tents or temporary shelters. Instead, caravanners sleep on the ground next to their packs and piles of salt blocks. Cooking and other activities take place in the same area, resulting in an accumulation of residues on the ground surface. The accumulation of animal dung and hearths and the presence of distinctive round bread stones for cooking are characteristic signs of caravan camps. Long-term campsites are the most important sites for studies of caravan activity because of their location, high traffic, redundancy of materials, and length of occupation.

Overnight campsites near permanent pastoralist villages in the lowlands also accumulate an abundance of material culture. Such camping grounds are fixed areas. There are very few large flat sites close to villages or water suitable for camping. Villagers take advantage of the trade by provisioning caravanners but prefer that they camp at the edges of town to reduce the risk of disturbance resulting from the presence of so many strangers. Houses are also very close to each other, and it is thus not possible for caravanners to enter the villages with their herds—especially as the caravanners at overnight camps often number in the thousands. Herders cannot leave animals unattended because of the dangers of straying, predation, and theft. Even in the highlands, where houses are more dispersed, caravanners stay out of towns and villages to watch over their herds (which they brand to deter theft and assist in animal recovery). Caravanners are also mindful of the need not to disturb planted fields.

Material concentrations at short-term rest areas are less dense than those at long-term encampments. Here, caravanners usually camp for one or two hours in wide-open spaces with opportunities for grazing and perhaps shade trees. Natural rock shelters in the lowland portion of the route may accumulate abundant refuse due to their fixed positions on the landscape.

The single most readily identifiable signatures of the caravan trade are cooking hearths and stones. Caravanners use two types of hearths: small ones for making tea and coffee and larger ones for making bread. Today, bread is the fundamental meal of all caravanners and traders. Although caravanners from both the highlands and the lowlands start their journey with ready-made food, these rations only last two to three days. For the rest of the trip, the caravanners have to prepare fresh food or purchase provisions from highland or lowland settlements found along the route. They make fresh *birkuta* and *gogo* bread at long-term campsites. In the annual caravan setting, men cook for themselves on the trail—this is the only context in which highland Tigray or lowland Afar men cook.

Bread making is a group activity for Arho, and everyone in the group participates in the process. *Birkuta* is a round bread the size of a small soccer ball, and *gogo* is a flatbread about 5 cm thick made from unleavened dough. Most caravanners make *birkuta*, but only a few people make *gogo* on the route. *Birkuta*—made from flour (wheat, barley, or sorghum), water, and salt—is baked in an open-air fire over preheated, round sandstone cobbles (about 20) and smaller stones (about 150 to 200). Bakers place one preheated cobble inside the dough and then place the dough on top of the remaining stones (figure 5.8a, b). Fresh, hot charcoal is used to maintain the stones' heat until the bread is fully cooked, which takes twenty to thirty minutes. *Gogo* is also baked on top of preheated rocks. *Birkuta* is completely distinctive of caravan journeys and is never made at home. *Gogo* is cooked at home but usually on clay griddles. Members of the caravans I camped with told me that food cooks faster in the desert than it does in the highlands due to the difference in altitude.

 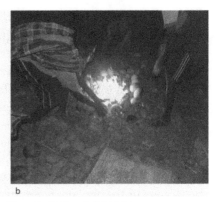

a b

FIGURE 5.8A, B. Birkuta *bread baking in camp. Photo by Helina S. Woldekiros.*

Material traces of the salt caravan can also be seen on the salt flats, but these wood or metal artifacts are perishable. Mining and cutting tools include *godama* (metal axes) and *godma* and *hodu* (thick sticks). Residues that accumulate along the trail include donkey, mule, and camel bones and dung; cloth; *sorit* (water sack containers); salt; rope, plastic, or fiber sacks (*madaberia*); and plastic bags. Warehouses also accumulate material residue from the salt trade. Modern warehouses are made of cement or rock block or are brick-walled buildings with corrugated iron roofs. The location of warehouses in the market and their proximity to the salt route constitute a useful proxy.

Finally, extensive material accumulation can be observed at the exit points of towns, in transitional places between the highlands and the lowlands, and at tax points. For example, the exit point of Hamed Ela accumulates a lot of dung, as well as cloth, ropes, bones, and *madaberia*.

Both short- and medium-term processes (Brooks and Yellen 1987; Nielsen 2000) create artifact clusters and activity areas on the landscape that are distinctive of the salt caravan trade. However, overnight (long-term) campsites demonstrate the highest concentration of material.

I identified the modern caravan route and feeder trails as well as state and local participants and social networks involved in the movement of perishable goods along the Afar trading route. The Afar trade route from the highlands to the lowland salt flats of the Danakil Depression was followed by a series of *chaînes opératoires* (sequences of operation). Participants included caravanners, brokers, warehouse owners, shop owners, salt miners, and residents of villages and towns. The functioning of a salt niche economy reveals the numerous advantages it provides both for farmers and herders as small-scale, seasonal participants and for brokers, more prominent traders, and the state as larger-scale, year-round participants. Participation in the Afar salt caravan trade makes up for subsistence farming and herding shortfalls. Many of these incentives for a salt niche economy and participation in the salt trade were also relevant in the Aksumite period. Ethnoarchaeological data discussed here also reveal that the trade route and the location of towns and villages are materialized in geographically predictable locales, demonstrating that particular artifacts such as bread stones provide strong indicators of the location of the salt route that allow archaeologists to recognize ancient caravan sites. Caravanners set up camp near sources of water and food, leaving traces of artifacts directly related to traders.

6

THE ARCHAEOLOGY OF THE SALT TRADE

Settlement Patterns and Features

To make salt trade feasible from the highlands to the Afar sources, it is clear—given geographic and cultural variability—that participation is needed from several categories of stakeholders. These categories include a range of traders and residents of settlements, towns, and villages from both highland and lowland areas. My contemporary research documented a structured but complex pack-based trade network that continues to this day and, as I will demonstrate, that has existed in one form or another for at least two millennia.

In this chapter, I turn to the archaeological evidence to examine the pathways and organization of the ancient salt route. Data on ancient caravan sites and settlements document the long-term nature of the salt trade between the highlands and the lowlands. To rank and typify resource utilization within sites, I discuss stratigraphic data, structures, and the interpretation of artifacts. After presenting these data sets, I examine their implications for elucidating the complex power relations within the Aksumite polity and among non-state and non-elite agents.

One of the particular contributions this research makes is its comparison of the location and structure of ancient settlements, churches, and campsites in

https://doi.org/10.5876/9781646424733.c006

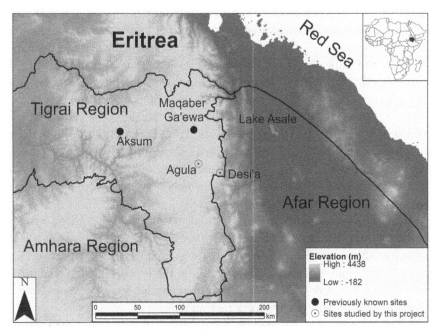

FIGURE 6.1. *Archaeological sites discovered by this project*

relation to the modern salt trail. These spatial data provide important insights concerning regional clients and participants. At a macro level, their strategic position indicates the nature of the links between the Aksumite state and the towns on the fringes of its polity. Through discussions of this spatial and material evidence, I demonstrate the existence and complexity of the ancient organization of local trade and its archaeological signature on the landscape, towns, and campsites.

SETTLEMENTS

Location and Macro-regional Patterns

The main regional Aksumite trade route ran from near Aksum northward toward the port of Adulis and the Red Sea. The Aksumites' exploitation of the lowland salt basin in the Afar and the organization of the salt trade resulted in towns and settlements in the eastern highlands far from the main Aksumite trade route, along long-distance and local trails leading eastward to the Afar salt flats, as well as distinctive settlements located in transitional zones between the highlands and the lowlands.

I discovered through survey and excavation that most of the contemporary towns on the salt trade route—Agula, Usot, and Desi'a—also have ancient components. In addition, the well-known pre-Aksumite sites Addi Kaweh and

Maqaber Ga'ewa lie close to the salt trade route (Dugast and Gajda 2014). All of these ancient towns are located 100 km south or east of Aksum—the center of the Aksumite state—along the edges of the eastern highlands, most densely concentrated in the districts of Atsbi Wonberta and Kelete Awulaelo (figure 6.1).

It is significant that the locations of ancient towns and churches in direct contact with the Afar salt route do not resemble those of nearby contemporary and ethnographically documented trader towns and churches. The contemporary buildings recorded in the ethnoarchaeological phase of this study lie on the tops of mountains or steep slopes and are hidden from view when one looks up from the present caravan trail. In contrast, the ancient Aksumite and medieval towns and churches near the trail were located closer to it, in landscapes where the slopes were less steep.

Ancient and modern caravan trails usually parallel rivers. Ancient villages and towns were situated on gentle slopes facing the trail, the river, and ancient churches. Ethnoarchaeological data indicate geographic and social reasons for this pattern. I found Aksumite church ruins on the lowest-elevation landforms, more than 1 km away from the ancient settlements but less than 100 m from a river and the ancient/contemporary caravan trail.

My research revealed that modern towns are sited in steep areas due to agricultural intensification and increased demand for flat areas for farming by a growing population. Today, even the sides of mountains are farmed in the northern Ethiopian highlands. The ancient salt trader towns on the eastern edges of the Ethiopian highlands form a north-south settlement ribbon on moderate slopes near the passes and paths of the trade route. Their placement speaks to the role of salt-related niche economies in the lives of highlanders and the subsistence strategy in places closer to the lowlands leading to the Afar salt sources versus better-watered areas with greater farming potential. The prominent modern towns in these districts—Haiki Mesihal (3,069 m asl [meters above sea level]), Atsbi (2,630 m asl), and Agula (1,930 m asl)—all overlie ancient towns. Today, these towns also have larger market centers than those in other regions, as well as rich oral histories and texts that refer to the historic salt trade (Pankhurst 1968). The lower-elevation towns Usot (500 m asl) and Desi'a (803 m asl), which overlay the ancient settlements I excavated, are smaller and lie in transitional zones between the northeastern highlands and the Afar lowlands (figure 6.1). Desi'a is a node, or articulation point, on the caravan trail where trails from at least five highland villages merge to descend along a single route to the salt flat. Today, both Usot and Desi'a towns are key camping and provisioning areas for caravanners descending from highland passes and caravan crossroads.

These border towns Usot and Desi'a are located close enough to the lowland salt flats and pastoral resources (within 70 km) and the highlands (within 35 km) to facilitate trade and exchange. The difference between these towns and those farther west in the highlands, like Agula and Atsbi, is that at the eastern edge of the highlands where Usot and Desi'a lie, the environment is not rich enough to allow year-round farming. This environmental variation has implications for both modern and ancient farmers and the organization of the ancient salt route.

Today, border towns far from the hubs of the Ethiopian highlands and close to ecotones also tend to utilize economic niches that are physically distant from their home environment. People in Desi'a, who live in a semiarid environment and are mostly smallholder farmers, are an example. They take advantage of the large caravan traffic that passes through their town by providing logistics (food, water, hay) and labor services to supplement their farming way of life. People who live in towns near the agricultural heartland of highland Ethiopia, in contrast, tend to use resources within their environment, such as rainfed agriculture and agricultural products, as well as trade by taking advantage of their proximity to large urban markets. This economic strategy is also found in other regions of the world and is often referred to by anthropologists as an *ecotone strategy* (Nicholson 1987, 1988; Senft 2009; Spengler, Frachetti, and Fritz 2013). The significance of ecotones and altitudinal variability in the location of ancient centers for trade and exchange has been particularly emphasized in the Andes (Berenguer 1994; Browman 1981; Nielsen 2000).

Since farming was not productive in the lower-altitude edges of the eastern Ethiopian highlands and could not support large, dispersed populations, the development of ancient towns at Agula, Atsbi, and Desi'a was unexpected. It is probable that these ancient towns arose as people settled near the trails to the Afar salt flats to profit from trade, as they continue to do today.

The towns Wukro, Agula, and Desi'a are located at the intersection of the local and regional trade routes and are key to understanding the extent of participation of the Aksumite state in the Afar salt trade. Wukro lies squarely on the major north-south Aksumite trade route leading north to the capital city Aksum and, farther, to the northern escarpment and port of Adulis. The other two sites lie farther east. Previous archaeological studies have shown that Wukro was a major religious center as early as the pre-Aksumite period (Wolf and Nowotnick 2010). These studies were mainly concerned with investigating the nature of a pre-Aksumite religious temple in Wukro named Maqaber Gawa and dedicated to the Sabean god Almaqah. However, the town's presence directly on the salt trade route leading from the highlands to the Afar Salt Lake suggests that the Aksumite state may have had an interest in the Afar salt trade—far from the center of power—as early as ca. 700 BC.

The landscape-scale settlement data presented in this book provide a basis for predicting the location of other ancient sites that may have played a role in the Aksumite salt trade from the Afar Depression. The data also suggest reasons people would have participated in local trade and how the Aksumite state may have played a direct role in the ancient salt trade. Information on the structure of ancient towns and caravan camps complements this larger-scale picture of the organization of ancient salt trading on the Afar route.

The Structure of Ancient Towns and Camps on the Afar Route

Excavation at the highland trader town ancient Agula and the ancient border town Desi'a yielded contextual information on ancient border and trader towns between the highlands and the lowlands, their role in the salt trade, and the life-ways of ancient towns and caravan campsites. To highlight the archaeological significance of these two types of towns and settlements to our understanding of the organization of the Afar salt trade, I first compare the stratigraphic signatures of the settlement sites Ona Adi Agway in ancient Agula and Ona Hahaile in ancient Desi'a. Common to both of these towns are the presence of ordinary houses or domestic structures and a lack of large, finely made elite buildings such as those found at Aksum, Yeha, and other northern highland towns. I argue that we do not see spectacular elite architecture in these locations because—like the present-day inhabitants of border towns in the region—members of the ancient communities Agula and Desi'a were involved in the salt industry on a subsistence basis. The people profiting from the salt trade were more likely located in distant highland Aksumite towns such as the capital Aksum or Yeha, where elite architecture, hierarchy, and elite status are well represented in the landscape. This study provides information on ancient home construction on the lower salt route and in the Agula and Desi'a areas. It also indicates that these towns were not elite settlements.

To characterize site types, activities, and artifact types related to caravan activities and settlements at the ancient towns Agula and Desi'a, I present data from different contexts within each site: household settlements, caravan campsites, and churches. The sites selected for excavation were especially well preserved and located on plains that lay adjacent to the caravan trail, campsites, and settlements. Ona Adi Agway (Unit 1) in the ancient town of Agula and Ona Hahaile (Units 2 and 3) in the town Desi'a are household settlement sites. Caravan campsites include Meda Ble'at (Unit 2) in Agula and Ona Adi Abobay (Unit 1) in Desi'a. I focus on the excavation of one Aksumite church site, Cherkos Agula (Unit 3) in Agula, although others were identified. The stratigraphy and features associated with each level are illustrated in the following sections.

These excavations supply important information on the nature of deposits expected from caravan campsites, settlement sites, and religious centers found on the trade route. They also provide a broader understanding of the formation of these types of sites and the ceramic and stone artifacts from stratified deposits. The depth of deposits varied considerably among the three site types, with the stratigraphy resulting from the occupation of the settlement site and the ancient

Aksumite church ruins about 1.35 m deep. The caravan campsite, in contrast, was only about 45 cm deep. Below, I detail the stratigraphic contexts of these three excavated contexts (caravan campsites, settlement sites, and religious centers).

Given the broad distribution of surface materials and the large settlements and campsites discovered by the project, I excavated only the densest areas. The size of the excavation units was designed to obtain enough material to date and sample the distinct architectural features and stratigraphies of the ancient towns and campsites. The largest unit was 5 m² and the smallest was 2 m². Here, levels represent the smallest excavation sediments, at arbitrary levels of 5 cm or, if possible, following the natural soil color change. Phases represent different periods of architectural construction and chronological similarities in material culture.

Agula: Highland Traders' Town

Some of the most revealing findings regarding the complex nature of the ancient Aksumite political and economic structure came from excavations at Agula, one of two ancient towns, along with Wukro, located at the top of the highland escarpment bordering the low deserts of the Danakil Depression. Agula was one of the main intersection points for salt traders, salt caravanners, and state tax officials in medieval times and is still actively involved in the contemporary salt trade. Located at the intersection of the local and regional trade routes, Agula and the ancient town of Desi'a—which I discuss shortly—are key to understanding the extent of the Aksumite state's participation in the salt trade.

Archaeological excavation of several types of sites in the town Agula provided information about various regional agents who participated in trade on the ancient salt route. My research assistants and I excavated the sites Ona Adi Agway (Unit 1, a settlement site), Meda Ble'at (Unit 2, a caravan campsite), and Cherkos Agula (Unit 3, an ancient church) in the modern town of Agula (see figure 6.2). All of the sites were discovered in 2010 by survey and surface collections and revealed pre-Aksumite, Aksumite, and medieval occupations.

Excavating Agula: Insights into a Salt Trading Community
Ona Adi Agway: Settlement Site

Ona Adi Agway dated to the Aksumite and medieval periods. Unit 1 consists of a settlement located on an elevated mound adjacent to a major contemporary Arho caravan route and the Agula River, which runs east-west (figure 6.2). It is sited on what today is farmland, covering an area of about 2 ha (hectares) (figure 6.3). The site has not been plowed, however, and was well preserved. Unit 1 was a 5-m² trench, subdivided into four quadrants—each measuring 2.5 m², with a depth of 90 cm.

The spatial data, stratigraphy, and features uncovered at Ona Adi Agway indicate that this building was used to support more than a single household. A hearth and other features reveal use of this space for intensive cooking activity

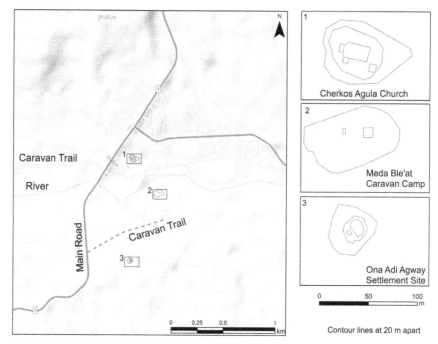

FIGURE 6.2. *The ancient town of Agula, with settlement area, caravan camp, and church*

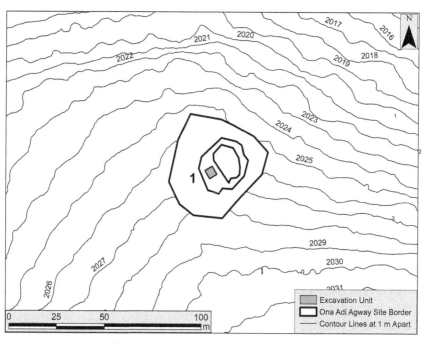

FIGURE 6.3. *Site Ona Adi Agway: Excavation Unit 1*

over a long period. Based on my findings, I argue that Ona Adi Agway was a settlement that provided logistical support to traders on the Afar trade route.

The building structure we uncovered at Ona Adi Agway was a medium-sized domestic building. The wall construction, building techniques, and plans showed two distinct phases of building construction and eight levels of cultural deposits that reflected three phases of occupation of the building. The early building structure was rectangular, with one semi-complete room and a cobbled paved surface. The later phase structure was circular (figure 6.4a, b). Two walls belonging to the northeast corner of a room were also excavated in the early phase. Results from stratigraphic, radiocarbon, and ceramic analyses showed that the early-phase wall dated to the Aksumite period (200–500 CE) and the later-phase wall dated to the medieval period (1270–1527 CE). The ancient occupation at Ona Adi Agway accumulated up to 1 m of sediment. The area was subsequently leveled, leaving a thick layer of silty fill composed of material from a collapsed wall, rubbish fills, buildings, and occupation levels.

In Phase I (levels 6, 7, and 8), we uncovered a rectangular room made of semi-worked, rectangular sandstone, with larger stones used in the later phases. The structure was built directly on the bedrock and ran in four courses. Based on the amount of wall collapse in this phase, it seems likely that several courses were missing. It is hard to tell how tall the original building was from the assemblage. However, the walls had been plastered with clay, and smaller angular stones had been used for chinking.

The section revealed that the sediment was compacted with organic material, which was probably dung. There was also a lot of clay plaster or burned clay paste present. Signs of trash burning were present throughout the phase. The ceramics of Phase I differed from those of Phase II, and I consider Phase I to be Aksumite based on the presence of Redware Aksumite pottery and sherds of other pottery typical of the Aksumite period (figure 6.5).

Use of the site Ona Adi Agway varied through time. Before the construction of the early-phase building, the site was used for domestic waste disposal. Refuse uncovered from the site contained significant cultural remains dated to Aksumite times, such as the early building. The waste disposal phase was followed by a phase in which the area was used for cooking and food preparation (figure 6.6). At least four circular hearth features of different sizes (present in levels 3, 4, 5, and 8) were revealed, as was a complex depositional sequence showing the reuse of space and rooms. Cooking hearths were found in all three phases of occupation, including the phase in between the upper and lower architectural phases (see figure 6.4.a, b). The cooking hearths were marked by alignments of uncut stones that contained a great deal of wood, charcoal, and ash. We found pieces of ceramic bowls, jars, cups, and clay griddles, as well as green, black, and brown obsidian (figures 6.7a, b, c, d, e, f, g; 6.8). We also found grinding stones

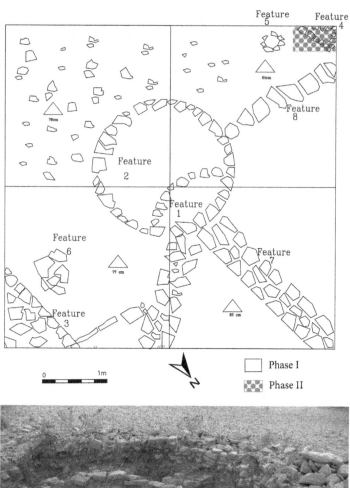

Feature 5   Feature 4

Feature 8

Feature 2

Feature 1

Feature 6

Feature 7

Feature 3

0   1m

□ Phase I

▨ Phase II

FIGURE 6.4A, B. *Plan showing early and later building phase of the settlement site Ona Adi Agway in Agula town*

FIGURE 6.5. *Redware Aksumite pottery*

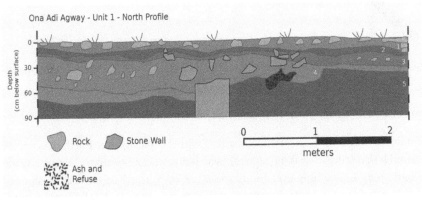

FIGURE 6.6. *Site Ona Adi Agway, stratigraphic sequence, north wall, Unit 1*

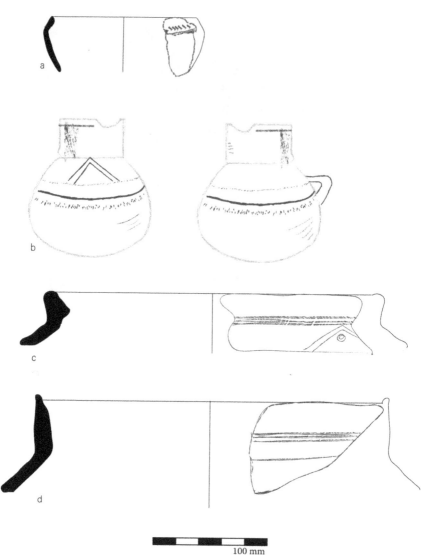

100 mm

FIGURE 6.7A–D. *Pottery jars, bowls, and cups from the site Ona Adi Agway*

on top of and near the hearths, consistent with a cooking area. Furthermore, we found *birkuta* (bread-making stones), which link the sites with the caravan trade (figure 6.9). I have only ever found these cooking stones in modern or ancient salt caravan food preparation areas, so they represent a clear link to salt caravan traders. A bovine cranial fragment was also found in Phase I.

Phase II included a thin layer of soft clay silt sediment and a distinct ash layer mixed with organic material and clay plaster (probably from the wall collapse). A cooking hearth was also present (Feature 2). This phase contained many

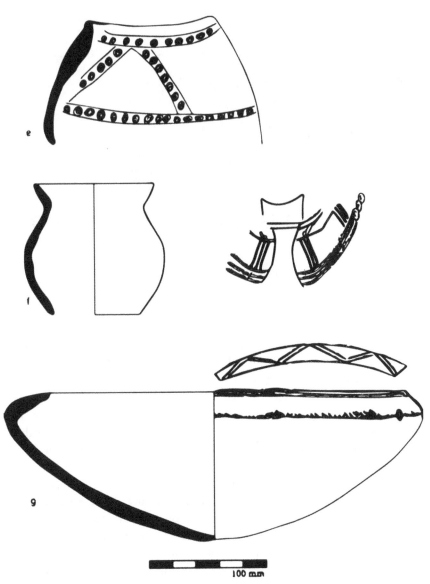

FIGURE 6.7E–G. *Pottery jars, bowls, and cups from the site Ona Adi Agway*

artifacts, including Aksumite ceramics, obsidian and chert lithics, charcoal, and bone. We also found cowry shells, which can be associated with long-distance trade (figure 6.10).

Phase III (levels 1, 2, and 3) contained topsoil (level 1) and wall collapse. Significant levels were levels 2 and 3. The chronological and cultural features found in these levels provided information about the types of activities that

FIGURE 6.8. *Obsidian and chert tools from the site Ona Adi Agway*

occurred at the site. Two walls, Features 3 and 4, were exposed. Phase III is also where the later circular building phase was uncovered. The building continued to be used as a domestic space or cooking area at this time, with two circular stone alignments—hearth features—present. The pottery sherds recovered from this phase are distinct from those of the site's early phase. The 14C radiocarbon date (cal 720–1643 CE, ISGS-6816, U1/NE/L5) supports these distinctions by showing a clear continuity with Phase II and the medieval occupation of the site.

This phase of architectural collapse and post-abandonment (levels 1 and 2) yielded a circular hearth and grinding stone, evidence that the site was still heavily used for cooking. A radiocarbon date places level 2 of this phase at cal 1412–1643 CE (ISGS-6817, U1/NW/L2). Having artifacts this old be obtained this close to the surface shows that the site was well sealed by the roof and wall collapse. Plant remains were also recovered, predominantly wheat and barley.

Desi'a: Foothill Town
Excavating Desi'a: Building Techniques and Construction Materials
The ancient town of Desi'a was an important foothill town strategically located to take advantage of the Afar salt trade. Its physical location at a node point on the caravan trail, where key routes from the highlands merge, influenced caravan traffic through this town. As in Agula, excavation at Desi'a sampled a settlement site (Ona Hahaile) and a caravan campsite (Ona Adi Abobay). The

FIGURE 6.9. Birkuta, or bread-making stones, from the site Ona Adi Agway

history of ancient settlement at this location ties development of the local community to the salt trade, since even today, this area is not sufficiently productive to support a farming community of this size.

Ona Hahaile: Settlement Site

The ancient town of Desi'a is about 5 km from the modern town center of Desi'a. It is located on top of a flat hill, about 200 m from the major river and 50 m from the caravan trail—which passes right by the ruins of the ancient St. Georgis church (Emba Georgis), located about 1 km east of the site. Like the settlement Ona Adi Agway in the town Agula, the settlement Ona Hahaile in

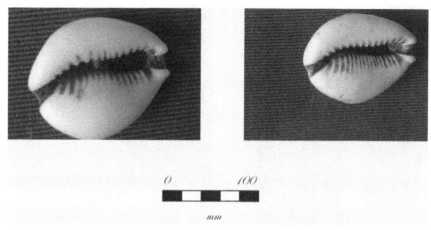

FIGURE 6.10. Cowry shells recovered from the site Ona Adi Agway

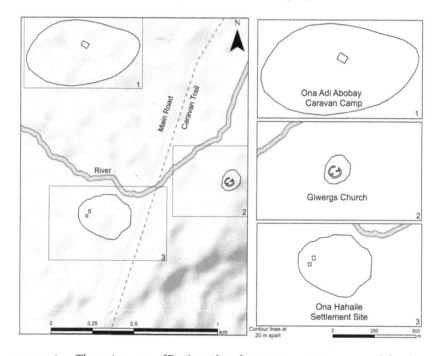

FIGURE 6.11. The ancient town of Desi'a, with settlement area, caravan camp, and church

Desi'a lies just a few meters from the major salt caravan on the Desi'a Salt Route, the Desi'a River, campsites, and the ruins of Emba Georgis (figure 6.11).

The settlement is in the direct viewshed of the church, with the river and the caravan trail lying between them. The hill slope is steep to the north and moderately steep to the west. Scatters of wall collapse, ceramic sherds, and lithic

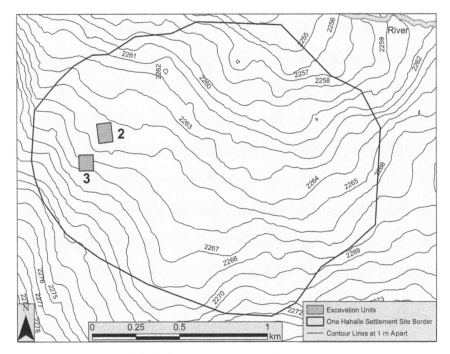

FIGURE 6.12. *Site Ona Hahaile: Excavation Unit 2 and Unit 3*

material cover about 4 ha, but the settlement site only extends over ca. 1 ha. As in Agula, the volume of wall collapse made it problematic for an ox-drawn plow; thus, the site is well preserved.

Two discrete units (Unit 2 and Unit 3) were excavated at Ona Hahaile, with each trench measuring 3 m² (figure 6.12). I chose two adjacent mounds for excavation, which were clearly ruins of different room structures. Unit 2 was a rectangular building that might have been a portion of an isolated residential building or part of a larger building (figure 6.13a, b). The exterior sediment contained a high concentration of organic residue, probably mostly dung resulting from caravan traffic. Accumulation of ash outside the building walls also reflected cooking activity outside the structure. Unit 3, which lay 3 m west of Unit 2, was a circular structure with a different architectural style and function. This building, unlike the rectangular building, was made of large, vertically oriented flat stones (figure 6.14a, b). Inside the room, a wall divided the circle in half. The significant amount of charred wheat and barley seeds found in the circular building, together with charcoal deposits, indicate the use of the space as a crop processing area. This unit dated to a later time period than the rectangular building (cal 1444 CE).

Excavation of Unit 2 and Unit 3 at Ona Hahaile provided information on the functions of buildings at foothill towns on the ancient trade route as well as

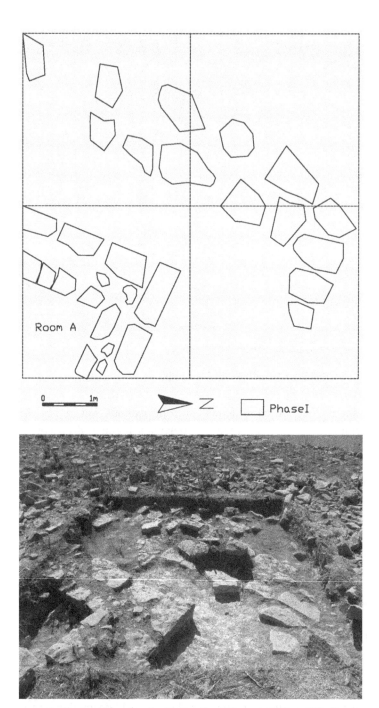

Room A

0   1m

N   ☐ Phase I

FIGURE 6.13A–B. *Plan showing Unit 2, the settlement site Ona Hahaile in Desi'a town*

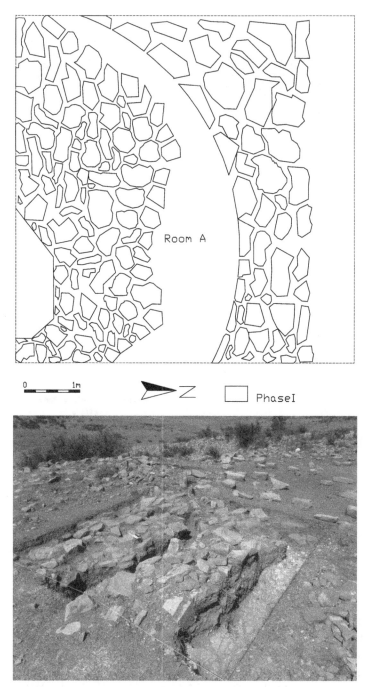

Room A

0   1m   N   ☐ PhaseI

FIGURE 6.14A–B. *Plan showing Unit 3, the settlement site Ona Hahaile in Desi'a town*

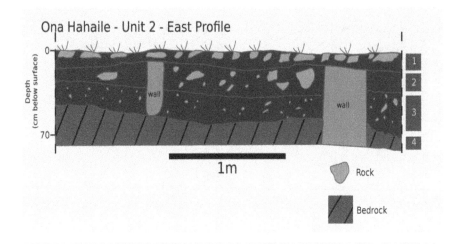

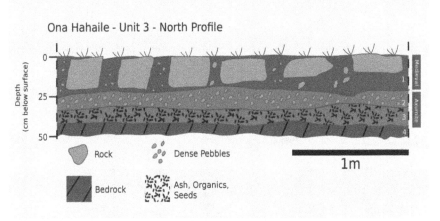

FIGURE 6.15A–B. *Settlement site Ona Hahaile—(a) Unit 2 stratigraphy, (b) Unit 3 stratigraphy*

architectural change. Like the Ona Adi Agway settlement, Ona Hahaile had a complex history, with continuous occupation over a long period and two building phases corresponding to the mid-Aksumite and medieval periods. The matrix for the first of these two phases (Phase I, or the early period) was the deepest (ca. 60 cm) (figure 6.15a, b). The second phase represented the later phase of occupation and included levels made up of rubble from wall and roof collapse (see figure 6.13a, b). One significant architectural similarity between the two ancient towns at Desi'a and Agula is the change from a rectangular building that dominated the early-phase architectural style of the settlements to a round building that seemed to be a feature of the later phase, especially during the medieval period. In both towns, stone walls made of shaped architectural stones, paved floors, postholes, and domestic spaces preserved traces of cooking hearths, grinding stones, and carbonized seeds (barley and wheat).

Construction materials and building techniques used at the foothill town Ona Hahaile in Desi'a were non-elite compared to known elite Aksumite sites such as Aksum, Matara, and Yeha—where fine masonry work and the use of diverse materials such as fired brick have been recorded. There were slight differences in construction techniques within the settlement. Limestone, readily available near Desi'a, was used for wall construction. This limestone was mostly unshaped, and both large and small rocks were used. In Unit 2, some of the wall stones of the rectangular structure were relatively large (63 cm long) and rectangular; smaller stones (25 cm) were flatter (cut). The circular structure in Unit 3 was formed of three faces and one course at the base of the building made of smaller rectangular stones (28 cm). Wood beams were also used in construction at Unit 3, and the remains of cedar were recovered from the site. Postholes (16 cm diameter) were found south of the trench at this phase, outside the building structure. Dark brown mud was used as mortar to bind the stones. The reason for the difference in construction techniques within the settlement is not apparent, but it might relate to a difference in function between buildings and rooms.

Radiocarbon dates and ceramic styles show continued use of the site during the medieval period. Cultural materials found in the settlement include dung, ceramic sherds (particularly jars and bowls), bread-cooking stones, fired hearthstones, lithics, and cowry shells. A great deal of charcoal and ash was also present in each phase. The site was abandoned at the end of Phase II, for unknown reasons. People may have abandoned ancient Desi'a to intensify agriculture, as historically documented, but it may also have been abandoned for security-related reasons. The modern settlement resides on top of the mountain north of the site.

Phase I (levels 3, 4, and 5) was early and included the architectural level. This architectural phase includes rooms built directly on top of the bedrock. The lower-level fill was formed by a light olive-brown lime and clay soil that was very coarse and friable and had silky inclusions. This deposit also contained cultural material. Above this was yellowish-brown clay soil. The earliest feature in this phase was an ash surface that contained charcoal and ceramic sherds. Walls that formed a T-shape were also found. This T-shape ran southwest, with the tail running slightly east-west. The walls disappeared in their respective directions, outside the border of the trench.

Clearing this phase exposed four walls: Feature 1 and Feature 2. These walls had two courses and two faces, respectively, and formed portions of the insides of rooms. Feature 1 faced north, and Feature 2 was oriented to the east and south of the trench. Readily available limestone rocks (large and small, 19–47 cm) were used for the wall construction. The prevalence of flat stones, particularly in the eastern quadrant, suggests that there had been a stone-lined floor or that wall collapse had occurred directly onto this surface. The ash surface in the southwest quadrant also showed that the space between buildings had been used for cooking and rubbish disposal. The position of Features 1 and 2 (portions of a building wall separated by half a meter) delineated the rooms.

Both the interior sediment and the floor deposits surrounding the features were pale brown, silty, and softer than later levels. There was, however, a noticeable difference between the interior and exterior sediment. The exterior sediment—especially in the northeast quadrant—and exterior surface contained a higher concentration of organic sediment and a high volume of dung.

The second phase (levels 1 and 2), ca. 25 cm thick, was made up of rubble from wall and roof collapse as well as cultural materials and represented the later phase of occupation. Before excavation began, the ground surface had been cleared of collapsed rubble and vegetation, but there were no standing walls aboveground.

CHURCHES

The presence and strategic location of ancient church ruins (Ethiopian Orthodox churches) at the ancient towns of Agula and Desi'a evidence institutional involvement in the Afar salt trade route far from the political center of the Aksumite polity. During the medieval period, historical texts indicate that churches on the salt route were associated with state control of trade through tax collection (Huntingford 1989). Aksumite and post-Aksumite churches were built, some of which were carved out of solid rock (rock-hewn) (D. Phillipson 2009a). The shape of Aksumite churches resembled elite structures and was usually rectangular, except for some that were shaped like crosses. I identified three Aksumite churches along the salt route: Cherkos Agula, St. Georgis, and Michael Amba. Cherkos Agula was located in Agula town, St. Georgis in Desi'a, and Michael Amba near Haiki Mesihal. Cherkos Agula and St. Georgis were stone churches, whereas Michael Amba was rock-hewn. Cherkos Agula and Michael Amba were previously known Aksumite churches (D. Phillipson 2009a), but the ruin of St. Georgis church in Desi'a was first reported during this project. Cherkos Agula was a rectangular building associated with an elite style of architecture. St. Georgis Church in Desi'a was a round building built in a non-elite style. Due to the sacred nature of these churches today, archaeological excavation was conducted only at Cherkos Agula. Below, I discuss the main archaeological features of this church.

The Archaeology of Cherkos Agula Church: Evidence for Institutional Involvement on the Trade Route

Cherkos Agula is an ancient Aksumite church ruin in the town Agula, strategically located about 100 m from the Agula River and 1 km from the caravan trail that leads from the salt flat to the highlands. It lies northeast of the ancient town

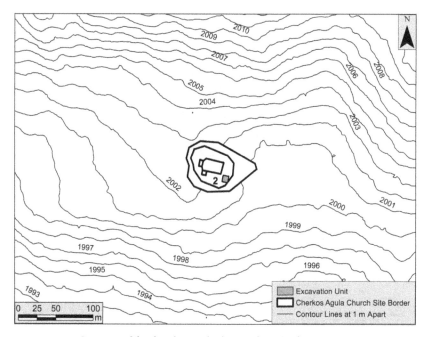

FIGURE 6.16. *Location of the church site Cherkos Agula in Agula town*

and adjacent to hilly terrain. The church occupies about 0.65 ha of an ancient floodplain, made up of dark, reddish-brown silt and clay soil that is suitable for growing maize, wheat, and barley (figure 6.16). We found earthen mounds, ceramics, lithic scatters, and wall collapse on about 1 ha surrounding the ruin. The church at Agula has been described by archaeologists Francis Anfray (1970) and David W. Phillipson (2009a); however, prior to this project, there had been no archaeological excavation of the site. D. Phillipson (2009a) suggests that the church at Agula dated to the late Aksumite period based on the style. The radio-carbon results of this study are consistent with this dating and indicate use in the late Aksumite (cal 778–1161 CE; ISGS-6818) and medieval (cal 1297–1625 CE; ISGS-6819) periods. However, artifacts suggest that the church was also active during mid-Aksumite times.

Cherkos Agula was named after Saint Cherkos in Ge'ez (Quiricus or Kērykos in Greek). According to legends, Saint Cherkos was martyred with his mother, Julitta, in 304 CE in Tarsus, Turkey (De Voragine 2012). The church was first mentioned by the Portuguese priest Francisco Alvares during his visit to Ethiopia in 1520, at the time of Emperor Lebna-Dengel (Beckingham and Huntingford 1961). It seems to have been functional and in good condition during Alvares's visit. He commented on the architecture and stone platform on which the church was built. The church was mentioned again in 1868, when it was described by

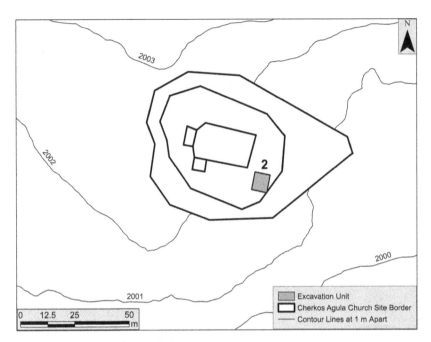

FIGURE 6.17. *Site Cherkos Agula: Unit 3*

members of the British Napier Expedition to Ethiopia (Acton 1868; Stanley 1874). Their description indicates that the church was in ruins and that it had been destroyed by treasure seekers sent by King Sabagadis (ca. 1770–1831 CE), rival of the then-ruling king Wolde Selassie (ca. 1736–1816 CE) (Pankhurst 1982).

Architectural Features and Trade Activities at Cherkos Agula Church

The preservation of the remains of this ancient Aksumite church structure is remarkable, and it is clear that it was once an imposing structure. The building was originally 14 m wide and 18.5 m long and was made up of three types of cut stone: limestone, sandstone, and marble. In the church compound, near the church ruin, rectangular cut sandstone pillars and throne bases are present. A unique material was used for the floor surface, made of a bright white paste that probably includes lime. Local legend suggests that bird eggs were used to mix the mortar, which is why it is bright white and brittle. The base platform and three entrance stairs are located on the ruin's west, north, and south sides. The steps of the main public entrance are on the west side of the building; two narrower stairs, probably reserved for the priests, are located on the south and north sides.

The ruin is of religious significance to people in the town. I was granted permission to examine a mound located about 1 m from the eastern entrance for excavation. This mound is in the direct viewshed of the caravan campsite (Meda

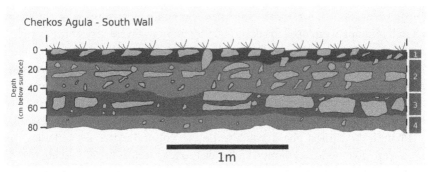

FIGURE 6.18. Site Cherkos Agula, stratigraphic sequence, south wall, Unit 3

FIGURE 6.19. A small, bell-shaped artifact found in Cherkos Agula, similar to a pendant used in modern Ethiopian Orthodox Church ceremonies

Ble'at) and settlement (Ona Adi Agway) to the north (see figure 6.2). The excavation trench of 3 m² (Unit 3) covered the southern half of the mound (figure 6.17). My objectives were to describe the architecture and obtain dates for the site without disturbing the standing ruin and to collect empirical information and artifacts related to church sites on the salt trail. I was interested in the relationship of the church to the town and the ancient salt route, and I also wished to compare it to other sites examined during this research.

My excavation of Unit 3 shows that the mounds/structures near the main church building were used for domestic functions and were probably destroyed at the same time as the main church building. One radiocarbon sample taken from this site dated to cal 778 CE; ISGS-6818. However, Aksumite-type ceramics recovered suggest that this area was also in use earlier. Wall collapse, material accumulation, architectural change, and artifacts recovered revealed that the site had been used continually over at least three phases of occupation (figure 6.18).

Phase I, the earliest phase, contained much cultural material—including cattle, sheep/goat bones, ceramics, and lithic tools, as well as bread-making stones. The lithics provided evidence for changes in raw material use through time. No brown and tan chert lithic tools were found in the earlier phases, for example, but they were used abundantly in later phases. A small bell-shaped artifact was found in this context, similar to a pendant used in modern Ethiopian Orthodox Church ceremonies (figure 6.19). Charcoal was found in all phases.

Phase II was distinguished by its architecture. Based on the ceramics and other artifacts, this phase dates to the Aksumite period, which is consistent with the results of radiocarbon dating of this phase based on excavated charcoal. We found many burned rocks, as well as cattle and sheep/goat bones. We also located a large grinding stone next to an ash-filled circular stone hearth. This grinding stone was similar to those used by contemporary priests to prepare communion bread, which is usually bread made from freshly ground wheat and barley.

Phase II of Cherkos Agula was very similar to the second phase of the Ona Adi Agway settlement at Agula. The same processes seem to have taken place, with intense cooking activity represented by a thin ash layer and cultural activity found sandwiched between two phases. The high level of activity at this time suggests that the apex of the salt trade and greatest caravan traffic occurred during the Aksumite rather than the medieval period.

Phase III represented the later phase of the site, or the late Aksumite period. The topsoil and building collapse material at this phase was similar to that of the big Aksumite church ruin aboveground. During this phase, people used at least three types of rock for building construction. We identified the raw materials as sandstone, bluestone (probably volcanic), and marble. The mortar used to plaster stone columns was the same as the material used in the church construction, a very compact white material. Ceramic and lithic artifacts were recovered from this phase, including charcoal and land-snail shells.

The third phase in Unit 3 at Cherkos Agula differed from the third phase at the Agula settlement Ona Adi Agway (Unit 1). Unlike the Agula settlement, where limestone was the only raw material used, Cherkos Agula used three types of stones for construction. Limestone is found in most parts of the Tigray region, but granite (which is locally called *ketsela* stone) is rare in the Agula area and must be transported from a long distance. The third type was sandstone. In building construction at Cherkos Agula, different sizes and shapes of cut and uncut rocks were employed. Some blocks were rectangular, and some were asymmetrical. We found angular cobblestones with mortar/paste still attached to them. The granite and suite of building materials used at Cherkos Agula are similar to those found at elite Aksumite highland sites. In the following section, I move from discussing the permanent buildings, towns, and churches to considering the more ephemeral residues left by the ancient caravans.

CARAVANNERS

Uncovering Distinctive Archaeological Features of Caravan Campsites
In many parts of the world, caravans and caravan transport developed to fill a niche, to connect arid regions with resource-rich areas, and to connect resource areas with consumers as more and more complex economies developed (Clarkson et al. 2017). But how do we identify caravan activity in the archaeological record in areas where natural resources contributed to the evolution of polities and centralized states? Few archaeological and anthropological studies have differentiated caravan behavior from that of other mobile groups, such as pastoralists who create sites with short-term and long-term activity signatures on the landscape. Based on ethnoarchaeological findings discussed in chapter 5, I argue that the caravan campsites on the Afar salt trade route are distinctive and leave archaeological features that can be used to link prehistoric trade activities of resources in bulk both here and in other parts of the world.

Ancient Salt Caravan Sites on the Afar Salt Route
During the archaeological survey of sites on the Afar salt trade route, I identified at least two ancient caravan campsites: Meda Ble'at, in the ancient town of Agula, and Ona Adi Abobay, in ancient Desi'a (see figures 6.3 and 6.11). The location, internal structure, and artifact repertoire of these sites were very similar. At both sites, my team and I sampled excavated areas from an ancient campground that covered between 1 and 4 ha. At all the towns surveyed, ancient caravan campsites were found in the floodplain tucked between shallow rivers and trade routes going to the salt flat and back (figure 6.20). Today, caravanners camp in the lower plains, near the river and farmlands. One reason for this is the huge gathering of people and animals on the caravan trail campsites, which might see up to 6,000 animals in a single night. This requires a more expansive space than can be provided by villages, where houses are very close to each other. Caravanners also do not wish to disturb the daily lives of villagers, whose logistical assistance is critical for their journey. The villagers themselves have concerns about the presence of so many strangers in town. These social and logistical factors relating to the logistics of pack caravans may well have been at play in earlier times.

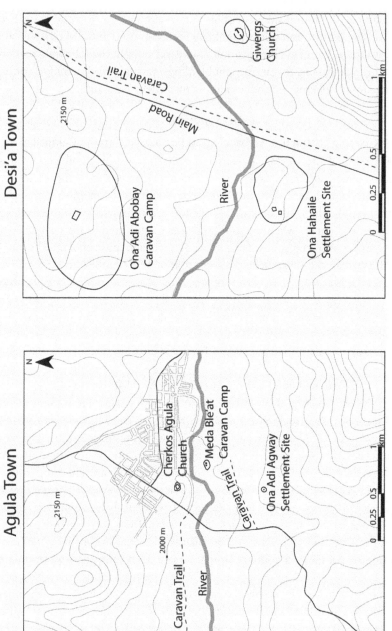

FIGURE 6.20. Location of caravan campsites in the floodplain tucked between shallow rivers and trade routes going to the salt flat and back

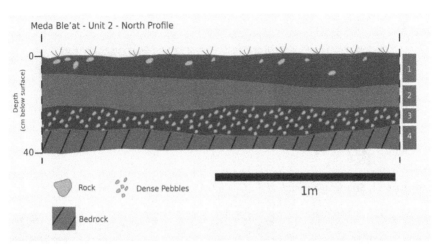

FIGURE 6.21. *Stratigraphy profile of site Meda Ble'at, Agula town, north wall*

FIGURE 6.22. *Site Meda Ble'at: Excavation Unit 2*

The caravan campsites in the towns Agula and Desi'a were key to this investigation. I excavated a 2 m² unit at Meda Ble'at (figures 6.21 and 6.22) and a 3 m² unit at Ona Adi Abobay (figures 6.23 and 6.24). These ancient caravan campsites had similar features. The most distinctive was a high density of previously heated bread-making stones on and around the camps. Another common feature

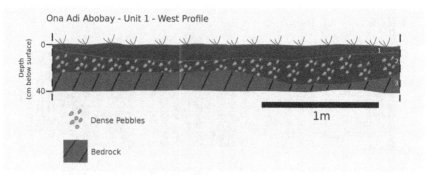

FIGURE 6.23. *Stratigraphy profile of site Ona Adi Abobay, Desi'a town, west wall*

FIGURE 6.24. *Site Ona Adi Abobay: Excavation Unit 1*

was the slopes (0.1768°–0.3536°) and very shallow depth of deposits (30–40 cm). The top levels of both sites preserved organic animal dung, very fine charcoal fragments, and cultural artifacts. The early phases of these campsites contained lithic artifacts and highly fragmented ceramic sherds. The last level before the bedrock at both sites was culturally sterile. Macrobotanical remains indicate the importance of barley and wheat in the caravanners' diet, which were probably used to make bread. Faunal remains were rare at both sites relative to macro-botanical remains. Since foodways play an important role in distinguishing the caravanners and other participants on the route, they are discussed in more detail in the next section.

Space was not formally organized within ancient campsites. Large areas made up of many smaller campsites along with shallow stratigraphy indicated repeated short-term occupation of the areas. The campsites were consistently located near ancient towns, settlements, and rivers situated along the ancient and modern salt trade route. Lithics, highly fragmented ceramics, and dung indicate the presence of people and large numbers of livestock. While this combination could indicate either caravanners or pastoralists, the cuisine here emphasized cereals and stone cooking on a fire, which is particularly distinctive of caravanners.

FOODWAYS ON TRADE ROUTES: EVIDENCE FOR REGIONAL PARTICIPATION AND PEER NETWORK

The Role of Food in Group Identity on Trade Routes

In addition to the hard and challenging journey and navigation of the trade route, the daily routine of cooking and the practice of group eating habitually socialize participants with peers/communities on the route. Foodways are powerful symbols of group identity (Anderson 2014, 199–200). Identities are conveyed through food not only in terms of ethnicity and gender but also in terms of taste and preference, as well of food processing, consumption, and the sorts of equipment used in the preparation of food (Twiss 2012). Individuals or groups may alter their identities in response to their contexts. For example, many of the people who work on the current Afar trade route come from households where women are responsible for the majority of the cooking. On the Afar trade route, in contrast, all of the men, regardless of their nationality or religion, prepare their own meals.

Caravanners on the modern-day trade route also use food as a means of expressing their sense of group identity or belonging by eating with other caravan members from their respective villages and cities. During fasting seasons, the Afar and highland caravanners display different food preferences based on their religious affiliation. The majority of caravanners from both groups observe fasts in accordance with their respective Muslim and Ethiopian Orthodox faiths. Muslim caravanners fast during the day and can break their fast in the evening with whatever food is available on the trail, which may include meat if they are near towns and villages. Ethiopian Orthodox caravanners, in contrast, are only permitted to eat vegetarian/vegan food during all fasting seasons, including winter; they are not permitted to consume meat or dairy items.

Cooking and eating habits and the general diet of caravanners and traders on the route provide a snapshot of regional cuisine preferences and culturally and functionally acceptable foods on the road. Ceramic and lithic evidence in the archaeological record of contextualized utensils and foodways also provides a strong correlation between cuisine and regional identity.

Regional Cooking Technology in the Past: Archaeological Evidence from the Afar Salt Trade Route

Well-documented food resources in the Ethiopian highlands during the pre-Aksumite and Aksumite periods include locally grown wheat, barley, finger millet, sorghum, flax, linseed, *noog*, and *te'f* (D'Andrea 2008; Marshall and Hildebrand 2002). Small- and larger-scale farmers also kept cattle, sheep, goats, and chickens (Cain 2000; Chaix 2013; Woldekiros and D'Andrea 2017).

Although more research needs to be done into the preparation and consumption of these foodstuffs during the Aksumite period, we do know that the Aksumites used both ovens and griddles to make bread (Lyons and D'Andrea 2003). They made leavened bread from wheat and barley and unleavened/fermented bread from *te'f*. It is possible that the present highland cuisine was first established during the Aksumite phase, as bread making was central to Aksumite cuisine and continues to be today.

Excavations on the Afar trade route give us a good indication of what was eaten in the past in caravan campsites (Meda Ble'at and Ona Adi Abobay), in settlement sites (Ona Adi Agway and Ona Hahaile), and by members of the church (Cherkos Agula). The faunal and botanical evidence recovered from all five sites was dominated by domestic species—including wheat, barley, *te'f*, sheep, goats, and cattle—but there was a contrast in the representation of animal and plant remains among the settlements sites, church site, and caravan campsites. The macrobotanical remains as a whole included 5,348 domestic cereal seeds (85%), 556 unidentified domestic cereals (9%), 196 wild edible seeds (3%), 134 unidentified wild seeds (2%), and 29 unknown wild seeds (< 1%). The domestic cereals included free-threshing bread wheat (*Triticum* sp.), likely emmer wheat (*Triticum* cf. *dicoccum*) (figure 6.25a, b), hulled barley (*Hordeum* sp.) (likely six-row), and *te'f* (*Eragrostis te'f*) (appendix D). Ethnographic and ethnoarchaeological studies have shown that these crops were traditionally used for making flat and round breads in the Ethiopian highlands (Lyons and D'Andrea 2003). Wheat was ubiquitous at all sites except the caravan campsite Meda Ble'at. Barley was found at all sites and was the most abundant cereal recovered from the caravan sites.

Seven types of wild plant seeds were identified at each site; the most abundant of these, Malvaceae, were undigested flowering plants, usually found in animal dung. The Poaceae (grasses) found were those common to open fields, where pastoralists grazed their livestock (Kuznar 1993; Yager 2009). Other wild plants recovered include Apiaceae cf. *Carum* sp., Brassicaceae cf. *Brassica* sp., Fabaceae, Polygonaceae cf. *Rumex* sp., and Solanaceae. These plants provide good proxy data for the presence of pack animals on the route and the likely components of

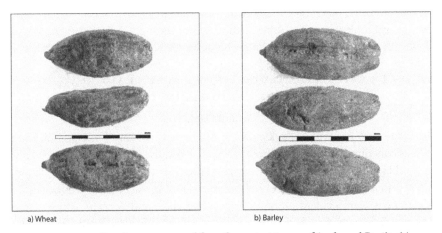

a) Wheat   b) Barley

FIGURE 6.25A–B. *Cereal crops recovered from the ancient towns of Agula and Desi'a, (a) wheat, (b) barley*

their diet. Today, salt caravanners traveling from the highlands usually let camels forage for themselves but carry water and straw for their donkeys and mules, since grazing land is scarce on the trail.

As mentioned, there was a marked contrast between sites in terms of the representation of animal remains relative to plant remains. Meat did not seem to represent a significant portion of the traders' diet. However, more bones were present at the settlement sites than at caravan sites. Similar to other Aksumite sites, the animals commonly present were cattle, sheep, goats, camels, and chickens. There were no wild animal remains in the assemblages, suggesting that hunting did not supplement traders' diets. Through time, there was a decrease in fauna present (appendix E).

People ate more meat at the settlement sites and the church than they did at caravan sites. The numbers of identifiable specimens (NISP) of animal remains were as follows: Ona Adi Agway (NSIP = 514), Ona Hahaile (NSIP = 281), and Cherkos Agula (NSIP = 166). It is likely that people did not eat much meat at the campsites Meda Ble'at and Ona Adi Abobay because they did not have plans to spend more than a night or two there. Furthermore, animals are cumbersome to carry, time-consuming to butcher and prepare, and expensive to purchase. The ethnoarchaeological research suggested that meat was not commonly eaten on the route; faunal data from the ancient caravan campsites indicate that this was also the case in the past.

In the ancient town of Agula, beef seems to have been preferred, followed by mutton and goat meat (appendix E). In the ancient town of Desi'a, mutton and goat were more common, followed by beef. One reason for the predominance of sheep and goats in Desi'a is that they are easy to keep and require less water and grass than cattle do (Dahl and Hjort 1976). Whereas Agula town is located in the wetter and cooler ecological zone on the edges of the highland escarpment, Desi'a town lies in the drier transitional zone between the highlands and lowlands.

CERAMICS AND LITHICS ON THE AFAR TRADE ROUTE: EVIDENCE FOR REGIONAL INVOLVEMENT

Ceramic Data

In addition to food refuse, evidence of cooking and serving from ceramics and lithics contributes useful evidence on foodways on the trade route. The ceramic assemblage also provides particularly good proxy data on regional social identity and participation on the salt route from the towns Agula and Desi'a. Once more, differences were evident among villages, churches, and caravan camps—with the ceramic and lithic artifacts indicating that highland villagers from different regions participated in the caravan trade as early as the Aksumite period.

The ancient settlement at the town Agula (Ona Adi Agway) had the largest number of ceramic sherds (n = 1,288), followed by the settlement at Desi'a (Ona Hahaile) (n = 978) and the church at Agula (Cherkos Agula) (n = 717) (appendix F). Potsherds were also present at the caravan campsites Ona Adi Abobay (n = 25) in Desi'a and Meda Ble'at (n = 15) in Agula. Smaller quantities of highly fragmented ceramics were present at caravan sites. Specialized culinary vessels at the settlement sites and Cherkos Agula included cooking bowls, jars, cups, and griddles (see figure 6.6a–g, appendix G). Analysis of attributes and surface treatments recovered fifteen ceramic types at Agula and fourteen at Desi'a. This variety of wares provides strong evidence for links to other regions as well as information on activities in settlements, campsites, and church sites.

The most significant finding relating to vessel function is the domestic nature of the assemblages. At Aksumite and pre-Aksumite sites, vessel function is usually subdivided according to domestic or ceremonial use. At Aksumite sites, ceremonial ceramics are distinctive and represented by very few types (D. Phillipson 2009b). In this study, vessel function was correlated with vessel type. All of the ceramics recovered from these sites were handmade, with some showing coiling as the technique used to make the pottery; further, all of the vessels found at the Afar salt caravan project sites were domestic in nature. Griddles were used for dry cooking, whereas cups, bowls, and jars were used for wet cooking or food consumption. This interpretation is based on the wear on artifacts and the presence of soot from cooking and storage.

All of the excavations at Agula and Desi'a demonstrated a patterned distribution of two types of serving/cooking bowls, which is particularly significant because these vessels match those found at major pre-Aksumite and Aksumite trading towns on the main Aksumite trade routes leading to the Red Sea (figures 6.26 and 6.27a–e). Bowls found at the settlement sites in Agula and Desi'a were

FIGURE 6.26. *Decorated pottery from the ancient town of Agula*

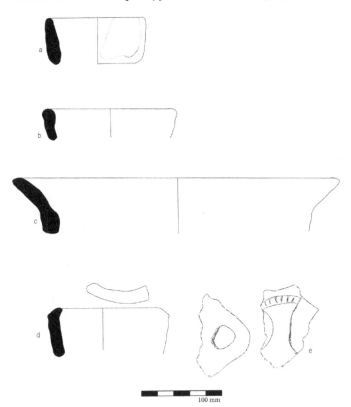

FIGURE 6.27. *Decorated and plain pottery from the ancient town of Desi'a*

distinctive in terms of both surface treatment and attributes. The first type was a medium-sized open bowl with a thick, flat rim that was either a light grayish-brown burnished ceramic or a fine redware. Decoration on the rim consisted of a chevron, a cross-hatch, or an incision or finger impression on the carina (figure 6.26). Redware of this type has been found in pre-Aksumite and Aksumite sites as far as the port of Adulis on the Red Sea and the town Matara in the northern Aksumite territory. These sites lie about 200 km from the sites excavated on the salt trail (see Anfray 1966; Peacock and Blue 2007). The second distinctive vessel type was a large, red, coarse-ribbed bowl indicating shared meals; it is well-known by scholars working in northern Ethiopia (see D'Andrea et al. 2008, 163). This ware had a lot of mineral inclusions and possibly an organic temper. Its distribution extended to towns east of Aksum, including Yeha and Ona Adi (see D'Andrea et al. 2008; Fattovich 2009).

Other vessel forms found at the settlement site at Agula (Ona Adi Agway), such as decorated jars with direct vertical rims and decorated handles, were broadly distributed across the Aksumite highlands. Similar jars were discovered by Francis Anfray (1966, 46) at Matara on the major international trade route from Aksum to the Red Sea port of Adulis (Anfray 1974; Munro-Hay 1991, 48). This indicates regional participation in the salt trade with ties to different parts of the Aksumite highland littorals.

The difference between the ceramics found in the towns Agula and Desi'a can be seen in the painted, fine redware found in small quantities in Agula. These fine wares, which required skill to make, suggest that people of high status visited the town. State agents traveling with a caravan party would be the sort of people who might have used these vessels.

Remains of griddles were recovered from settlements sites in both towns. The presence of flat griddles (30–48 cm) indicates that dry cooking occurred at these sites. Bread making has a long tradition in the cuisine of the Ethiopian highlands. The sites date to the mid- and late Aksumite periods, but the earliest date for ceramic griddles and dry-cooking methods is in the northern Ethiopian highlands and dates to 520 BCE (Dombrowski 1971).

The most common griddle type found in the archaeological record of the northern Ethiopian highlands is the *mogogo* griddle. The *mogogo* is made from one portion of clay and one portion of sand. It has a smooth black surface and a reddish bottom and is usually about 58 cm in diameter and 2–3 cm thick (Lyons and D'Andrea 2003). This type of griddle is still used in Ethiopia today. A variety of flatbreads are cooked by preheating the *mogogo* with wood or charcoal prior to spreading batter on the glossy upper surface. Flatbreads are cooked for two to three minutes, whereas thicker breads (such as *embasha*) are baked for up to thirty or forty minutes.

The ceramic sherds recovered from the caravan campsites at Desi'a (Ona Adi Abobay) and Agula (Meda Ble'at) were the first to have been collected from caravan campsites in the Horn of Africa. Only one jar rim sherd was found at Ona Adi Abobay. Small ceramic body sherds probably reflected intense trampling at the sites. The ceramics from these caravan campsites were dominated by ca. fifth-century CE Aksumite brownware, indicating heavy use at this time by highlanders. There were also redwares, blackwares, and graywares in the assemblage. Some of the body sherds were decorated, but most were plain. Decorations included incisions in the form of horizontal bands, cross-hatches, and inverted V-shapes.

Lithics

Stone tools, especially sharp obsidian knives, were used in northern Ethiopia during the Aksumite and medieval periods (Curtis 2009; D'Andrea et al. 2008; D. Phillipson 2000b). Obsidian sources have not been discovered in the Ethiopian highlands, but they have been documented in southern Afar (Negash, Brown, and Nash 2011). Since obsidian sources are rare in the Ethiopian highlands, the presence of obsidian is significant and suggests that the salt route was also used for obsidian exchange. A total of 121 lithic artifacts were recovered from excavations of sites at Agula and Desi'a (appendix G). Most of them came from the settlement and church site Agula and from the caravan campsite at Desi'a. Their presence on the Afar trade route reflects the need for knives and other tools on the route.

Other stone artifacts (n = 40) found in the assemblage reflected cooking. They included bread stones (43%, n = 17), river pebbles (40%, n = 16), and grinding stones (18%, n = 7). The river pebbles could have been used as ceramic burnishers. The bread stones (*birkuta* stones) were used to make bread on the caravan route and are still used by caravanners today. They are unknown in highland Aksumite assemblages.

The lithic analyses show at least six types of raw materials in the overall assemblage. The raw material with the highest frequency was obsidian (46%), followed by chert (42%). Quartzite (8%), granite (2%), chalcedony (1%), and basalt (1%) were also present. The diversity of obsidian sources at the sites suggests that obsidian was likely to have been acquired from the Afar region and that salt was not the only good traded on the route. The XRF results show obsidian from at least five sources and of three colors: black, brown, and green. A regional comparison of lithic artifacts could be used to examine exchange patterns in the northern Ethiopian highlands. Increased utilization of obsidian might indicate the intensification of regional exchange networks between the lowlands and the highlands. Obsidian in the highlands could also be tied to interactions between lowland and highland communities through the salt trade.

Studies of lithic assemblages from the Afar Salt Caravan Route had never been undertaken prior to ours. This assemblage shows a high frequency of obsidian. The lack of angular or flake trimming waste for obsidian indicates that initial core reduction took place elsewhere. These artifacts were likely transported from highland collections or sources in the Afar. Obsidian lithic artifacts from at least five sources suggest regional or local diversity in the use of sources and could reflect regions from which Afar participants came. There was relatively constant obsidian raw material utilization over time, and obsidian artifacts were the smallest artifacts in the assemblage. Interestingly, the majority of the unshaped informal tools were recovered from caravan site components, and 85 percent were made of obsidian. This suggests that caravanners' logistics, travel costs, or both did not allow them to make formal tools on the trail. These informal obsidian lithic tools were likely used for food preparation or maintenance activities during rest periods. Archaeological research is needed at obsidian source sites to examine the hypothesis suggested by these data: that obsidian was collected in the Afar and prepared for transport.

Cowry Shells

Cowry shells discovered at Ona Adi Agway and Ona Hahaile suggest that the regional salt trade route was closely connected to the long-distance trading route through the Red Sea port of Adulis, which is roughly 400 km north of Agula and Desi'a. Shell fragments and worked marine shells were unearthed at sites in both of the towns Agula and Desi'a, and they were found in a variety of conditions. No freshwater shells were discovered. Two kinds of marine shells, *Monetaria annulus* (Linnaeus 1758) (n = 3) and *Cypraea erythraeensis* (n = 1), appear to have been preferred on these trade routes. When it comes to *Monetaria annulus* species, dorsum removal was a significant part of the shell alteration process.

Radiocarbon dates taken above and below the levels where the shells were discovered, as well as ceramic types, indicate that the marine shells from the Red Sea area arrived in Agula during the mid- to late Aksumite phase, whereas the shell from Desi'a was a result of medieval period activity.

Peoples' preference for *M. annulus* cowry species has been observed in later-period sites in Ethiopia at Harlaa (Insoll 2021), as well as in other sub-Saharan African countries (Haour and Christie 2019). This demonstrates the significance and preference for this specific type of cowry shell from the Aksumite period to medieval Ethiopia. *M. annulus* was most likely used as a form of exchange, as well as worn as a necklace, a bracelet, or an ornament for hair or clothing. Until recently, rural women adorned traditional infant sling carriers with hundreds of cowry shells (personal observation). Sling carriers adorned with cowry shells are typically made of leather and are passed down from generation to generation.

Taken together, information on the location of ancient trading towns and caravan campsites, site structures, ceramics, lithics, and cowries indicates the regions from which ancient regional trade between the highlands and the lowlands stemmed and the presence of participants from both regions trading in salt and possibly also obsidian.

The caravan campsites were distinctive, located on slightly sloping ground favorable for pack travel and in open areas close to water sources and settlements. Consistent with sites created by mobile and pastoral people, these overnight sleeping areas were characterized by shallow occupation phases, nonformalized usage of space, and fragmented ceramic and lithic artifact scatters. The presence of bread-cooking stones was also distinctive. With the exception of a few that are now used for irrigated farming, these campsites are still used by modern caravanners.

The excavation of settlement sites at the previously unrecorded ancient towns of Agula and Desi'a contributes to our understanding of life in ancient towns on the salt route and in non-elite settlements in the Aksumite and medieval periods. These settlements were strategically located adjacent to the trade route at distances ranging from 100 m to 500 m. The location of settlements indicates the importance of these towns in providing logistical support and food for traders traveling to the lowland resources. The church buildings were very similar to the elite buildings at previously studied Aksumite sites. This was especially true for Cherkos Agula. My archaeological study of ancient churches in these towns demonstrates the significance of churches in monitoring the routes and caravan traffic up and down to the lowlands. This finding is important for understanding the role of the Aksumite elite in the economic organization of the salt trade.

The ceramics and chert and obsidian artifacts collected from the ancient towns of Agula and Desi'a revealed intensive Aksumite and medieval activity along the Afar route and provide information on the highland regions to which the trade was linked and from which participants came. The implications of these results for understanding the organization of trade and the participation of local rural communities and the Aksumite state are discussed in chapter 7 and the conclusion.

7

HETERARCHIES, HIERARCHIES, AND PEER NETWORKS

Afar Salt Caravan Trade and Aksumite Political Economy

Archaeologists have long argued that elite control of long-distance trade and agricultural wealth led to complex hierarchical socioeconomic and political institutions in the northern Ethiopian highlands and to the rule of powerful Aksumite kings (Anfray 1974; Chittick 1974; D'Andrea and Haile 2002; D'Andrea et al. 1999; Fattovich 1977; Harrower, McCorriston, and D'Andrea 2010; Michels 2005; Munro-Hay 1991; D. Phillipson 2009c). One can observe vertical power structures and institutionalized inequality in the hierarchically structured mortuary and residential architecture at ancient Aksum and other Aksumite cities, as well as in the symbols of power such as thrones and luxury imports found there. There is also good evidence for elite control of resources and much of the main trade route from Aksum to the Red Sea. Recent research on the spatial organization of Aksumite settlements, however, challenges a simple view of centralized Aksumite power and argues for independent administration of some of the prominent Aksumite cities and towns (Harrower and D'Andrea 2014). Archaeologists have not often explored the variety of relationships, participants, and contexts—spatial, ideological, technological, and administrative—that

https://doi.org/10.5876/9781646424733.c007

might have existed in the ancient Aksumite state. This book examines evidence of heterarchical structures in the Aksumite state by investigating the role of the local salt trade—and multiple agents of that trade—in the complex sociopolitical organization and relationships of early polities in the north Ethiopian and Eritrean highlands.

In this chapter, I discuss archaeological insights regarding the role of the Afar salt and obsidian trade in the Aksumite political economy. I start by summarizing the organization of ancient trade on the Afar route, focusing on the relative roles of individuals, local traders, the Aksumite elite, and the state. Contexts for heterarchical and peer networks are examined, as well as social and political structures that may have coexisted with a hierarchical social organization found at the core of the Aksumite state. I argue that control of the source and distribution of salt—an essential dietary ingredient—created cooperative relationships within and among networks and horizontal and vertical power structures at both the core and the fringes of the Aksumite polity.

CONTEXT AND OPPORTUNITIES FOR PARTICIPATION OF MULTIPLE AGENTS IN THE POLITICAL ECONOMY

Because the lowland salt source is located in one of the hottest, driest, and harshest environments on earth and is accessed from mountainous regions with few passes, caravanners likely followed only a few practical routes. This study has identified the major ones. It has also documented for the first time that there was caravan activity on the trade routes to the Afar during the Aksumite period and that there were accessible paths through the highlands and passes of the escarpment to the lowland Danakil Depression and salt sources. Pastoralists have a long history in this region of the Horn of Africa, and the lowland portion of the route would have required their cooperation. The presence of Afar obsidian from several sources in the ancient highland town of Agula and the foothill town of Desi'a on the salt route and the degree of effort required for highlanders to travel the Afar salt route also indicate that highlanders' relations with lowland pastoralists were good enough to allow trade or exchange interactions during the Aksumite period.

Branching routes from a number of northern Ethiopian highland locales meet at a few key places such as Usot, Agula, and Desi'a. The presence of alternative routes from different parts of the highlands to the lowlands demonstrates that people living in several highland regions participated in the ancient Afar trade. This is supported by the presence along the routes of utilitarian, non-elite ceramics from diverse highland regions, which also points to the operation of small-scale regional caravans. This study's work on the previously unreported Aksumite-period towns of Agula and Desi'a—located respectively at a confluence point in the highlands and a transitional zone between the highlands and lowlands—contributed valuable information in this regard. These sites are strategically located for local participation in the trade and the provisioning of caravanners. In addition to local participation, these towns also provided opportunities for state control of the salt trade, as revealed by the location of ancient Christian churches right on the caravan trail at Desi'a, Agula, and Haiki Meshail.

The clergy occupied leadership roles in the Aksumite state, and the presence of Aksumite churches in towns on the Afar route—as well as the orientation of church doors toward the caravan trail—suggest that they may have acted as agents of the church and the state in the organization of ancient trading activity on the route. Aksumite churches outside of Aksum and major cities are usually found on top of mountains, sited in intentionally hard-to-reach places. However, this is not true of the churches of St. Georgis in Desi'a and Cherkos in Agula, which are located in the lowest-elevation areas of the valley, facing the caravan routes to and from the salt plains. Furthermore, ethnohistorical accounts document that the church in Agula collected salt taxes from caravanners in the sixteenth century during the time of Emperor Eyasu II (Crawford 1958; Huntingford 1989). This provides a model for the church as an agent of the state during the Aksumite period, although whether churches actually taxed the Aksumite trade or fulfilled other state functions is unclear.

The lack of elite structures in the border town of Desi'a and its location in an arid transitional lowland point on the salt trail and not in the productive high-elevation agricultural land commonly settled by Aksumite farmers is intriguing and provides a counterpoint to narratives of state control. Today, farmers from the marginal eastern highlands are able to survive there by supplementing their resources through participation in the salt trade. The archaeological record indicates that farmers may have used similar strategies in the past. The suboptimal location of Desi'a strongly suggests that some of the border escarpment towns may have been formed by farmers who supplemented a marginal agricultural livelihood with participation in a salt-based niche economy rather than through any direct initiative of the Aksumite state. The presence of non-elite domestic structures and coarsely constructed churches at Agula and Desi'a also indicates a non-elite community and participation of non-elite groups or individuals in the local salt trade in these towns. The abundance of subsistence resources such as barley and wheat and the relative absence of meat further support this indication.

A complex picture emerges of the church and probably the state structuring aspects of the salt trade and the trading activity of border towns, combined with an array of independent actors—including residents and farmers from small-scale highland farming communities and lowland pastoral communities who undertook seasonal salt trading on the Afar route. Evidence of multiple participants in the ancient Afar salt and obsidian trade—including non-elites and traders from the eastern highlands—fits with Cosmas Indicopleustes's assertion that in the sixth century, individual traders played a role in the Sasu gold trade south of the Aksumite territory, together with the governor of the region and agents of the king (Kobishchanov 1979; D. Phillipson 2012; Wolska-Conus 1962). This is a far cry from the state domination of trade envisioned by earlier Aksumite scholars.

The location of the Afar route and the data obtained from the excavation of archaeological sites along that route suggest that the ancient trade involved both obsidian and salt. Exploration of Afar obsidian quarry sites and large-scale excavations at other towns located at nodes where caravans meet are needed to test this hypothesis and further explore relationships between residents and seasonal traders. In the next section, I discuss the ideas raised here in the context of ethnohistorical data and archaeological information on the organization of trade in the Aksumite state.

As discussed in chapter 2, I use different lines of evidence—including ethnoarchaeology and historical texts along with archaeology—to provide a more textured account of the role of the salt trade in the socioeconomic and political organization of the Aksumites, as well as the periods that followed. I use ethnoarchaeology as an illustrative model rather than a comparative model of the organization of salt trade on the Afar trade route.

We can discern the dynamic nature of the Afar salt trade, differentiated through time and location, by employing complementary approaches that cross-examine one line of evidence against another and one time period against another. Ethnoarchaeological data must be used with caution and in conjunction with archaeological data to be effective. It should not be assumed that the present-day societies under investigation are the same as they were in the past or that they are similarly affected by local or global events. The rapid social and technological changes we are witnessing today can assist us in better understanding the dynamic nature of product creation and distribution in the past.

HORIZONTAL DIFFERENTIATION: OPPORTUNITIES FOR DIVERSE FORMS OF INDIVIDUAL AND STATE PARTICIPATION ON THE ANCIENT TRADE ROUTE

Based on this study, I predict that the organization of the salt trade during the Aksumite period differed in interesting ways from both its medieval form and its present form, chiefly in the array of participants and the entities that exercised control. The ethnographic data I collected show that a variety of stakeholders are involved in the contemporary salt trade. They include individual participants from the Danakil and subsistence farmers from a number of different highland areas and intermediate zones. Higher administrative levels are also involved, including the regional government in the Afar, highland middlemen, and larger traders. Today, salt production and trade in the Danakil are independently organized by individual farmers and herders who work the trade part-time as a niche economy. The role of individual small-scale traders ends once they unload their salt at warehouses and markets. The value and price of salt increase with distance from the salt flats and are determined by people higher up in the trade than the salt caravanners. These people—the middlemen, warehouse owners, and larger traders—benefit the most from the trade. The Afar regional government gains from the trade by taxing traders per the number of pack animals at the salt flat, and the state government profits from taxes paid by middlemen and salt warehouses in highland towns. In general, the profit from the salt trade, whether through tax collection or direct market sales, is gained only after the salt has reached urban areas.

This part-time collective participation by the state and independent individuals may have been similar throughout the Aksumite period. Thus, the question emerges: were Aksumite rulers the only ones who mobilized labor to gain access to the salt source, or were other non-elite agents involved? Further research is needed to examine the surplus accumulation of subsistence goods and their conversion into storable commodities such as grain, animals, salt, and oil. Although existing research has focused mainly on the import and export of sumptuary goods, these subsistence goods could also have played a role in wealth accumulation, the establishment of prestige, and the emergence of complex institutions in the northern Ethiopian highlands (D'Andrea 2008; D. Phillipson 2000a, 2012). Ancient trade in subsistence goods, especially salt, would have provided additional mechanisms for political leadership that were independent of central power and stemmed from the organization of individuals and the administration of resources traded between ecological zones.

To better understand the organization of the Afar trade and Aksumite motivations for acquiring salt from the lowlands, it is crucial to understand who the caravanners or traders were and how they were organized. The organization of large-scale movement of caravans on the route by any individual or group would have required access to major trade routes and state-controlled markets. Large caravans also needed access to significant numbers of pack animals and protection from thieves and predatory animals along the route. Decisions must have been made at family, town, and regional levels about who went to the salt flat and who did not. The incentive for a salt-based niche economy and for small-scale farmers and herders to participate part-time to acquire salt for households and trade items is clear. Historical and ethnographic data on Oromo salt traders also suggest that highland elites with access to a large number of laborers or human porters might have organized large-scale caravans to provision their areas and to gain influence (Baxter 1991).

In the early nineteenth century, caravanners from the central and southern Tigray region operated under the supervision of big men called *ba'algada*, who were more integrated into the state system than were outside traders or local traders at the periphery of the state (Munzinger 1869). The *ba'algada* were district governors and were given that title by the emperor. *Ba'algada* were responsible for scheduling trips to the salt flats, providing protection for caravanners, and collecting tax (Gebrelibanos 2009; Pankhurst 1966). They did this with the help of officials called *shumbahri*, who worked under them and accompanied the caravanners to the salt flat (see chapter 4 for a detailed discussion of nineteenth-century salt caravan organization). Caravanners were expected to load and drive the *ba'algada's* pack animals in addition to their own. This was a common practice in the eighteenth and nineteenth centuries (Pankhurst 1966) when highland elites controlled the caravan traffic in much of the territory of present-day Ethiopia. Among the Oromo pastoralists of southern Ethiopia, big men still acquire prestige by organizing caravans to collect salt for their areas from southern salt sources (Baxter 1991). However, *ba'algada* systems no longer operate in northern Ethiopia; Afar salt caravans are organized entirely by subsistence farmers and part-time small-scale traders from the highlands and the lowlands.

Did Aksumite caravans operate under the supervision *of ba'algada* or other elite individuals tied to the state, as they did in the early nineteenth century, or were they organized by independent small-scale subsistence agriculturalists and pastoralists, as they are today? To understand the organization of ancient caravans, we must understand the conditions under which they operated.

During the Aksumite period—as in the eighteenth and nineteenth centuries—it is possible that *ba'algada* commissioned by the state scheduled journeys to salt flats and towns like Agula or Desi'a to balance salt source access between elites and small-scale caravanners. During the eighteenth and nineteenth centuries, caravanners had to pay the elite or *ba'algada*. I hypothesize that given what is known about stratification and slave ownership during the Aksumite period, this might have been different. Aksumite nobles or other powerful men may have owned their own caravans, including the pack animals and their drovers. It is also possible that human porters or enslaved people were used during the early phases of the trade.

Issues of scale and the location of markets would also have created incentives for elite involvement in the Aksumite salt trade. To profit from the salt trade today, traders must transport and sell salt in bulk. Participation in salt caravans is very costly in terms of pack animals and energy. To acquire wealth from bulky or heavy subsistence goods such as salt or obsidian, traders need access to markets close to urban areas with considerable demand. Specialized salt traders also need storage space to stockpile salt for the season when it is too hot to mine, as well as capital to pay taxes and fees for protection on the trail for multiple trips. Salt's potential as a currency and exchange medium—corroborated by Cosmas Indicopleustes—provides further initiative for elite involvement in the trade. This currency value would have provided participation incentives for the king and elite Aksumites beyond subsistence markets or the patronage value of salt (Wolska-Conus 1962).

Given the difficulty of the journey, profit margins from the sale of salt or obsidian in rural areas, where demand was not as great as in urban areas, would have been minimal. Thus, ancient participants on the Afar trade route who sold or exchanged salt in villages and farming areas must have done so on a subsistence basis. I would anticipate that non-elite small-scale traders or farmers and other individuals participating in a salt niche economy provided most of the salt in smaller villages and rural areas.

Ethnographic and archaeological data from this study indicate that participation in salt production and salt (and obsidian) trade on the Afar route required logistical investment by the elite and non-elite alike; however, the larger the amount traded, the more significant the investment needed.

AKSUMITE TRADE: A CONTEXT FOR
PREHISTORIC SOCIAL DIFFERENTIATION

Information on the organization of Aksumite long-distance trade provides a broad framework for understanding the organization and contribution of regional trade to Aksumite societies. It also provides perspective on the role of elite resources and logistical participation in trade on the Afar salt route. During the first millennium BCE, agro-pastoral Aksumites discovered that products they lacked in the highlands could be found farther south, east, and west (Kobishchanov 1979; Pankhurst 1968; Selassie 1972; Taddesse 1968). They also profited from regional and international demand for highland goods. The exotic nature of goods from the highlands—including ivory, skins, and gold—and their demand in the world system spawned long-distance trade. Excavation of burial chambers at Aksumite sites has shown that royalty and powerful members of society were buried with Egyptian and Mediterranean imports, including Egyptian blue glass, amphorae, and copper tools (D. Phillipson 2012). It is clear that elite Aksumites were involved in the larger Nile trade and, like the ancient Nubians, were middlemen between the African hinterland and the world system. Stuart C. Munro-Hay (1991) and other scholars also believe the accumulation of sumptuous goods played a role in establishing and maintaining elite prestige.

The Aksumites were interested in limiting wealth to a few individuals. Clear evidence of this is found in the construction by kings and nobles of mega-stelae, burial grounds, temples, and churches for their exclusive use and the acquisition of local and exotic goods for their pleasure. The Aksum stelae park contains some of the largest single blocks of carved stone ever made and must have required an enormous number of laborers to construct (D. Phillipson 1998). Aksumite kings even took the title of *neguse* ("king of kings") to show the divine status of their power (Munro-Hay 1991).

The Aksumite elite were organizing forces in many aspects of life in the northern Ethiopian highlands. In addition to mobilizing labor for construction, they were also engaged in feeding people. Evidence in ancient texts, for example, suggests that the Aksumites paid for services and loyalty with bread, meat, and cattle (Kobishchanov 1979; Littmann 1907). Comparatively little is known about the daily lives of the non-elite and their interactions with the powerful elite.

At the end of the first millennium BCE, Adulis (the Aksumite port town and market) became the chief town and market center for African goods from inland and exotic goods from the Red Sea and the Indian Ocean regions. Aksum, the center of the Aksumite polity, was a ten-day walk from Adulis by caravan (Munro-Hay 1991). By controlling trade at Adulis, the Aksumites took advantage of the Egyptian ships coming down the Red Sea and ships coming across the Indian Ocean from West Asia. From Adulis, goods were transferred to Aksum by caravans (Littmann 1907; Munro-Hay 1991; Taddesse 1968).

One distinctive aspect of caravans is their ability to travel long distances, passing through local and non-local territories settled and controlled by diverse groups of people—including local elites, sedentary farmers, mobile pastoralists, and hunter-gatherers (Clarkson et al. 2017). As a result, control of the caravan trade route can fall into the hands of a variety of social institutions. The Aksumite elite and traders were accustomed to using trade as a source of wealth and prestige and to organizing caravans across the highlands and through several key escarpment passes, such as from the city Qohaito (2,500 m asl) in the northern lowlands to the coastal port Adulis (Anfray 1974). Highland traders served as middlemen for the long-distance trade between the Horn of Africa and the Red Sea. But little is known about how the participants were organized on the long-distance trade route.

Scholars do not know how united the surrounding regions were with the Aksumite polity, but it is clear that the Aksumites' trading partners had their own languages and identities. Aksumite inscriptions mention different ethnic groups with which the Aksumites interacted, such as the Beja pastoralists to the west. There is also textual evidence such as that regarding the Sasu gold trade to suggest that the Aksumites traded with people whose language they could not speak (Kobishchanov 1979). Security was certainly an issue on such trade routes—as it is today—and was often state-controlled. In ancient Nubia and Egypt, it was common for the state government to construct forts to protect caravan routes (Hafsaas-Tsakos 2009; Kendall 1997). Unlike their northern counterparts, the Aksumites did not build walls to protect trade routes or towns. Textual evidence from the period, however, indicates that Aksumite rulers used warriors to protect trading parties traveling to remote regions south and north of Aksum (Kobishchanov 1979; Munro-Hay 1991). Historical texts also record that the Aksumites sent soldiers and generals all the way to Yemen to protect their long-distance interests (Robin 1981).

It is possible that traders on the Afar route faced hostility at times from some of the diverse people found along the long-distance and local trade routes during the Aksumite period. Based on their actions on the route to Adulis, securing the economic corridor to the east toward the lowland salt and obsidian sources would have been a significant preoccupation of Aksumite rulers. Security concerns would have created an opportunity for collaboration with local leaders and thus more horizontal power structures.

Both the terrain and the scarcity of supplies make salt caravan travel unpredictable. Good political relations with pastoralists for logistical supplies and protection in the lowlands were essential. Today, caravanners carry enough food from their villages and towns in the highlands to last the entire journey to the Afar salt flat, but they rely on good relations with pastoralist villages in the lowlands for logistical supplies on their return. Resources are scarce, especially in the route's hot, dry, low portion. In addition, there are only a few viable passes on the salt trail for pack caravans to travel from the highlands to the lowlands. There may have been a role for the state in these relationships in ancient times. While I did not discover any forts or defensive structures on the route I traveled, further exploration is needed to determine if evidence of state participation can be found in other passes.

In medieval times, the state used local elites and churches to levy taxes. The terrain on the salt route provided Aksumite elites with the opportunity to erect tax polls at strategic locations such as valleys or passes through which all caravans had to travel. The ancient Aksumite state could similarly have taxed the trade by enrolling local elites or elders or by sending state agents to major passes as far along the route as the present-day Afar tax collection site at Hamed Ela. The location of Aksumite churches on the Afar route in ancient trading settlements and the documented role of medieval churches in tax collection strongly suggest that the church did, in fact, play such a role in Aksumite times.

Cuisine and cooking technology are good markers for regional participation and identity on the ancient salt trade route. Contemporary highland caravanners make wheat, barley, and sorghum stone-baked bread on the trail, whereas lowland caravanners prefer only sorghum bread. The presence of barley in large quantities in roughly built rooms dating to the Aksumite period in the foothill town Desi'a on the salt trade route suggests that it was the preferred food of the non-elite salt traders and their livestock. Sorghum was not recovered from the ancient salt trail, which could reflect greater use of these mid-elevation towns by farmers than by pastoralists. However, it may also relate to the history of sorghum and changing dietary preferences.

In summary, the archaeology of the salt route indicates that the Aksumite elite used the Afar trade to maintain their power and expand into new territories and also demonstrates that it would have been advantageous for Aksumite leaders to create alliances with competing regional elites in the northern highlands and the Afar lowlands. I suggest that the Aksumite state mediated security and political relations among diverse highlanders and between highlanders and lowlanders. The state benefited from the trade in a variety of ways—including the provision of highlanders with salt, which was dietarily significant, and obsidian, a key raw material for craft production. The Aksumite state would have benefited from the accumulation of wealth by any members of the elite who participated in organizing trade caravans and probably also from taxation mediated by churches on the route. Small-scale farmers and traders, specialized artisans, and residents of settlements along the trade route participated in the annual trade—as evidenced by the location on the route of towns such as Agula and Desi'a, the presence of non-elite architecture, and the nature of the ceramics found in trading towns in the borderlands between the highlands and the lowlands. As a result, trade on the Afar route during Aksumite times is likely to have contributed to the wealth and prestige of elite individuals and mitigated agricultural uncertainty among small-scale farmers and herders.

CONCLUSION

The Aksumite state was among the most influential civilizations in the period between 450 BCE and 900 CE, and it controlled trade in the Red Sea region (Fattovich 1977; Munro-Hay 1993; D. Phillipson 2012). Cattle wealth, indigenous agriculture, and long-distance trade played a well-documented role in the economy, elite accumulation of power, and development of the centralized, hierarchical Aksumite state. The dynamic nature of northern Ethiopia's regional salt trade acknowledges vertical power structures but emphasizes the complexity and variability of ancient political systems in Aksumite times. In northern Ethiopia, hierarchical, heterarchical, and cooperative power relationships have functioned concomitantly across time and space, existing side by side in Aksumite times as they do today and in regions spanning highland to lowland and urban to rural.

Salt trade and caravan organization on the Afar route are key to contextualizing the structure of Aksumite power and the use of the salt trail from the Afar lowlands to the northern Ethiopia highlands during the Aksumite period. Ethnoarchaeological fieldwork in Tigray and the Afar region documents that the salt caravan trade serves as a niche economy for small-scale traders who

https://doi.org/10.5876/9781646424733.c008

rely on farming and pastoralism during a portion of the year. Caravans from various highland areas follow dendritic pathways defined by mountain passes, converging in the lowlands with travelers from different parts of the highlands and Afar pastoralist caravanners. This study's archaeological survey and excavation uncovered three major towns with associated settlements, churches, and caravan campsites located in transitional zones/ecotones on the Afar trade route that connected the local and long-distance routes. Ceramics, obsidian artifacts, and characteristic bread-making stones from caravan campsites, settlements, and churches revealed the diversity of participants in the trade, including highlanders and lowlanders as well as elites and non-elites from different areas. Based on the location of settlements in the highlands and ecotonal areas, the presence and orientation of churches in settlements on the Afar route, and elite ceramics and building materials, I have argued that the elite were involved in organizing large-scale trade on the Afar route. The salt obtained filled the demand from urban areas and provided an avenue for patronage and a source of wealth. Small-scale traders and subsistence farmers and herders were able to create a niche economy, collecting salt on a part-time subsistence basis. The location of a non-elite farming town such as Desi'a in the arid foothills on the salt trail—which, though important, was seasonal—demonstrates farmers' investment in the ancient salt trade.

By studying domestic comestibles rather than international luxury trade to the Red Sea, I have approached trade from a broader point of view than have other Aksumite studies. This research sheds new light on simultaneous hierarchical and heterarchical relationships in Aksumite trade by collecting data at different levels of the economic ladder. Control of trade has often been attributed to the elite in a top-down manner because it is the elite architecture and impressive monuments that survive and have been the most studied; this is certainly true of the Aksumites. This book details the role of informal economies on the ancient Afar trade route and argues that local power brokers such as urban salt merchants and pastoralist community leaders also played a role in regional trade and, ultimately, in shaping and maintaining the state's power. Ethnoarchaeological and archaeological data from Ethiopia's eastern highlands and Afar lowlands show how trade and exchange have structured relationships between pastoralists and agriculturalists as well as highlanders and lowlanders over time. Differential power has been a factor in these relations, but so too have cooperation and interdependence. These perspectives allow us to depart from the dominant theories of the last 100 years that give precedence to hierarchical or vertical power control in ancient Ethiopia and to more effectively explore new evidence from the region.

The archaeology of the Afar salt trail discussed in this book provides the basis for future studies of varied interactions between highland and lowland communities, direct and indirect exchange, and the complexity of Aksumite and other ancient regional economies and political structures. Large-scale excavations of settlements that I have identified along the routes and in transition zones have great potential to illuminate other aspects of ancient trade both in northern Ethiopia and worldwide. My research examined a portion of the vast Afar salt route; future archaeological research will be needed to explore the remainder of the route and test the hypotheses I have proposed in this book.

These Aksumite data on the roles of non-elite local and state actors on the Afar salt route prompt an examination of concepts and models developed in other parts of the world regarding the political and social structures of early states and polities. One discussion forwarded here is whether it should be considered axiomatic that heterarchical and horizontal cooperative peer networks coexisted with vertical power structures in ancient polities. Scholars can continue to gain insights by comparing the similarities and differences of cases with diverse organizational settings, from the well-known diffuse heterarchical power structures at Jenne-Jeno in Mali (McIntosh 1999) to the more vertically structured trade in Old Kingdom Egypt (Förster 2007) and the flatter, more nomad-driven structure of the proto-Silk Roads (Frachetti et al. 2012).

Both hierarchical and more heterarchical organizations of salt trading are well-known among settled agricultural towns and production areas in ancient states in Central America (the Maya lowlands) and China (Han dynasty). The organization of the modern and ancient Afar salt trail has more in common with long-distance trade among pastoralists and small-scale agricultural farmers around the world than with large-scale agricultural-based polities. Nevertheless, the scale and rich detail of the contemporary Ethiopian salt trail to the Afar have much to offer scholars of ancient trade worldwide (see the Intraregional and Interregional Interaction and Political Landscapes section in chapter 2 for examples of cultures elsewhere where the model developed in this book can be tested). Future research will reveal more about the role of small-scale actors in ancient Aksumite trade and the diversity of individuals and institutions that contributed to the wealth and power of ancient societies globally.

This study of the modern and ancient Afar salt route also contributes to documenting the deep cultural heritage of the salt trade in northern Ethiopia, where it has functioned as a sustainable economic strategy for thousands of years. This practice reflects indigenous knowledge of the environment passed on from generation to generation. It provides information for studies of animal use in small-scale technology today and research on relations between increases in household income and pack animal ownership (Gebreab et al. 2005; Wilson 1991). The Afar salt route also encourages us to think in terms of concrete historical processes rather than in abstract terms, as well as to consider the unique local and regional biodiversity of pack animals that may be lost if the long-term effects of ancient trade and exchange are not evaluated.

Each caravan—which originates in a different hamlet connected by the Afar trade's dendritic network—spreads news, forges connections between people living in the highlands and those living in the lowlands, and works as a unique catalyst for cultural exchange. As one of the last remaining pack animal–based systems, it also serves as a living example of how commerce functioned in much of the world before the invention of the steam engine. In many parts of the world, pack animal–based caravans are being replaced by trucks and modern roads; this also applies to the Afar salt route. Since my fieldwork, new roads cutting through mountains in northern Ethiopia have been built to open up the Afar Desert to tourists and investors. This project hopes to help preserve this rich northern Ethiopian tradition.

APPENDIX A

UTENSILS AND PERSONAL POSSESSIONS

FOOD PREPARATION

Utensils

- Metal, wooden, or plastic bowl for mixing *shiro* with bread crumbs and salt
- Spoon (metal or horn)
- Teacup (plastic or gourd)
- Sandstone cobbles for bread making
- *Sorit* (sack made of goat skin) for storing water
- *Madaberia* (plastic or fiber sack for storing flour)
- Knife (metal)
- Jerry can (5–10 liter)
- Plastic or gourd jar (1 liter)

Food

- Wheat, barley, or sorghum flour to make bread (*birkuta*, *gogo*)
- *Shiro* powder (spiced chickpea and fava bean powder used to make a sauce)

https://doi.org/10.5876/9781646424733.c009

- Sugar, tea, and coffee
- Hay for the pack animals
- Chaf (*te'f*, wheat, barley) from the highlands
- Wild grass from the lowlands and the highlands

PERSONAL POSSESSIONS

- Wooden comb
- *Mefakia* (wooden toothbrush)
- *Gabi* (blanket made of cotton)
- Scarf to protect head from the heat (wool)
- Shoes (sandals or flip-flops made of plastic or leather)
- Flashlight, D-cell batteries
- Knife (for protection against predators)
- Cloth shorts or wraparounds
- T-shirts and long-sleeved shirts
- Wooden stick for herding

PACK GEAR

- Pack pads—*gula* and *kuda*
- Pack hooks—*anabu*, *koree*, and *koyeta*
- Ropes and straps made of grass fiber and leather for strapping the load on packs

APPENDIX B
STANDARD SIZES OF SALT BLOCKS

| No. | Salt Type | Salt Size | |
		Cm (w × h × d)	Weight (kg)
1.	Gole'o	24 × 36 × 6	8
2.	Gerawayni	23 × 30 × 6	6
3.	Ankarabe	22 × 30 × 5	5

https://doi.org/10.5876/9781646424733.c010

APPENDIX C

SUMMARY OF PARTICIPANTS

No.	Category of Participants	Number of Participants per Region		Grand Total
		Tigray	*Afar*	
1	Caravanners	117	41	158
2	Salt miners	5	0	5
3	Salt cutters	0	8	8
4	Warehouse owners	10	2	12
5	Middlemen	5	0	5
6	Shop owners	18	0	18
7	Residents	16	11	27
8	*Sar* makers	0	3	3
	Total	171	65	
	Grand Total			230

https://doi.org/10.5876/9781646424733.c011

APPENDIX D

DOMESTIC CEREALS

Taxon	Latin Binomial and Authority	Count	Ubiquity (percent)	Count (percent)
Te'f	Eragrostis teff	41	38	1
Te'f	Eragrostis cf. teff	2	15	<1
Barley	Hordeum cf. vulgare	4,908	62	83
Barley	Hordeum sp.	246	23	4
Wheat	Triticum sp.	141	46	2
Wheat	Triticum cf. dicoccum spikelet fork	10	23	<1
Unidentifiable cereals	Unidentifiable cereals	556	69	9
	Total	5,904		100

https://doi.org/10.5876/9781646424733.c012

APPENDIX E

SUMMARY OF FAUNAL REMAINS IN NISP (NUMBER OF IDENTIFIED SPECIMENS) BY SITE AND CONTEXT

Taxa	Ona Adi Agway	Cherkos Agula	Ona Hahaile U2	Ona Hahaile U3	Ona Adi Abobay	Meda Ble'at	Grand Total
?*Camelus dromedarius* (cf. camel)	0	0	2	0	0	0	2
Caprini (sheep/goat)	43	25	72	6	0	0	146
Capra hircus (goat)	0	0	2	0	0	0	2
Bos taurus/indicus (cattle)	156	67	49	16	1	0	289
?*Madoqua* cf. Dik-Dik	1	0	0	0	0	0	1
Rodent	1	1	0	0	0	0	2
Bovid	49	22	52	0	0	0	123
Large bovid	110	2	1	0	0	0	113
Medium bovid	60	0	0	1	0	0	61
Small bovid	3	0	0	0	0	0	3
PID mammal	89	49	49	8	0	0	195
Gallus gallus D. (chicken)	1	0	0	0	0	0	1
Aves (birds)	1	0	0	0	0	0	1
Total NISP	514	166	227	31	1	0	939

https://doi.org/10.5876/9781646424733.c013

APPENDIX F

SHERD COUNT BY SITE AND PHASE

Site	Exc. Units	Phases	Levels	Areas (m²)	Number Decorated	Number Undecorated	Number Indeterminate
Ona Adi Agway	1	1	6, 7, 8	75	110	376	–
		2	4, 5	50	85	342	–
		3	1, 2, 3	75	104	271	–
Cherkos Agula	1	1	6	18	17	65	16
		2	4, 5	18	26	168	53
		3	1, 2, 3	18	41	231	100
Ona Hahaile	2	1	3, 4, 5	27	16	162	76
		2	1, 2	18	124	277	195
	3	1	3, 4	18	4	24	6
		2	1, 2	18	6	66	22
Ona Adi Abobay	1	1	2	9	2	10	–
		2	1	9	1	12	–
Meda Ble'at	1	1	3	4	–	1	–
		2	2	4	–	6	–
		3	1	4	–	8	–
Grand Total					536	2,019	468

https://doi.org/10.5876/9781646424733.c014

APPENDIX G

INVENTORY OF LITHICS STUDIED FROM EXCAVATION OF ALL SITES

Lithics	Ona Adi Agway				Cherkos Agula			Ona Hahaile U2		Ona Hahaile U3	
	Ph I	Ph II	Ph III	Survey	Ph I	Ph II	Ph III	Ph I	Ph II	Ph I	Ph II
Core	0	0	2	0	0	0	1	0	0	0	0
Recycled core	0	0	0	0	0	0	0	0	0	0	0
Bipolar core fragment	0	1	0	0	0	0	0	0	0	0	0
Bipolar core	1	0	0	0	0	0	0	0	0	0	0
Core trimming flake	0	0	0	0	0	1	0	4	0	0	0
Single platform core	0	0	0	0	1	0	0	0	0	0	0
Opposing platform core	0	0	0	0	0	0	0	0	0	0	0
Burin spall	0	0	0	0	0	0	0	0	0	0	0
Shatter	0	0	0	0	0	0	0	0	0	0	0
Angular waste	0	0	0	0	3	0	1	0	0	0	0
Flake	2	2	2	1	2	1	1	0	1	0	0
Flake fragment	1	0	0	1	3	1	0	0	0	1	0
Trampled	0	0	0	0	0	0	0	0	0	0	0
Bipolar flake	0	0	0	0	0	0	0	0	0	0	0
Bipolar flake fragment	0	0	0	0	0	0	0	0	0	0	0
Utilized unshaped	1	1	0	0	0	0	0	0	0	0	0
Shaped tool	1	0	0	0	0	0	1	0	0	0	0
Modified unshaped	0	0	0	0	1	0	0	0	0	0	0
Partially backed	0	0	0	0	0	0	0	0	0	0	0
Curved backed	0	0	0	0	0	0	0	0	1	0	0
Grand Total	6	4	4	2	10	3	4	4	2	1	0

https://doi.org/10.5876/9781646424733.c015

	Meda Ble'at			Ona Adi Abobay				Desi'a C. Camp	Usot	Grand Total	
	Ph I	Ph II	Ph III	Ph I	Ph II	Ph III	Survey	Survey	Survey	Total N	%
	0	0	0	0	0	2	0	0	I	6	6
	0	0	I	0	0	0	0	0	0	I	I
	0	0	0	0	0	0	0	0	0	I	I
	0	0	0	0	0	0	0	0	I	2	2
	0	0	0	0	0	0	0	0	0	5	5
	0	I	0	0	0	0	0	0	0	2	2
	0	0	0	0	0	0	I	0	0	I	I
	0	0	0	0	0	0	I	0	0	I	I
	0	0	0	0	0	0	0	2	0	2	2
	0	0	I	0	I	I	0	0	0	7	6
	0	0	3	0	0	0	0	I	3	19	17
	0	I	I	0	4	0	0	4	I	18	17
	0	I	I	0	0	0	0	0	0	2	2
	0	0	0	0	0	0	0	0	3	3	3
	0	0	0	0	I	0	0	0	0	I	I
	0	0	0	0	6	2	I	14	3	28	26
	0	0	0	0	I	0	0	0	0	3	3
	0	0	I	0	0	0	I	I	I	5	5
	0	0	0	0	0	0	0	0	I	I	I
	0	0	0	0	0	0	0	0	0	I	I
	0	3	8	0	13	5	2	20	12	109	74

REFERENCES

Abbink, Jon. 1990. "'The Enigma of Beta Esra'el Ethnogenesis: An Anthro-Historical Study." *Cahiers d'études Africaines* 30 (120): 397–449. doi: 10.3406/cea.1990.1592.

Abir, Mordechai. 1966. "Salt, Trade, and Politics in Ethiopia in the 'Zämänä Mäsafent.'" *Journal of Ethiopian Studies* 4 (2): 1–10. https://www.jstor.org/stable/41965738.

Abir, Mordechai. 1968. *Ethiopia, the Era of the Princes: The Challenge of Islam and Reunification of the Christian Empire, 1769–1855.* Westport, CT: Praeger.

Abir, Mordechal. 1992. "Mohammed Hassen, The Oromo of Ethiopia: A History 15701860, African Studies Series No. 66 (Cambridge: Cambridge University Press, 1990). Pp. 270." *International Journal of Middle East Studies* 24 (2): 344–46. https://doi-org.libproxy.wustl.edu/10.1017/S0020743800021784.

Abungu, George H. O., and Henry W. Mutoro. 1993. "Coast-Interior Settlements and Social Relations in the Kenya Coastal Hinterland." In *The Archaeology of Africa: Food, Metals, and Towns,* ed. Thurstan Shaw, Paul Sinclair, Bassey Andah, and Alex Okpoko, 694–704. New York: Routledge.

Acton, Roger. 1868. *The Abyssinian Expedition and the Life and Reign of King Theodore.* London: Office of the Illustrated London News.

https://doi.org/10.5876/9781646424733.c016

Adams, Robert M. 1975. "The Emerging Place of Trade in Civilizational Studies." In *Ancient Civilization and Trade*, ed. Jeremy A. Sabloff and Cyrus Clarke Lamberg-Karlovsky, 451–466. Albuquerque: University of New Mexico Press.

Adams, Robert M. 1992. "Anthropological Perspectives on Ancient Trade." *Current Anthropology* 33 (1): 141–160. doi: 10.1086/204022.

Ahmed, Abdullahi M. 1990. "A Survey of the Harar Djugel (Wall) and Its Gates." *Journal of Ethiopian Studies* 23:321–334.

Ahmed, Hussein. 1992. "The Historiography of Islam in Ethiopia." *Journal of Islamic Studies* 3 (1): 15–46.

Alagoa, Ebiegberi Joe. 1970. "Long-Distance Trade and States in the Niger Delta." *Journal of African History* 11 (3): 319–329. doi: 10.1017/S0021853700010173.

Alemseged, Zeresenay, Fred Spoor, William H. Kimbel, René Bobe, Denis Geraads, Denné Reed, and Jonathan G. Wynn. 2006. "A Juvenile Early Hominin Skeleton from Dikika, Ethiopia." *Nature* 443 (7109): 296–301. doi.org/10.1038/nature05047.

Alexander, John. 1975. "The Salt Industries of Africa: Their Significance for European Prehistory." In *Salt, the Study of an Ancient Industry: Report on the Salt Weekend Held at the University of Essex 20–22 September 1974*, ed. Kay W. De Brisay and Kathleen A. Evans, 81–83. Colchester: Colchester Archaeological Group.

Alexander, John. 1982. "The Prehistoric Salt Trade in Europe." *Nature* 300 (5893): 577–578. doi.org/10.1038/300577a0.

Alexander, John. 1985. "The Production of Salt and Salt Trading Networks of Central and Western Europe in the First Millennium BC." In *Studi di paletnologia in onore di Salvatore M. Puglisi*, ed. Rita Scopacasa, 563–569. Rome: Università di Roma "La Sapienza."

Alexander, John. 1993. "The Salt Industries of West Africa: A Preliminary Study." In *The Archaeology of Africa: Food, Metals, and Towns*, ed. Thurstan Shaw, Paul Sinclair, Bassey Andah, and Alex Okpoko, 652–657. New York: Routledge.

Alexianu, Marius, and Olivier Weller. 2009. "The Ethnosal Project: Ethnoarchaeological Investigation at the Moldavian Salt Springs." *Antiquity* 83 (321): 1–3.

Almathen, Faisal, Pauline Charruau, Elmira Mohandesan, Joram M. Mwacharo, Pablo Orozco-terWengel, Daniel Pitt, Abdussamad M. Abdussamad, Margarethe Uerpmann, Hans-Peter Uerpmann, and Bea De Cupere. 2016. "Ancient and Modern DNA Reveal Dynamics of Domestication and Cross-Continental Dispersal of the Dromedary." *Proceedings of the National Academy of Sciences* 113 (24): 6707–6712. doi.org/10.1073/pnas.151950811.

Ambrose, Stanley H. 1984. "The Introduction of Pastoral Adaptations to the Highlands of East Africa." In *From Hunters to Farmers: The Causes and Consequences of Food Production in Africa*, ed. John Desmond Clark and Steven A. Brandt, 212–239. Berkeley: University of California Press.

Anderson, Eugene Newton. 2014. *Everyone Eats: Understanding Food and Culture*. New York: New York University Press.

Andrews, Anthony P. 1980. "Salt and the Maya: Major Prehispanic Trading Spheres." PhD diss., University of Arizona, Tucson.

Anfray, Francis. 1966. "La Poterie de Matara: Esquisse typologique." *Rassegna di studi etiopici* 22:5–74. https://www.jstor.org/stable/41299562.

Anfray, Francis. 1968. "Les Rois d'Axoum d'après la numismatique." *Journal of Ethiopian Studies* 6 (2): 1–5. https://www.jstor.org/stable/41960897.

Anfray, Francis. 1970. "Notes archéologiques." *Annales d'Ethiopie* 8:31–56. doi: 10.3406/ethio.1970.881.

Anfray, Francis. 1972. "Fouilles de Yeha." *Annales d'Ethiopie* 9:45–64.

Anfray, Francis. 1974. "Deux villes Axoumites: Adoulis et Matara." In *IV Congresso internazionale de studi etiopici*, ed. Taddese Beyene, 745–765. Rome: Academia Nazionale dei Lincei.

Anfray, Francis. 1990. *Les Anciens Ethiopiens: Siècles d'histoire*. Paris: Armand Colin.

Apaak, Clement Abas. 2008. "The Socio-economic Role of Salt in Northern Highland Ethiopia." PhD diss., Simon Fraser University, Burnaby, BC.

Appadurai, Arjun. 1988. *The Social Life of Things: Commodities in Cultural Perspective*. Cambridge: Cambridge University Press.

Aquilea, Rufinus, and Tyrannius Rufinus. 1997. *The Church History of Rufinus of Aquileia, Books 10 and 11*. Edited and translated by Philip R. Amidon. New York: Oxford University Press.

Asfaw, Berhane, Yonas Beyene, Sileshi Semaw, Gen Suwa, Tim White, and Giday WoldeGabriel. 1991. "Fejej: A New Paleoanthropological Research Area in Ethiopia." *Journal of Human Evolution* 21 (2): 137–143. doi.org/10.1016/0047-2484(91)90004-F.

Asfaw, Berhane, Yonas Beyene, Gen Suwa, Robert C. Walter, Tim D. White, Giday WoldeGabriel, and Tesfaye Yemane. 1992. "The Earliest Acheulean from Konso-Gardula." *Nature* 360 (6406): 732–735. doi.org/10.1038/360732a0.

Atici, Levent. 2014. "Tracing Inequality from Assur to Kültepe/Kanesh: Merchants, Donkeys, and Clay Tablets." In *Animals and Inequality in the Ancient World*, ed. Benjamin S. Arbuckle and Sue Ann McCarty, 231–250. Boulder: University Press of Colorado.

Bard, Kathryn A., Mauro Coltorti, Michael C. DiBlasi, Francesco Dramis, and Rodolfo Fattovich. 2000. "The Environmental History of Tigray (Northern Ethiopia) in the Middle and Late Holocene: A Preliminary Outline." *African Archaeological Review* 17 (2): 65–86. doi: 10.1023/A:1006630609041.

Bard, Kathryn A., Rodolfo Fattovich, Andrea Manzo, and Cinzia Perlingieri. 1997. "Archaeological Investigations at Bieta Giyorgis (Aksum), Ethiopia: 1993–1995 Field Seasons." *Journal of Field Archaeology* 24 (4): 387–403. doi: 10.1179/jfa.1997.24.4.387.

Barfield, Thomas J. 2001. "The Shadow Empires: Imperial State Formation along the Chinese-Nomad Frontier." In *Empires: Perspectives from Archaeology and History*, ed.

Susan E. Alcock, Terence N. D'Altroy, Kathleen D. Morrison, and Carla M. Sinopoli, 10–41. Cambridge: Cambridge University Press.

Barnett, Tertia. 1999. *The Emergence of Food Production in Ethiopia*. Oxford: Archaeopress (British Archaeological Reports S. 763).

Barrett-Gaines, Kathryn. 2004. "The Katwe Salt Industry: A Niche in the Great Lakes Regional Economy." *African Economic History* 32:15–49. jstor.org/stable/3601616.

Barth, Fritz Eckart. 1967. "Prähistorische Knieholzschäftungen aus dem Salzberg zu Hallstatt, OÖ." *Mitt(h)eilungen der Gesellschaft für Salzburger Landeskunde* 115 (2): 313–320.

Barth, Heinrich. 1896. *Travels and Discoveries in North and Central Africa: Being a Journal of an Expedition Undertaken under the Auspices of HBM's Government, in the Years 1849–1855*. Vol. 3. Drallop.

Batterson, Mark, and William W. Boddie. 1972. *Salt, the Mysterious Necessity*. Midland, MI: Dow Chemical Company.

Bauer, Dan Franz. 1975. "For Want of an Ox . . . : Land, Capital, and Social Stratification in Tigre." In *Proceedings of the First United States Conference on Ethiopian Studies, Michigan State University, 2–5 May 1973*, ed. Harold G. Marcus and John T. Hinnant, 235–248. East Lansing: African Studies Center, Michigan State University.

Bauer, Dan Franz. 1977. *Household and Society in Ethiopia: An Economic and Social Analysis of Tigray Social Principles and Household Organization*. East Lansing: African Studies Center, Michigan State University.

Baxter, Paul Trevor William. 1991. *When the Grass Is Gone: Development Intervention in African Arid Lands*. Vol. 25. Uppsala: Nordic Africa Institute.

Beckingham, Charles Fraser, and George Wynn Brereton Huntingford. 1961. *The Prester John of the Indies, a True Relation of the Lands of the Prester John, Being the Narrative of the Portuguese Embassy to Ethiopia in 1520 Written by Father Francisco Alvares*. London: Hakluyt Society.

Beckingham, Charles Fraser, and George Wynn Brereton Huntingford. 1962. "The Prester John of the Indies (Cambridge, 1961)." *History* 47 (159): 60–61.

Behrens, Sven. 1971. *Physical Environment and Its Significance for Economic Development*. Lund: Department of Geography, Royal University of Lund.

Beldados, Alemseged, and Lorenzo Costantini. 2011. "Sorghum Exploitation at Kassala and Its Environs, Northeastern Sudan, in the Second and First Millennium BC." *Nyame Akuma* 75:33–39.

Bent, James Theodore. 1893. *The Sacred City of the Ethiopians: Being a Record of Travel and Research in Abyssinia in 1893*. London: Longmans, Green.

Berenguer, José. 1994. "Asentamientos, caravaneros y tráfico de larga distancia en el norte de Chile: El caso de Santa Bárbara." In *Taller de costa a selva: Intercambio y producción en los Andes Centro Sur*, ed. María Eester Albec, 17–50. Provincia de Jujuy, Argentina: Instituto Interdisciplinario de Tilcara.

Bernand, Etienne, Abraham Johannes Drewes, and Roger Schneider. 1991. *Recueil des inscriptions de l'Ethiopie des périodes pré-Axoumite et Axoumite*. 3 vols. Paris: Académie des Inscriptions et Belles-Lettres.

Bernus, Edmond, and Suzanne Bernus. 1972. *Du Sel et des dattes; Introduction a l'étude de la communauté d'In Gall et de Tegidda-n-Tesemt*. Centre nigérien de recherches en sciences humaines. http://www.worldcat.org/oclc/828805.

Berry, Sara. 2004. "Value and Ambiguity: Evidence and Ideas from African 'Niche Economies.'" *African Economic History* 32:143–151. jstor.org/stable/3601622.

Beyin, Amanuel. 2011a. "Early to Middle Holocene Human Adaptations on the Buri Peninsula and Gulf of Zula, Coastal Lowlands of Eritrea." *Azania: Archaeological Research in Africa* 46 (2): 123–140. doi: 10.1080/0067270X.2011.580139.

Beyin, Amanuel. 2011b. "Upper Pleistocene Human Dispersals Out of Africa: A Review of the Current State of the Debate." *International Journal of Evolutionary Biology* 2011 (2011): 1–17. doi: 10.4061/2011/615094.

Beyin, Amanuel. 2013. "A Surface Middle Stone Age Assemblage from the Red Sea Coast of Eritrea: Implications for Upper Pleistocene Human Dispersals Out of Africa." *Quaternary International* 300:195–212. doi: 10.1016/j.quaint.2013.02.015.

Biginagwa, Thomas John. 2012. "Historical Archaeology of the Nineteenth-Century Caravan Trade in Northeastern Tanzania: A Zooarchaeological Perspective." *Azania: Archaeological Research in Africa* 47 (3): 405–406. doi.org/10.1080/0067270X.2012.707482.

Birmingham, David, and Richard Gray. 1970. "Early African Trade in Angola and Its Hinterland." In *Pre-colonial African Trade: Essays on Trade in Central and Eastern Africa before 1900*, ed. Richard Gray and David Birmingham, 163–173. London: Oxford University Press.

Blanton, Richard E. 2010. "Collective Action and Adaptive Socioecological Cycles in Premodern States." *Cross-Cultural Research* 44 (1): 41–59. doi.org/10.1177/1069397109351684.

Blanton, Richard E., Gary M. Feinman, Stephen A. Kowalewski, and Peter N. Peregrine. 1996. "A Dual-Processual Theory for the Evolution of Mesoamerican Civilization." *Current Anthropology* 37 (1): 1–14. doi: 10.1086/204471.

Bohannan, Paul, and George Dalton, eds. 1962. *Markets in Africa*. Vol. 9. Evanston, IL: Northwestern University Press.

Bouanga, Ayda. 2014. "The Kingdom of Damot: An Inquiry into Political and Economic Power in the Horn of Africa (13th c.)." *Annales d'Éthiopie* 29 (1): 261–264. https://doi.org/10.3406/ethio.2014.1572.

Bovill, Edward William. 1970. *The Golden Trade of the Moors, 1958*. London: Oxford University Press.

Brandt, Steve Andrew. 1982. "A Late Quaternary Cultural/Environmental Sequence from Lake Besaka, Southern Afar, Ethiopia." PhD diss., University of California, Berkeley.

Brandt, Steven Andrew. 1986. "The Upper Pleistocene and Early Holocene Prehistory of the Horn of Africa." *African Archaeological Review* 4 (1): 41–82. doi.org/10.1007/BF01117035.

Brandt, Steven Andrew, Andrea Manzo, and Cinzia Perlingieri. 2008. "Linking the Highlands and Lowlands: Implications of a Test Excavation at Kokan Rockshelter, Agordat, Eritrea." In *The Archaeology of Ancient Eritrea*, ed. Peter R. Schmidt, Matthew C. Curtis, and Zelalem Teka, 33–47. Trenton, NJ: Red Sea Press.

Bray, Tamara L. 2005. "Multi-ethnic Settlement and Interregional Exchange in Pimampiro, Ecuador." *Journal of Field Archaeology* 30 (2): 119–141. doi: 10.1179/00934690 5791072369.

Brigand, Robin, and Olivier Weller. 2015. *Archaeology of Salt: Approaching an Invisible Past.* New York: Routledge.

Brooks, Alison S., and John E. Yellen. 1987. "The Preservation of Activity Areas in the Archaeological Record: Ethnoarchaeological and Archaeological Work in Northwest Ngamiland, Botswana." In *Method and Theory for Activity Area Research: An Ethnoarchaeological Approach*, ed. Susan Kent, 63–106. New York: Columbia University Press.

Browman, David L. 1981. "New Light on Andean Tiwanaku: A Detailed Reconstruction of Tiwanaku's Early Commercial and Religious Empire Illuminates the Processes by which States Evolve." *American Scientist* 69 (4): 408–419. https://www.jstor.org/stable/27850533.

Brumfiel, Elizabeth M. 1995. "Heterarchy and the Analysis of Complex Societies: Comments." *Archeological Papers of the American Anthropological Association* 6 (1): 125–131. doi: 10.1525/ap3a.1995.6.1.125.

Budge, Ernest A. Wallis. 1970. *A History of Ethiopia, Nubia, and Abyssinia: According to the Hieroglyphic Inscriptions of Egypt and Nubia, and the Ethiopian Chronicles.* New York: Dover.

Buxton, David Roden. 1947. "The Christian Antiquities of Northern Ethiopia." *Archaeologia* 92:1–42. doi: 10.1017/S0261340900009863.

Buxton, David Roden. 1967. *Travels in Ethiopia.* New York: Praeger.

Buxton, David Roden. 1971. "II.—the Rock-Hewn and Other Medieval Churches of Tigré Province, Ethiopia." *Archaeologia* 103:33–100. doi: 10.1017/S0261340900013850.

Cain, Chester. 2000. "Animals at Axum: Initial Zooarchaeological Research in the Later Prehistory of the Northern Ethiopian Highlands." PhD diss., Washington University, St. Louis, MO.

Capriles, José M., and Nicholas Tripcevich. 2016. *The Archaeology of Andean Pastoralism.* Albuquerque: University of New Mexico Press.

Carey, Sorcha. 2006. *Pliny's Catalogue of Culture: Art and Empire in the Natural History.* Oxford: Oxford University Press.

Carpenter, Rhys. 1956. "A Trans-Saharan Caravan Route in Herodotus." *American Journal of Archaeology* 60 (3): 231–242. doi.org/10.2307/500150.

Casson, Lionel. 1989. *The Periplus Maris Erythraei: Text with Introduction, Translation, and Commentary.* Princeton, NJ: Princeton University Press.

Casson, Lionel, and Ramsay MacMullen. 2012. *The Periplus Maris Erythraei: Text with Introduction, Translation, and Commentary.* Princeton, NJ: Princeton University Press.

Chaix, Louis. 2013. "The Fauna from the UNO/BU Excavations at Bieta Giyorgis (Aksum) in Tigray, Northern Ethiopia: Campaigns 1995–2003; Pre-Aksumite, 700–400 BC to Late Aksumite, AD 800–1200." *Journal of African Archaeology* 11 (2): 211–241. doi: 10.3213/2191-5784-10244.

Chalfin, Brenda. 2004. "Old Commodities in New Niches: The Shea Economy as Frontier." *African Economic History* 32:51–63. jstor.org/stable/3601617.

Chavaillon, Jean, and Marcello Piperno. 2004. *Studies on the Early Paleolithic Site of Melka Kunture, Ethiopia.* Turin, Italy: Istituto italiano di preistoria e protostoria.

Chedeville, Edouard. 1966. "Quelques faits de l'organisation sociale des 'Afar." *Africa* 36 (2): 173–196. doi: 10.2307/1158203.

Chittick, Neville. 1974. "Excavations at Aksum, 1973–4: A Preliminary Report." *AZANIA: Journal of the British Institute in Eastern Africa* 9 (1): 159–205. doi: 10.1080/00672709511721.

Christie, A. Catherine, and Anne Haour. 2018. "The 'Lost Caravan' of Ma'den Ijafen Revisited: Re-appraising Its Cargo of Cowries, a Medieval Global Commodity." *Journal of African Archaeology* 16 (2): 125–144. doi.org/10.1163/21915784-20180008.

Clark, Gracia. 2004. "Managing Transitions and Continuities in Ghanaian Trading Contexts." *African Economic History* 32:65–88. jstor.org/stable/3601618.

Clark, John Desmond, and Rosamond Glynis Prince. 1978. "Use-Wear on Later Stone Age Microliths from Laga Oda, Haraghi, Ethiopia, and Possible Functional Interpretations." *Azania: Journal of the British Institute in Eastern Africa* 13 (1): 101–110.

Clark, John Desmond, Kenneth D. Williamson, Joseph W. Michels, and Curtis A. Marean. 1984. "A Middle Stone Age Occupation Site at Porc Epic Cave, Dire Dawa (East-Central Ethiopia)." *African Archaeological Review* 2 (1): 37–71. https://www.jstor.org/stable/23617468.

Clarkson, Persis B. 2019. "Caravans of the North: A Comparison of 20th Century Caravans in Northern Canada and Northern Chile 1." *Chungara* 51 (1): 57–69. doi.org/10.4067/S0717-73562019005000101.

Clarkson, Persis B., Calogero M. Santoro, Thomas E. Levy, Lautaro Núñez, Axel Nielsen, Steven Rosen, Frank Förster, José M. Capriles, Anatoly M. Khazanov, Michael Frachetti, Daniela Valenzuela, Vivien G. Standen, Barbara Cases, Gonzalo Pimentel, Patrice Lecoq, Ximena Medinacelli, Luis Briones, André Wink, Nicholas

Tripcevich, Heiko Riemer, Enelidolfo O'Ryan, Ximena Loayza, Thomas F. Lynch, and Helina Woldekiros. 2017. "A Worldwide Network for Comparative Studies on Caravans: Past, Present, and Future." *Chungara, Revista de antropología Chilena* 49 (3). http://www.redalyc.org/resumen.oa?id=32652868001.

Cohen, Abner. 1966. "Politics of the Kola Trade: Some Processes of Tribal Community Formation among Migrants in West African Towns." *Africa* 36 (1): 18–36. doi.org/10.2307/1158126.

Cohen, Abner. 2018. "Cultural Strategies in the Organization of Trading Diasporas." In *The Development of Indigenous Trade and Markets in West Africa: Studies Presented and Discussed at the Tenth International African Seminar at Fourah Bay College Freetown December 1969*, ed. Claude Meillassoux, 266–281. London: Oxford University Press for the International African Institute.

Cohen, Ronald. 1965. "Some Aspects of Institutionalized Exchange: A Kanuri Example." *Cahiers d'études Africaines* 5 (Cahier 19): 353–369. https://www.jstor.org/stable/4390902.

Connah, Graham. 1987. *African Civilizations: Precolonial Cities and States in Tropical Africa, an Archaeological Perspective*. Cambridge: Cambridge University Press.

Connah, Graham. 1991. "The Salt of Bunyoro: Seeking the Origins of an African Kingdom." *Antiquity* 65 (248): 479–494. doi: 10.1017/S0003598X0008008X.

Connah, Graham. 2001. *African Civilizations: An Archaeological Perspective*. 2nd ed. Cambridge: Cambridge University Press.

Connah, Graham, Ephraim Kamuhangire, and Andrew Piper. 1990. "Salt Production at Kibiro." *AZANIA: Journal of the British Institute in Eastern Africa* 25 (1): 27–39. doi.org/10.1080/00672709009511406.

Cowgill, George L. 1997. "State and Society at Teotihuacan, Mexico." *Annual Review of Anthropology* 26 (1): 129–161. doi: 10.1146/annurev.anthro.26.1.129.

Crawford, Osbert Guy Stanhope. 1958. *Ethiopian Itineraries, circa 1400–1524*. Cambridge: Cambridge University Press.

Crumley, Carole L. 1979. "Three Locational Models: An Epistemological Assessment for Anthropology and Archaeology." *Advances in Archaeological Method and Theory* 2:141–173. https://www.jstor.org/stable/20170145.

Crumley, Carole L. 1995. "Heterarchy and the Analysis of Complex Societies." *Archaeological Papers of the American Anthropological Association* 6 (1): 1–5. doi: 10.1525/ap3a.1995.6.1.1.

Crummey, Donald. 2000. *Land and Society in the Christian Kingdom of Ethiopia: From the Thirteenth to the Twentieth Century*. Urbana: University of Illinois Press.

Cumming, Graeme S. 2016. "Heterarchies: Reconciling Networks and Hierarchies." *Trends in Ecology and Evolution* 31 (8): 622–632. doi: 10.1016/j.tree.2016.04.009.

Cunningham, Jerimy J., and Kevin M. McGeough. 2018. "The Perils of Ethnographic Analogy: Parallel Logics in Ethnoarchaeology and Victorian Bible Customs Books." *Archaeological Dialogues* 25 (2): 161–189. doi.org/10.1017/S1380203818000181.

Curtin, Philip D. 1984. *Cross-cultural Trade in World History.* Cambridge: Cambridge University Press.

Curtis, Matthew C. 2008. "New Perspectives for Examining Change and Complexity in the Northern Horn of Africa during the First Millennium BCE." In *The Archaeology of Ancient Eritrea*, ed. Peter Ridgway Schmidt, Matthew C. Curtis, and Zelalem Teka, 329–348. Trenton, NJ: Red Sea Press.

Curtis, Matthew C. 2009. "Relating the Ancient Ona Culture to the Wider Northern Horn: Discerning Patterns and Problems in the Archaeology of the First Millennium BC." *African Archaeological Review* 26 (4): 327–350. doi: 10.1007/s10437-009-9062-4.

Daaku, Kwame Y. 2018. "Trade and Trading Patterns of the Akan in the Seventeenth and Eighteenth Centuries." In *The Development of Indigenous Trade and Markets in West Africa: Studies Presented and Discussed at the Tenth International African Seminar at Fourah Bay College Freetown December 1969*, ed. Claude Meillassoux, 81–168. London: Oxford University Press for the International African Institute.

Dahl, Gudrun, and Anders Hjort. 1976. *Having Herds: Pastoral Herd Growth and Household Economy.* Stockholm: Department of Social Anthropology, University of Stockholm.

D'Andrea, A. Catherine. 2008. "T'ef (*Eragrostis Tef*) in Ancient Agricultural Systems of Highland Ethiopia." *Economic Botany* 62 (4): 547–566. doi: 10.1080/00380768.2011.593482.

D'Andrea, A. Catherine, and Mitiku Haile. 2002. "Traditional Emmer Processing in Highland Ethiopia." *Journal of Ethnobiology* 22 (2): 179–218.

D'Andrea, A. Catherine, Diane Lyons, Mitiku Haile, and Ann Butler. 1999. "Ethnoarchaeological Approaches to the Study of Prehistoric Agriculture in the Highlands of Ethiopia." In *The Exploitation of Plant Resources in Ancient Africa*, ed. Marijke van der Veen, 101–122. New York: Springer.

D'Andrea, A. Catherine, Andrea Manzo, Michael J. Harrower, and Alicia L. Hawkins. 2008. "The Pre-Aksumite and Aksumite Settlement of NE Tigrai, Ethiopia." *Journal of Field Archaeology* 33 (2): 151–176. doi: 10.1179/009346908791071268.

D'Andrea, A. Catherine, Linda Perry, Laurie Nixon-Darcus, Ahmed G. Fahmy, and Elshafaey A. E. Attia. 2018. "A Pre-Aksumite Culinary Practice at the Mezber Site, Northern Ethiopia." In *Plants and People in the African Past*, ed. Anna Maria Mercuri, A. Catherine D'Andrea, Rita Fornaciari, and Alexa Höhn, 453–478. Cham, Switzerland: Springer.

D'Andrea, A. Catherine, Michael P. Richards, Laurence A. Pavlish, Shannon Wood, Andrea Manzo, and Helina S. Wolde-Kiros. 2011. "Stable Isotopic Analysis of Human and Animal Diets from Two Pre-Aksumite/Proto-Aksumite Archaeological Sites in Northern Ethiopia." *Journal of Archaeological Science* 38 (2): 367–374. doi.org/10.1016/j.jas.2010.09.015.

D'Andrea, A. Catherine, Peter R. Schmidt, and Matthew C. Curtis. 2008. "Paleoethno-botanical Analysis and Agricultural Economy in Early First Millennium BCE Sites around Asmara." In *The Archaeology of Ancient Eritrea*, ed. Peter R. Schmidt, Matthew C. Curtis, and Zelalem Teka, 207–216. Trenton, NJ: Red Sea Press.

Davies, Matthew I. J. 2009. "Wittfogel's Dilemma: Heterarchy and Ethnographic Approaches to Irrigation Management in Eastern Africa and Mesopotamia." *World Archaeology* 41 (1): 16–35. doi: 10.1080/00438240802666465.

De Blois, François. 1984. "Clan-Names in Ancient Ethiopia." *Die Welt des Orients* 15: 123–125. https://www.jstor.org/stable/25683145.

Denton, Derek. 1984. *The Hunger for Salt: An Anthropological, Physiological, and Medical Analysis*. Heidelberg: Springer-Verlag.

De Villiers, Marq, and Sheila Hirtle. 2007. *Timbuktu: The Sahara's Fabled City of Gold*. New York: Walker.

De Voragine, Jacobus. 2012. *The Golden Legend: Readings on the Saints*. Princeton, NJ: Princeton University Press.

Dillian, Carolyn D., and Carolyn L. White. 2010. "Introduction: Perspectives on Trade and Exchange." In *Trade and Exchange: Archaeological Studies from History and Prehistory*, ed. Carolyn D. Dillian and Carolyn L. White, 3–14. New York: Springer.

Di Salvo, Mario. 2016. *The Basilicas of Ethiopia: An Architectural History*. London: Bloomsbury.

Di Salvo, Mario, and Carolyn Gossage. 2017. *The Basilicas of Ethiopia: An Architectural History*. London: I. B. Tauris.

Dombrowski, Joanne Carol. 1970. "Preliminary Report on Excavations in Lalibela and Natchabiet Caves, Begemeder." *Annales d'Ethiopie* 8 (1970): 21–29. doi: 10.3406/ETHIO.1970.880.

Dombrowski, Joanne Carol. 1971. "Excavations in Ethiopia: Lalibela and Natchabiet Caves, Begemeder Province." PhD diss., Boston University, Boston.

Domínguez-Rodrigo, Manuel, Travis Rayne Pickering, Sileshi Semaw, and Michael J. Rogers. 2005. "Cutmarked Bones from Pliocene Archaeological Sites at Gona, Afar, Ethiopia: Implications for the Function of the World's Oldest Stone Tools." *Journal of Human Evolution* 48 (2): 109–121. doi: 10.1016/j.jhevol.2004.09.004.

Doresse, Jean. 1959. *Ethiopia: Ancient Cities and Temples*. London: Elek Books.

Douin, Georges. (1869–1873) 1933. *Histoire du règne du Khédive Ismaïl*. Vol. 3. Cairo: Publications spéciales, Société Royale de Géographie d'Égypte.

Drewes, Abraham Johannes. 1962. *Inscriptions de l'Ethiopie antique*. Leiden: E. J. Brill.

Dueppen, Stephen A. 2014. *Egalitarian Revolution in the Savanna: The Origins of a West African Political System*. Sheffield, UK: Equinox.

Dugast, Fabienne, and Iwona Gajda. 2014. "Prospections archéologiques dans la région de Meqele et les contreforts orientaux du Tigray." *Annales d'Éthiopie* 29 (1): 179–197. doi: 10.3406/ethio.2014.1564.

Dunnavant, Justin. 2017. "Representation, Heritage, and Archaeology among the Wolaita of Ethiopia." PhD diss., University of Florida, Gainesville. https://ufdc.ufl.edu/UFE0051041/00001.

Earle, Timothy K. 1982. "Prehistoric Economics and the Archaeology of Exchange." In *Contexts for Prehistoric Exchange*, ed. Jonathon E. Ericson and Timothy K. Earle, 1–12. New York: Academic Press.

Earle, Timothy K. 1994. "Positioning Exchange in the Evolution of Human Society." In *Prehistoric Exchange Systems in North America.*, ed. Timothy G. Baugh and Jonathon E. Ericson, 419–437. New York: Plenum.

Earle, Timothy K. 2002. *Bronze Age Economics: The Beginnings of Political Economies.* Boulder, CO: Westview.

Earle, Timothy K., and Jonathon Ericson, eds. 1977. *Exchange Systems in Prehistory.* New York: Academic Press.

Edwards, David N. 1998. "Meroe and the Sudanic Kingdoms." *Journal of African History* 39 (2): 175–193. doi: 10.1017/S0021853797007172.

EGS (Ethiopian Geologic Survey). 1973. *Geology, Geochemistry, and Hydrology of Hot Springs of the East African Rift System within Ethiopia.* New York: United Nations.

Ehret, Christopher, and Merrick Posnansky. 1982. *The Archaeological and Linguistic Reconstruction of African History.* Berkeley: University of California Press.

Fagan, Brian M., and John E. Yellen. 1968. "Ivuna: Ancient Salt Working in Southern Tanzania." *AZANIA: Journal of the British Institute in Eastern Africa* 3 (1): 1–43. doi.org/10.1080/00672706809511486.

Falola, Toyin. 1991. "The Yoruba Caravan System of the Nineteenth Century." *International Journal of African Historical Studies* 24 (1): 111–132. doi: 10.2307/220095.

Fargher, Lane F., and Verenice Y. Heredia Espinoza. 2016. *Alternative Pathways to Complexity: A Collection of Essays on Architecture, Economics, Power, and Cross-Cultural Analysis.* Boulder: University Press of Colorado.

Fattovich, Rodolfo. 1977. "Pre-Aksumite Civilization of Ethiopia: A Provisional Review." In *Proceedings of the Seminar for Arabian Studies*, ed. James B. Phillips, vol. 7, 73–78. Oxford: Archaeopress.

Fattovich, Rodolfo. 1990. "Remarks on the Pre-Aksumite Period in Northern Ethiopia." *Journal of Ethiopian Studies* 23:1–33. https://www.jstor.org/stable/44324719.

Fattovich, Rodolfo. 2000. *The Aksum Archaeological Area: A Preliminary Assessment.* Vol. 1. Naples, Italy: Isituto Universitario Orientale, Centro Interdipartimentale di Servizi per l'Archeologia.

Fattovich, Rodolfo. 2008. *Kings and Farmers: The Urban Development of Aksum, Ethiopia, ca. 500 BC–AD 1500.* Boston: Program for the Study of the African Environment, African Studies Center, Boston University.

Fattovich, Rodolfo. 2009. "Reconsidering Yeha, c. 800–400 BC." *African Archaeological Review* 26 (4): 275–290. doi: 10.1007/s10437-009-9063-3.

Fattovich, Rodolfo. 2010a. "The Development of Ancient States in the Northern Horn of Africa, c. 3000 BC–AD 1000: An Archaeological Outline." *Journal of World Prehistory* 23 (3): 145–175. doi: 10.1007/s10963-010-9035-1.

Fattovich, Rodolfo. 2010b. "The Southern Red Sea in the Third and Second Millennia BC: An Archaeological Overview." In *Navigated Spaces, Connected Places: Proceedings of the Red Sea Project V Held at the University of Exeter, 16–19 September 2010*, ed. Dionisius A. Agius, John Cooper, Athena Trakadas, and Chiara Zazzaro. Oxford: British Archaeological Reports.

Fattovich, Rodolfo. 2012. "The Northern Horn of Africa in the First Millennium BCE: Local Traditions and External Connections." *Rassegna Di Studi Etiopici* 4:1–60.

Fattovich, Rodolfo, and Kathryn A. Bard. 2001. "The Proto-Aksumite Period: An Overview." *Annales d'Ethiopie* 17:3–24. doi: 10.3406/ethio.2001.987.

Fauvelle-Aymar, François-Xavier, Laurent Bruxelles, Amélie Chekroun, Romain Mensan, Olivier Onézime, Asnake Wubete, Deresse Ayenatchew, Hailu Zeleke, Bertrand Hirsch, and Ahmed Mohamed. 2006. "A Topographic Survey and Some Soundings at Nora, an Ancient Muslim Town of Ethiopia." *Journal of Ethiopian Studies* 39 (1–2): 1–11. http://www.jstor.org/stable/41966167.

Fawcett, A. H. 1973. "Katwe Salt Deposits." *Uganda Journal* 37:63–80. ISSN 0041-574X.

Fedele, Francesco G. 2014. "Camels, Donkeys, and Caravan Trade: An Emerging Context from Barāqish, Ancient Yathill (Wadi al-Jawf, Yemen)." *Anthropozoologica* 49 (2): 177–194. doi.org/10.5252/az2014n2a02.

Ferguson, Charles A. 1970. "The Ethiopian Language Area." *Journal of Ethiopian Studies* 8 (2): 67–80. http://www.jstor.org/stable/41965809.

Ferman, Louis A., Stuart Henry, and Michele Hoyman. 1987. "Issues and Prospects for the Study of Informal Economies: Concepts, Research Strategies, and Policy." *Annals of the American Academy of Political and Social Science* 493 (1): 154–172. http://www.jstor.org/stable/1046200.

Fewster, Kathryn J. 2006. "The Potential of Analogy in Post-processual Archaeologies: A Case Study from Basimane Ward, Serowe, Botswana." *Journal of the Royal Anthropological Institute* 12 (1): 61–87. doi.org/10.1111/j.1467-9655.2006.00281.x.

Finley, Moses I. 1985. *The Ancient Economy*. 2nd ed. Berkeley: University of California Press.

Finneran, Niall. 2007. *The Archaeology of Ethiopia*. London: Routledge.

Finneran, Niall, and Jacke Phillips. 2003. "The Prehistoric Settlement of the Shire Region, Western Tigray, Ethiopia: Some Preliminary Observations." *Nyame Akuma* 59:26–33. https://static1.squarespace.com/static/5bd0e66f8d97400eb0099556/t/5bd c5d3889858399c4c225ea/1541168441262/Nyame+Akuma+Issue+059-Article+05.pdf.

Flad, Rowan K. 2011. *Salt Production and Social Hierarchy in Ancient China: An Archaeological Investigation of Specialization in China's Three Gorges*. Cambridge: Cambridge University Press.

Flannery, Kent V. 1968. "The Olmec and the Valley of Oaxaca: A Model for Interregional Interaction in Formative Times." In *Dumbarton Oaks Conference on the Olmec*, ed. Elizabeth P. Benson, 79–110. Washington, DC: Dumbarton Oaks.

Flannery, Kent V. 1972. "Summary Comments: Evolutionary Trends in Social Exchange and Interaction." In *Social Exchange and Interaction, Anthropological Papers*, ed. Edwin N. Wilmsen, 129–136. Ann Arbor: University of Michigan Press.

Ford, Richard I. 1972. "Barter, Gift, or Violence: An Analysis of Tewa Intertribal Exchange." In *Social Exchange and Interaction, Anthropological Papers*, ed. Edwin N. Wilmsen, 21–45. Ann Arbor: University of Michigan Pres.

Förster, Frank. 2007. "With Donkeys, Jars, and Water Bags into the Libyan Desert: The Abu Ballas Trail in the Late Old Kingdom / First Intermediate Period." In *International Conference of Nubian Studies*, ed. Heiko Riemer, Frank Föster, Michael Herb, and Nadja Pöllath, vol. 7, 1–36. London: British Museum Studies in Ancient Egypt and Sudan (BMSAES).

Förster, Frank, and Heiko Riemer. 2013. *Desert Road Archaeology in Ancient Egypt and Beyond*. Cologne: Heinrich-Barth-Institut.

Foucher, Emile. 1994. "The Cult of Muslim Saints in Harar: Religious Dimension." In *Proceedings of the Eleventh International Conference of Ethiopian Studies*, ed. Bahru Zewde, Richard Pankhurst, and Tesfaye Beyene, 71–79. Addis Ababa: Institute of Ethiopian Studies, Addis Ababa University.

Frachetti, Michael D., David W. Anthony, Anatoly V. Epimakhov, Bryan K. Hanks, Robert C. P. Doonan, Nikolay N. Kradin, Clifford C. Lamberg-Karlovsky, Sandra L. Olsen, Daniel T. Potts, and John Daniel Rogers. 2012. "Multiregional Emergence of Mobile Pastoralism and Nonuniform Institutional Complexity across Eurasia." *Current Anthropology* 53 (1): 2–38.

Frachetti, Michael D., C. Evan Smith, Cynthia M. Traub, and Tim Williams. 2017. "Nomadic Ecology Shaped the Highland Geography of Asia's Silk Roads." *Nature* 543 (7644): 193–198. doi.org/10.1038/nature21696.

Franchetti, Raimondo. 1935. *Nella Dancàlia etiopica: Spedizione italiana 1928–29*. Milan: A. Mondadori.

Franklin, Kathryn, and Emily Boak. 2019. "The Road from Above: Remotely Sensed Discovery of Early Modern Travel Infrastructure in Afghanistan." *Archaeological Research in Asia* 18:40–54. doi.org/10.1016/j.ara.2019.02.002.

Freidel, David, and F. Kent Reilly III. 2010. "The Flesh of God: Cosmology, Food, and the Origins of Political Power in Ancient Southeastern Mesoamerica." In *Pre-Columbian Foodways: Interdisciplinary Approaches to Food, Culture, and Markets in Ancient Mesoamerica*, ed. John Staller and Michael Carrasco, 635–680. Chicago: Springer.

Frison, George C. 1972. "The Role of Buffalo Procurement in Post-altithermal Populations on the Northwestern Plains." In *Social Exchange and Interaction, Anthropological Papers*, ed. Edwin N. Wilmsen, 11–20. Ann Arbor: University of Michigan Press.

Fry, Robert E. 1980. *Models and Methods in Regional Exchange*. Washington, DC: Society for American Archaeology.

Gaudiello, Michela, and Paul Yule. 2017. *Miṣṣas Baḥri, a Late Aksumite Frontier Community in the Mountains of Southern Tigray: Survey, Excavation, and Analysis, 2013–16*. Oxford: British Archaeological Reports.

Gebreab, Feseha, A. Gebre Wold, Friew Kelemu, Abule Ibro, and Ketema Yilma. 2005. "Donkey Utilization and Management in Ethiopia." In *Donkeys, People, and Development*, ed. Denis Fielding and Paul Starkey, 46–52. Wageningen, the Netherlands: CTA

Gebrelibanos, Tsegaye Berhe. 2009. "The Ethiopian Salt Trading System in the Twentieth Century: A View from Mäqäla, Northern Ethiopia." In *Proceedings of the Sixteenth International Conference of Ethiopian Studies*, ed. Svein Ege, Harald Aspen, Birhanu Teferra, and Shiferaw Bekele, vol. 3, 185–201. Trondheim, Norway: NTNU-trykk.

Gebre-Meskel, Haddis. 1992. *A Survey of Representative Land Charters of the Ethiopian Empire (1314–1868) and Related Marginal Notes in Manuscripts in the British Library, the Royal Library, and the University Libraries of Cambridge and Manchester*. London: School of Oriental and African Studies, University of London.

Gerlach, Iris. 2012. "Yeha: An Ethio-Sabaean Site in the Highlands of Tigray (Ethiopia)." In *New Research in Archaeology and Epigraphy of South Arabia and Its Neighbors, Proceedings of the "Rencontrés sabéennes 15" Held in Moscow on May 25th–27th*, ed. Alexander Sedov, 215–240. Moscow: State Museum of Oriental Art.

Getachew, Kassa Negussie. 2001. *Among the Pastoral Afar in Ethiopia: Tradition, Continuity, and Socio-economic Change*. Utrecht: International Books.

Goldstein, Paul S. 2000. "Exotic Goods and Everyday Chiefs: Long-Distance Exchange and Indigenous Sociopolitical Development in the South Central Andes." *Latin American Antiquity* 11 (4): 335–361. doi: 10.2307/972001.

Goñalons, Guillermo L. Mengoni, and Hugo D. Yacobaccio. 2006. "The Domestication of South American Camelids." In *Documenting Domestication—New Genetic and Archaeological Paradigms*, ed. Melinda A. Zeder, 228–244. Berkeley: University of California Press.

Good, Charles M. 1972. "Salt, Trade, and Disease: Aspects of Development in Africa's Northern Great Lakes Region." *International Journal of African Historical Studies* 5 (4): 543–586. doi: 10.2307/217269.

Gouletquer, Pierre. 1975. *Niger, Country of Salt*. Colchester: Colchester Archaeological Group.

Grillo, Katherine Mary. 2012. "The Materiality of Mobile Pastoralism: Ethnoarchaeological Perspectives from Samburu, Kenya." *Azania: Archaeological Research in Africa* 47:540–541. doi: 10.7936/K79K487V.

Guedda, Mohamed. 1989. *Alternatives de développement des populations pastorales en République de Djibouti*. Rome: Organisation des Nations Unies pour l'Alimentation et l'Agriculture (FAO).

Gutherz, Xavier, Joséphine Lesur, Jessie Cauliez, Vincent Charpentier, Amélie Diaz, Mohamed Omar Ismaël, Jean-Michel Pène, Dominique Sordoillet, and Antoine Zazzo. 2015. "New Insights on the First Neolithic Societies in the Horn of Africa: The Site of Wakrita, Djibouti." *Journal of Field Archaeology* 40 (1): 55–68. doi.org/10.1179/0093469014Z.000000000110.

Guyer, Jane I. 1997. *An African Niche Economy: Farming to Feed Ibadan, 1968–88.* Edinburgh: Edinburgh University Press.

Hafsaas-Tsakos, Henriette. 2009. "The Kingdom of Kush: An African Centre on the Periphery of the Bronze Age World System." *Norwegian Archaeological Review* 42 (1): 50–70. doi: 10.1080/00293650902978590.

Haile-Selassie, Yohannes. 2001. "Late Miocene Hominids from the Middle Awash, Ethiopia." *Nature* 412 (6843): 178–181. doi: 10.1126/science.1092978.

Hailu, Berihun Kassa, and Jemal Abebe Jemere. 2017. "Recalling the History of Sultan Mohammed Hanfare Illalta: Was He a Democratic Sultan of Aussa in Afar, Ethiopia?" *African Journal of History and Culture* 9 (9): 72–77.

Han, Lu, Songbiao Zhu, Chao Ning, Dawei Cai, Kai Wang, Quanjia Chen, Songmei Hu, Junkai Yang, Jing Shao, and Hong Zhu. 2014. "Ancient DNA Provides New Insight into the Maternal Lineages and Domestication of Chinese Donkeys." *BMC Evolutionary Biology* 14 (1): article 246. doi.org/10.1186/s12862-014-0246-4.

Hansen, Valerie. 2012. *The Silk Road: A New History.* Oxford: Oxford University Press.

Haour, Anne, and Annalisa Christie. 2019. "Cowries in the Archaeology of West Africa: The Present Picture." *Azania: Archaeological Research in Africa* 54 (3): 287–321. doi.org/10.1080/0067270X.2019.1648726.

Harding, Anthony. 2013. *Salt in Prehistoric Europe.* Leiden: Sidestone.

Harlan, Jack R. 1969. "Ethiopia: A Center of Diversity." *Economic Botany* 23 (4): 309–314. doi.org/10.1007/BF02860676.

Harrower, Michael J., and A. Catherine D'Andrea. 2014. "Landscapes of State Formation: Geospatial Analysis of Aksumite Settlement Patterns (Ethiopia)." *African Archaeological Review* 31 (3): 513–541. doi: 10.1007/s10437-014-9165-4.

Harrower, Michael J., Ioana A. Dumitru, Cinzia Perlingieri, Smiti Nathan, Kifle Zerue, Jessica L. Lamont, Alessandro Bausi, Jennifer L. Swerida, Jacob L. Bongers, and Helina S. Woldekiros. 2019. "Beta Samati: Discovery and Excavation of an Aksumite Town—Corrigendum." *Antiquity* 94 (373): 1534–1552. doi.org/10.15184/aqy.2019.84.

Harrower, Michael J., Joy McCorriston, and A. Catherine D'Andrea. 2010. "General/Specific, Local/Global: Comparing the Beginnings of Agriculture in the Horn of Africa (Ethiopia/Eritrea) and Southwest Arabia (Yemen)." *American Antiquity* 75 (3): 452–472. doi: 10.7183/0002-7316.75.3.452.

Hecht, Elisabeth-Dorothea. 1982. "The City of Harar and the Traditional Harar House." *Journal of Ethiopian Studies* 15:57–78. http://www.jstor.org/stable/41965897.

Helm, Richard, Alison Crowther, Ceri Shipton, Amini Tengeza, Dorian Fuller, and Nicole Boivin. 2012. "Exploring Agriculture, Interaction, and Trade on the Eastern African Littoral: Preliminary Results from Kenya." *Azania: Archaeological Research in Africa* 47 (1): 39–63. doi: 10.1080/0067270X.2011.647947.

Henze, Paul B. 2000. *Layers of Time: A History of Ethiopia.* London: St. Martin's.

Hildebrand, Elisabeth A. 2007. "A Tale of Two Tuber Crops: How Attributes of Enset and Yams May Have Shaped Prehistoric Human-Plant Interactions in Southwest Ethiopia." In *Rethinking Agriculture: Archaeological and Ethnoarchaeological Perspectives,* ed. Timothy P. Denham, José Iriarte, and Luc Vrydaghs, 273–298. Walnut Creek, CA: Left Coast.

Hirth, Kenneth. 1984. *Trade and Exchange in Early Mesoamerica.* Albuquerque: University of New Mexico Press.

Hiskett, John. 1994. *The Course of Islam in Africa.* Islamic Surveys. Edinburgh: Edinburgh University Press.

Hopkins, Benjamin D. 2008. "Camels, Caravans, and Corridor Cities." In *The Making of Modern Afghanistan,* ed. Benjamin Hopkins, 110–135. New York: Palgrave Macmillan.

Hughes, Richard E. 1978. "Aspects of Prehistoric Wiyot Exchange and Social Ranking." *Journal of California Anthropology* 5 (1): 53–66. http://www.jstor.org/stable/25748368.

Huntingford, George Wynn Brereton. 1955. "Arabic Inscriptions in Southern Ethiopia." *Antiquity* 29 (116): 230–233. doi: 10.1017/S0003598X00021955.

Huntingford, George Wynn Brereton. 1980. *The Periplus of the Erythraean Sea.* London: Hakluyt Society.

Huntingford, George Wynn Brereton. 1989. *The Historical Geography of Ethiopia.* Oxford: Oxford University Press.

Insoll, Timothy. 1997. "An Archaeological Reconnaissance Made to Dahlak Kebir, the Dahlak Islands, Eritrea: Preliminary Observations." In *Ethiopia in Broader Perspective: Papers of the 13th International Conference of Ethiopian Studies,* ed. Katsuyoshi Fukui, Eisei Kurimoto, and Masayoshi Shigeta, 382–388. Kyoto: Japan Publications Trading Co.

Insoll, Timothy. 2003. *The Archaeology of Islam in Sub-Saharan Africa.* Cambridge: Cambridge University Press.

Insoll, Timothy. 2017. "First Footsteps in the Archaeology of Harar, Ethiopia." *Journal of Islamic Archaeology* 4 (2): 189–215. doi.org/10.1558/jia.35273.

Insoll, Timothy. 2021. "Marine Shell Working at Harlaa, Ethiopia, and the Implications for Red Sea Trade." *Journal of African Archaeology* 1: 1–24. doi: 10.1163/21915784-20210001.

Insoll, Timothy, and Thurstan Shaw. 1997. "Gao and Igbo-Ukwu: Beads, Interregional Trade, and Beyond." *African Archaeological Review* 14 (1): 9–23. doi: 10.1007/BF02968364.

Johanson, Donald, and Kate Wong. 2010. *Lucy's Legacy: The Quest for Human Origins.* New York: Harmony Books.

Kendall, Timothy. 1997. *Kerma and the Kingdom of Kush, 2500–1500 BC: The Archaeological Discovery of an Ancient Nubian Empire.* Washington, DC: National Museum of African Art, Smithsonian Institution.

Kessy, Emanuel T. 2003. "Iron Age Settlement Patterns and Economic Change on Zanzibar and Pemba Islands." In *East African Archaeology: Foragers, Potters, Smiths, and Traders,* ed. Chapurukha M. Kusimba and Sibel B. Kusimba, 117–131. Philadelphia: University of Pennsylvania Museum of Archaeology and Anthropology.

Khazanov, Anatoly M., and André Wink. 2001. *Nomads in the Sedentary World.* Richmond, UK: Curzon.

Kimura, Birgitta, Fiona Marshall, Albano Beja-Pereira, and Connie Mulligan. 2013. "Donkey Domestication." *African Archaeological Review* 30 (1): 83–95. doi.org/10.1007/s10437-012-9126-8.

Kirwan, Laurence Patrick. 1972. "The Christian Topography and the Kingdom of Axum." *Geographical Journal* 138 (2): 166–177. doi.org/10.2307/1795960.

Kitchen, Kenneth Anderson. 1971. "Punt and How to Get There." *Orientalia* 40 (2): 184–207. http://www.jstor.org/stable/43074450.

Kitchen, Kenneth Anderson. 1993. "The Land of Punt." In *The Archaeology of Africa: Food, Metals, and Towns,* ed. Thurstan Shaw, Paul Sinclair, Bassey Andah, and Alex Okpoko, 587–608. New York: Routledge.

Klein, Rebecca A. 2007. "We Do Not Eat Meat with the Christians: Interaction and Integration between the Beta Israel and Amhara Christians of Gonder, Ethiopia." PhD diss., University of Florida, Gainesville.

Kobishchanov, Yuri M. 1966. *Aksum.* Translated by Leonid T. Kapitanoff. University Park: Pennsylvania State University Press.

Kobishchanov, Yuri M. 1979. *Aksum.* Translated by Joseph W. Michels and Leonid T. Kapitanoff. University Park: Pennsylvania State University Press.

Kuper, Rudolph, and Stefan Kröpelin. 2006. "Climate-Controlled Holocene Occupation in the Sahara: Motor of Africa's Evolution." *Science* 313 (5788): 803–807. doi: 10.1126/science.1130989.

Kurlansky, Mark. 2002. *Salt: A World History.* New York: Walker.

Kürsten, Martin Otto. 1975. "Stratigraphic Units of Northern Afar." In *Afar Depression of Ethiopia: Proceedings of an International Symposium on the Afar Region and Related Rift Problems, Held in Bad Bergzabern FR Germany,* ed. Andreas Pilger and Artur Rösler, vol. 1: 168–169. Stuttgart: Nägele u. Obermiller.

Kusimba, Chapurukha Makokha. 1999. *The Rise and Fall of Swahili States.* Walnut Creek, CA: Altamira.

Kusimba, Chapurukha Makokha, and Sibel Barut Kusimba. 2003. *East African Archaeology: Foragers, Potters, Smiths, and Traders.* Philadelphia: University of Pennsylvania Press.

Kuznar, Lawrence A. 1993. "Mutualism between Chenopodium, Herd Animals, and Herders in the South Central Andes." *Mountain Research and Development* 13 (3): 257–265. doi.org/10.2307/3673655.

LaViolette, Adria, and Jeffrey Fleisher. 2005. "The Archaeology of Sub-Saharan Urbanism: Cities and Their Countrysides." In *African Archaeology: A Critical Introduction*, ed. Ann Brower Stahl, 327–352. Oxford: Blackwell.

LaViolette, Adria, and Jeffrey Fleisher. 2009. "The Urban History of a Rural Place: Swahili Archaeology on Pemba Island, Tanzania, 700–1500 AD." *International Journal of African Historical Studies* 42 (3): 433–455.

LaViolette, Adria, and Jeffrey Fleisher. 2018. "Developments in Rural Life on the Eastern African Coast, AD 700–1500." *Journal of Field Archaeology* 43 (5): 380–398. doi: 10.1080/00934690.2018.1489661.

Leakey, L. B. S. 1943. "The Industries of the Gorgora Rock Shelter, Lake Tana." *East Africa and Uganda Natural History Society and East Africa Natural History Society* 17: 199–208. http://creativecommons.org/licenses/by-nc-sa/3.0/.

Lesur, Joséphine, Elisabeth A. Hildebrand, Gedef Abawa, and Xavier Gutherz. 2014. "The Advent of Herding in the Horn of Africa: New Data from Ethiopia, Djibouti, and Somaliland." *Quaternary International* 343:148–158. doi.org/10.1016/j.quaint.2013.11 .024.

Levi, Scott. 1999. "India, Russia, and the Eighteenth-Century Transformation of the Central Asian Caravan Trade." *Journal of the Economic and Social History of the Orient* 42 (4): 519–548. doi.org/10.1163/1568520991201696.

Lewis, Ioan Myrddin. 1965. *Peoples of the Horn of Africa: Somali, Afar, and Saho*. London: Red Sea Press.

Liao, Chuan, Morgan L. Ruelle, and Karim-Aly S. Kassam. 2016. "Indigenous Ecological Knowledge as the Basis for Adaptive Environmental Management: Evidence from Pastoralist Communities in the Horn of Africa." *Journal of Environmental Management* 182:70–79. doi.org/10.1016/j.jenvman.2016.07.032.

Littmann, Enno. 1907. "Preliminary Report of the Princeton University Expedition to Abyssinia." *Zeitschrift für Assyriologie und Vorderasiatische Archäologie* 20 (1): 151–182. doi: 10.1515/zava.1907.20.1.151.

Lovejoy, Paul E. 1974. "Interregional Monetary Flows in the Precolonial Trade of Nigeria." *Journal of African History* 15 (4): 563–585. doi: 10.1017/S0021853700013888.

Lovejoy, Paul E. 1984. "Commercial Sectors in the Economy of the Nineteenth-Century Central Sudan: The Trans-Saharan Trade and the Desert-Side Salt Trade." *African Economic History* 13:85–116. doi: 10.2307/3601480.

Lovejoy, Paul E. 1986. *Salt of the Desert Sun: A History of Salt Production and Trade in the Central Sudan*. Cambridge: Cambridge University Press.

Lydon, Ghislaine. 2008. "Contracting Caravans: Partnership and Profit in Nineteenth-and Early Twentieth-Century Trans-Saharan Trade." *Journal of Global History* 3 (1): 89–113. doi.org/10.1017/S1740022808002453.

Lyons, Diane E. 2007. "Building Power in Rural Hinterlands: An Ethnoarchaeological Study of Vernacular Architecture in Tigray, Ethiopia." *Journal of Archaeological Method and Theory* 14 (2): 179–207. doi: 10.1007/s10816-007-9031-7.

Lyons, Diane E., and A. Catherine D'Andrea. 2003. "Griddles, Ovens, and Agricultural Origins: An Ethnoarchaeological Study of Bread Baking in Highland Ethiopia." *American Anthropologist* 105 (3): 515–530. doi: 10.1525/aa.2003.105.3.515.

Lyons, Diane, and Nicholas David. 2019. "To Hell with Ethnoarchaeology . . . and Back." *Ethnoarchaeology* 11 (2): 99–133. doi.org/10.1080/19442890.2019.1642557.

Machado, Maria J., Alfredo Pérez-González, and Gerardo Benito. 1998. "Paleoenvironmental Changes during the Last 4000 Yr in the Tigray, Northern Ethiopia." *Quaternary Research* 49 (3): 312–321. doi: 10.1006/qres.1998.1965.

Marshall, Fiona, Thomas P. Denham, José Iriarte, and Leïla Vrydaghs. 2007. "African Pastoral Perspectives on Domestication of the Donkey: A First Synthesis." In *Rethinking Agriculture: Archaeological and Ethnoarchaeological Perspectives*, ed. Timothy Pauketat and Patty Jo Watson, 371–407. Walnut Creek, CA: Left Coast Press.

Marshall, Fiona, Katherine Grillo, and Lee Arco. 2011. "Prehistoric Pastoralists and Social Responses to Climatic Risk in East Africa." In *Sustainable Lifeways: Cultural Persistence in an Ever-Changing Environment*, ed. Naomi F. Miller, Katherine M. Moore, and Kathleen Ryan, 39–74. Philadelphia: University of Pennsylvania Museum of Archaeology.

Marshall, Fiona, and Elisabeth Hildebrand. 2002. "Cattle before Crops: The Beginnings of Food Production in Africa." *Journal of World Prehistory* 16 (2): 99–143. doi: 10.1023/A:1019954903395.

Marx, Karl. 1977 [1867]. *Capital: A Critique of Political Economy.* Vol. 1. New York: Palgrave Macmillan.

McCann, James C. 1995. *People of the Plow: An Agricultural History of Ethiopia, 1800–1990.* Madison: University of Wisconsin Press.

McCrindle, John Watson. 1897. *The Christian Topography of Cosmas, an Egyptian Monk.* London: Hakluyt Society.

McDougall, E. Ann. 1990. "Salts of the Western Sahara: Myths, Mysteries, and Historical Significance." *International Journal of African Historical Studies* 23 (2): 231–257. doi: 10.2307/219336.

McDougall, E. Ann. 2004. "Exploring the 'Niche Economy': A Commentary." *African Economic History* 32:153–171. https://www.jstor.org/stable/3601623.

McIntosh, Susan Keech. 1999. "Pathways to Complexity: An African Perspective." In *Beyond Chiefdoms: Pathways to Complexity in Africa*, ed. Susan Keech McIntosh, 1–31. Cambridge: Cambridge University Press.

McKillop, Heather. 2002. *Salt: White Gold of the Ancient Maya*. Gainesville: University Press of Florida.

Michels, Joseph W. 2005. *Changing Settlement Patterns in the Aksum-Yeha Region of Ethiopia: 700 BC–AD 850*. BAR International Series 1446. Oxford: British Archaeological Reports.

Mitchell, Peter. 2005. *African Connections: Archaeological Perspectives on Africa and the Wider World*. New York: Altamira.

Mohr, Paul A. 1974. *Structural Setting and Evolution of Afar*. Cambridge, MA: Center for Astrophysics, Harvard College Observatory and Smithsonian Astrophysical Observatory.

Morgan, David R. 1974. "Salt Production in Tanzania: Past and Present." *Tanzania Notes and Records* 74:31–37.

Muller, Jon. 1984. "Mississippian Specialization and Salt." *American Antiquity* 49 (3): 489–507. doi: 10.2307/280356.

Munro-Hay, Stuart C. 1989. *Excavations at Aksum: An Account of Research at the Ancient Ethiopian Capital Directed in 1972–4 by the Late Dr. Neville Chittick*. London: British Institute in Eastern Africa.

Munro-Hay, Stuart C. 1991. *Aksum: An African Civilization of Late Antiquity*. Edinburgh: Edinburgh University Press.

Munro-Hay, Stuart C. 1993. "Development and Urbanism in Northern Ethiopia." In *The Archaeology of Africa: Food, Metals, and Towns*, ed. Thurston Shaw, Paul Sinclair, Bassy Andah, and Alex Okpoko, 609–621. London: Routledge.

Munro-Hay, Stuart C. 2002. *Ethiopia, the Unknown Land: A Cultural and Historical Guide*. London: I. B. Tauris.

Munzinger, Werner. 1868. "Journey across the Great Salt Desert from Hanfila to the Foot of the Abyssinian Alps." *Proceedings of the Royal Geographical Society of London* 13, no. 3 (1868): 219–224. doi.org/10.2307/1798935.

Munzinger, Werner. 1869. "Narrative of a Journey through the Afar Country." *Journal of the Royal Geographical Society of London* 39:188–232. doi: 10.2307/1798551.

Nadel, Siegfried Frederick. 1946. "Land Tenure on the Eritrean Plateau." *Africa: Journal of the International African Institute* 16 (1): 1–22. doi: 10.2307/1156534.

Negash, Agazi. 1997. "Temben's Place in the Neolithic of Northern Ethiopia." In *Ethiopia in Broader Perspective*, ed. Katsuyoshi Fukui, 389–398. Tokyo: Shoka.

Negash, Agazi, F. Brown, and Barbara Nash. 2011. "Varieties and Sources of Artefactual Obsidian in the Middle Stone Age of the Middle Awash, Ethiopia." *Archaeometry* 53 (4): 661–673. doi.org/10.1111/j.1475-4754.2010.00579.x.

Negash, Agazi, and Fiona Marshall. 2021. "Early Hunters and Herders of Northern Ethiopia: The Fauna from Danei Kawlos." *SINET: Ethiopian Journal of Science* 44 (2): 215–222.

Newbury, Colin W. 2018. "Prices and Profitability in Early Nineteenth-Century West African Trade." In *The Development of Indigenous Trade and Markets in West Africa: Studies Presented and Discussed at the Tenth International African Seminar at Fourah Bay College Freetown December 1969*, ed. Claude Meillassoux, 91–106. London: Oxford University Press for the International African Institute.

Nicholson, Beverley Alistair. 1987. "Human Ecology and Prehistory of the Forest/Grassland Transition Zone of Western Manitoba." PhD diss., Simon Fraser University, Burnaby, BC.

Nicholson, Beverly Alistair. 1988. "Modeling Subsistence Strategies in the Forest/Grassland Transition Zone of Western Manitoba during the Late Prehistoric and Early Historic Periods." *Plains Anthropologist* 33 (121): 351–365. doi: 10.1080/2052546.1988.11909413.

Nielsen, Axel. 2000. "Andean Caravans: An Ethnoarchaeology." PhD diss., University of Arizona, Tucson.

Nielsen, Axel. 2001. "Ethnoarchaeological Perspectives on Caravan Trade in the South-Central Andes." In *Ethnoarchaeology of Andean South America: Contributions to Archaeological Method and Theory*, ed. Lawrence A. Kuznar, 163–201. Ann Arbor, MI: International Monographs in Prehistory.

Núñez, Lautaro, Martin Grosjean, and Isabel Cartajena. 2010. "Sequential Analysis of Human Occupation Patterns and Resource Use in the Atacama Desert." *Chungara, Revista de antropología chilena* 42 (2): 363–391. https://repositorio.uchile.cl/handle/2250/121675.

Odess, Daniel. 1998. "The Archaeology of Interaction: Views from Artifact Style and Material Exchange in Dorset Society." *American Antiquity* 63 (3): 417–435. doi: 10.2307/2694628.

Oka, Rahul, and Chapurukha M. Kusimba. 2008. "The Archaeology of Trading Systems, Part 1: Towards a New Trade Synthesis." *Journal of Archaeological Research* 16 (4): 339–395. doi: 10.1007/s10814-008-9023-5.

Oman, Giovanni. 1974. "The Islamic Necropolis of Dahlak Kebīr in the Red Sea Report on a Preliminary Survey Carried Out in April 1972." *East and West* 24 (3–4): 249–295. http://www.jstor.org/stable/29756005.

Pankhurst, Richard. 1961. *An Introduction to the Economic History of Ethiopia, from Early Times to 1800*. London: Sidgwick and Jackson.

Pankhurst, Richard. 1966. *State and Land in Ethiopian History*. Vol. 3. Addis Ababa: Institute of Ethiopian Studies.

Pankhurst, Richard. 1968. *Economic History of Ethiopia, 1800–1935*. Addis Ababa: Haile Sellassie I University Press.

Pankhurst, Richard. 1982. "The Visit to Ethiopia of Yohannes To'umacean." *Journal of Ethiopian Studies* 15:79–104.

Pankhurst, Richard. 1990. *A Social History of Ethiopia*. Addis Ababa: Institute of Ethiopian Studies.

Pankhurst, Richard. 1998. *The Ethiopians*. Oxford: Blackwell.

Parsons, Jeffrey R. 2001. *The Last Salt Makers of Nexquipayac, Mexico: An Archaeological Ethnography*. Ann Arbor: University of Michigan Museum.

Peacock, David, and Lucy Blue. 2007. *The Ancient Red Sea Port of Adulis, Eritrea: Report of the Eritro-British Expedition, 2004–5*. Oxford: Oxbow Books.

Pearce, Nathaniel. 1831. *Life and Adventures of Nathaniel Pearce*. Vols. 1 and 2. London: Colburn and Bentley.

Phillipson, David W. 1998. *Ancient Ethiopia: Aksum, Its Antecedents and Successors*. London: British Museum Press.

Phillipson, David W. 2000a. "Aksumite Urbanism." In *Africa's Urban Past*, ed. David Anderson and Richard Rathbone, 52–65. Oxford: James Currey.

Phillipson, David W. 2000b. *Archaeology at Aksum, Ethiopia, 1993–97*. Vols. 1 and 2. London: British Institute in Eastern Africa and Society of Antiquaries.

Phillipson, David W. 2005. *African Archaeology*. Cambridge: Cambridge University Press.

Phillipson, David W. 2009a. "Aksum, the Entrepôt, and Highland Ethiopia, Third–Twelfth Centuries." In *Byzantine Trade, Fourth–Twelfth Centuries, the Archaeology of Local, Regional, and International Exchange: Papers of the Thirty-Eighth Spring Symposium of Byzantine Studies, St. John's College, University of Oxford, March 2004*, ed. Marlia Mundell Mango, 353–368. Farnham, UK: Ashgate.

Phillipson, David W. 2009b. *Ancient Churches of Ethiopia: Fourth–Fourteenth Centuries*. New Haven, CT: Yale University Press.

Phillipson, David W. 2009c. "The First Millennium BC in the Highlands of Northern Ethiopia and South-Central Eritrea: A Reassessment of Cultural and Political Development." *African Archaeological Review* 26 (4): 257–274. doi: 10.1007/s10437-009-9064-2.

Phillipson, David W. 2012. *Foundations of an African Civilisation: Aksum and the Northern Horn, 1000 BC–AD 1300*. Woodbridge, UK: James Currey.

Phillipson, David W., Jacqueline Sharon Phillips, and Ayele Tarekegn. 2000. *Archaeology at Aksum, Ethiopia, 1993–97*. Vols. 1 and 2. London: British Institute in Eastern Africa and Society of Antiquaries.

Phillipson, Laurel. 2000. "Aksumite Lithic Industries." *African Archaeological Review* 17 (2): 49–63. doi.org/10.1023/A:1006600324970.

Polanyi, Karl. 1947. "Our Obsolete Market Mentality." *Commentary* 13:109–117.

Polanyi, Karl, Conrad M. Arensberg, and Harry W. Pearson. 1957. *Trade and Market in the Early Empires: Economies in History and Theory*. Glencoe, IL: Free Press.

Potts, Daniel. 1984. "On Salt and Salt Gathering in Ancient Mesopotamia." *Journal of the Economic and Social History of the Orient* 27 (3): 225–271. doi: 10.2307/3631848.

Pradines, Stephane. 2017. "The Medieval Mosques of Nora: Islamic Architecture in Ethiopia." *Journal of Oriental and African Studies* 26. https://ecommons.aku.edu/uk _ismc_faculty_publications/6.

Renfrew, Colin. 1984. *Approaches to Social Archaeology*. Edinburgh: Edinburgh University Press.

Renfrew, Colin, Johnston R. Cann, and John E. Dixon. 1965. "Obsidian in the Aegean." *Annual of the British School at Athens* 60:225–247. doi: 10.1017/S0068245400013976.

Renne, Elisha P. 2016. "Craft, Memory, and Loss: *Babban Riga* Robes, Politics, and the Quest for 'Bigness' in Zaria City, Nigeria." In *Critical Craft: Technology, Globalization, and Capitalism*, ed. C. Michele Wilkinson-Weber and Anthony O. DeNicola, 217–238. London: Bloomsbury Academic.

Retsö, Jan. 1991. "The Domestication of the Camel and the Establishment of the Frankincense Road from South Arabia." *Orientalia Suecana* 40:187–219.

Riehm, Karl. 1961. "Prehistoric Salt Boiling." *Antiquity* 35 (139): 181–191. doi.org/10.1017 /S0003598X00036176.

Rivallain, Josette. 1977. "Le Sel dans les villages côtiers et lagunaires du Bas Dahomey: Sa fabrication, sa place dans le circuit du sel africain." *West African Journal of Archaeology* 7:143–167.

Robin, Christian-Julien. 1981. "Les Inscriptions d'Al-Mi'sâl et la chronologie de l'Arabie méridionale au IIIe siècle de l'ère chrétienne." *Comptes Rendus Des Séances de l'Académie Des Inscriptions et Belles-Lettres* 125 (125): 315–339.

Roe, Alan. 2005. "The Old 'Darb al Arbein' Caravan Route and Kharga Oasis in Antiquity." *Journal of the American Research Center in Egypt* 42:119–129. http://www.jstor .org/stable/27651804.

Rogers, Rhea J. 1995. "Tribes as Heterarchy: A Case Study from the Prehistoric Southeastern United States." *Archeological Papers of the American Anthropological Association* 6 (1): 7–16. doi: 10.1525/ap3a.1995.6.1.7.

Rosen, Steven. 2016. *Revolutions in the Desert: The Rise of Mobile Pastoralism in the Southern Levant*. New York: Routledge.

Rosen, Steven, and Benjamin A. Saidel. 2010. "The Camel and the Tent: An Exploration of Technological Change among Early Pastoralists." *Journal of Near Eastern Studies* 69 (1): 63–77. doi: 10.1086/654940.

Ross, Eric. 2010. "A Historical Geography of the Trans-Saharan Trade." In *The Trans-Saharan Book Trade: Manuscript Culture, Arabic Literacy, and Intellectual History in Muslim Africa*, ed. Graziano Krätli and Ghislaine Lydon, vol. 3, 1–34. Leiden: Brill.

Rossel, Stine, Fiona Marshall, Joris Peters, Tom Pilgram, Matthew D. Adams, and David O'Connor. 2008. "Domestication of the Donkey: Timing, Processes, and Indicators." *Proceedings of the National Academy of Sciences* 105 (10): 3715–3720. doi.org/10.1073/pnas .070969210.

Rossini, Carlo Conti. 1928. *Storia d'etiopia*. Bergamo: Istituto italiano d'arti grafiche.

Rossini, Carlo Conti, and Ignazio Guidi. 1907. *Historia Regis Sarṣa Dengel (Malak Sagad)*. Vol. 20. Paris: E typographeo reipublicae.

Ruiz-Giralt, Abel, Charlène Bouchaud, Aurélie Salavert, Carla Lancelotti, and A. Catherine D'Andrea. 2021. "Human-Woodland Interactions during the Pre-Aksumite and Aksumite Periods in Northeastern Tigray, Ethiopia: Insights from the Wood Charcoal Analyses from Mezber and Ona Adi." *Vegetation History and Archaeobotany* 30: 713–728. doi.org/10.1007/s00334-021-00825-2.

Sadr, Karim. 1991. *The Development of Nomadism in Ancient Northeast Africa*. Philadelphia: University of Pennsylvania Press.

Sahlins, Marshall. 1972. *Stone Age Economics*. Chicago: Aldine.

Saitta, Dean J., and Randall H. McGuire. 1998. "Dialectics, Heterarchy, and Western Pueblo Social Organization." *American Antiquity* 63 (2): 334–336. doi: 10.2307/2694702.

Santone, Lenore. 1997. "Transport Costs, Consumer Demand, and Patterns of Intraregional Exchange: A Perspective on Commodity Production and Distribution from Northern Belize." *Latin American Antiquity* 8 (1): 71–88. doi: 10.2307/971594.

Savard, Georges C. 1966. *Cross-cousin Marriage among the Patrilineal 'Afar*. Addis Ababa: Haile Sellassie I University.

Schmidt, Peter Ridgway, and Matthew C. Curtis. 2001. "Urban Precursors in the Horn: Early 1st-Millennium BC Communities in Eritrea." *Antiquity* 75 (290): 849–859. doi.org/10.1017/S0003598X00089420.

Schmidt, Peter Ridgway, Matthew C. Curtis, and Zelalem Teka. 2008. *The Archaeology of Ancient Eritrea*. Trenton, NJ: Red Sea Press.

Schneider, David M. 1979. *Livestock and Inequality in East Africa: The Economic Use for Social Structure*. Bloomington: Indiana University Press.

Schneider, Harold K., Melville J. Herskovits, and Edward E. LeClair. 1968. *Economic Anthropology: Readings in Theory and Analysis*. New York: Holt, Rinehart, and Winston.

Schneider, Madeleine. 1967. "Stèles funéraires arabes de Quiha." *Annales d'Ethiopie* 7:107–122. doi.org/10.3406/ethio.1967.867.

Schneider, Madeleine. 1970. "Stèles funéraires musulmanes de la province du Choa." *Annales d'Ethiopie* 8:73–78. doi.org/10.3406/ethio.1970.883.

Seland, Eivind Heldaas. 2014. "Early Christianity in East Africa and Red Sea/Indian Ocean Commerce." *African Archaeological Review* 31 (4): 637–647. doi: 10.1007/s10437-014-9172-5.

Selassie, Sergew Hable. 1972. *Ancient and Medieval Ethiopian History to 1270*. Addis Ababa: United Printers.

Senft, Amanda Ruth. 2009. "Species Diversity Patterns at Ecotones." PhD diss., University of North Carolina, Chapel Hill.

Sernicola, Luisa, and Laurel Phillipson. 2011. "Aksum's Regional Trade: New Evidence from Archaeological Survey." *Azania: Archaeological Research in Africa* 46 (2): 190–204. doi: 10.1080/0067270X.2011.580146.

Shackelford, Laura, Fiona Marshall, and Joris Peters. 2013. "Identifying Donkey Domestication through Changes in Cross-sectional Geometry of Long Bones." *Journal of Archaeological Science* 40 (12): 4170–4179. doi.org/10.1016/j.jas.2013.06.006.

Shea, John, John Fleagle, Frank Brown, and Zelalem Assefa. 2002. "Archaeological Reconnaissance of the Omo Kibish Formation, Ethiopia." *Journal of Human Evolution* 42 (2002): A33–A34.

Simoons, Frederick J. 1983. *Northwest Ethiopia: Peoples and Economy.* Westport, CT: Greenwood.

Smith, Andrew M., II. 2005. "Pathways, Roadways, and Highways: Networks of Communication and Exchange in Wadi Araba." *Near Eastern Archaeology* 68 (4): 180–189. doi: 10.1086/NEA25067624.

Southall, Aidan. 1956. *Alur Society: A Study in Types and Processes of Domination.* Cambridge: Heffer and Sons.

Southall, Aidan. 1988. "The Segmentary State in Africa and Asia." *Comparative Studies in Society and History* 30 (1): 52–82. doi.org/10.1017/S0010417500015048.

Southall, Aidan. 1999. "The Segmentary State and the Ritual Phase in Political Economy." In *Beyond Chiefdoms: Pathways to Complexity in Africa,* ed. Susan Keech McIntosh, 31–38. Cambridge: Cambridge University Press.

Spencer, Charles S. 1994. "Factional Ascendance, Dimensions of Leadership, and the Development of Centralized Authority." In *Factional Competition and Political Development in the New World: New Directions in Archaeology,* ed. Elizabeth M. Brumfiel and John W. Fox, 31–43. Cambridge: Cambridge University Press.

Spencer, Paul. 1965. *The Samburu: A Study in Geocentracy.* Berkeley: University of California Press.

Spengler, Robert N., Michael D. Frachetti, and Gayle J. Fritz. 2013. "Ecotopes and Herd Foraging Practices in the Steppe/Mountain Ecotone of Central Asia during the Bronze and Iron Ages." *Journal of Ethnobiology* 33 (1): 125–148. doi: 10.2993/0278-0771-33.1.125.

Stahl, Ann Brower. 1993. "Concepts of Time and Approaches to Analogical Reasoning in Historical Perspective." *American Antiquity* 58 (2): 235–260. doi.org/10.2307/281967.

Stahl, Ann Brower. 1994. "Innovation, Diffusion, and Culture Contact: The Holocene Archaeology of Ghana." *Journal of World Prehistory* 8 (1): 51–112. doi: 10.1007/BF02221837.

Stahl, Ann Brower. 1999. "Perceiving Variability in Time and Space: The Evolutionary Mapping of African Societies." In *Beyond Chiefdoms: Pathways to Complexity in Africa,* ed. Susan Keech McIntosh, 39–55. Cambridge: Cambridge University Press.

Stahl, Ann Brower. 2001. *Making History in Banda: Anthropological Visions of Africa's Past.* Cambridge: Cambridge University Press.

Stanley, Henry Morton. 1874. *Coomassie and Magdala.* London: Sampson, Low.

Stein, Burton. 1971. *The Segmentary State in South India History.* Tucson: University of Arizona Press.

Stevenson, Edward Luther. 1932. *Geography of Claudius Ptolemy: Based upon Greek and Latin Manuscripts and Important Late Fifteenth and Early Sixteenth Century Printed Editions, Including Reproductions of the Maps from the Ebner Manuscript, ca. 1460.* New York: New York Public Library.

Stout, Dietrich, Jay Quade, Sileshi Semaw, Michael J. Rogers, and Naomi E. Levin. 2005. "Raw Material Selectivity of the Earliest Stone Toolmakers at Gona, Afar, Ethiopia." *Journal of Human Evolution* 48 (4): 365–380. doi.org/10.1016/j.jhevol.2004.10.006.

Sutton, Ivor Bullard. 1981. "The Volta River Salt Trade: The Survival of an Indigenous Industry." *Journal of African History* 22 (1): 43–61. doi: 10.1017/S0021853700019598.

Sutton, John E. G. 1983. "West African Metals and the Ancient Mediterranean." *Oxford Journal of Archaeology* 2 (2): 181–188. doi: 10.1111/j.1468-0092.1983.tb00334.x.

Taddesse, Tamrat. 1968. *Church and State in Ethiopia, 1270–1527.* Oxford: Clarendon.

Tamrat, Taddesse. 1988. "Process of Ethnic Interaction and Integration in Ethiopian History: The Case of the Agaw." *Journal of African History* 29 (1): 5–18. http://www.jstor.org/stable/182235.

Tancredi, Alfonso Maria. 1903. "Notizie e studi sulla colonia Eritrea: Casa editrice italiana." *Bollettino della Società Geografica Italiana.* https://books.google.com/books?id=IBINAQAAMAAJ.

Terwilliger, Valery T., Zewdu Eshetu, Paul W. Adderley, Jérémy Jacob, Marylin L. Fogel, and Tsige Gebru Kassa. 2014. "Palaeoenvironmental Change and the Rise and Fall of D'MT and Aksum in Northern Ethiopia: How an Unambiguous Proxy for Rainfall Can Improve Interpretations of Micromorphological and Botanical Data." *Open PAGES Focus 4 Workshop.* Leuvain, Belgium. <insu-01060423>.

Tierney, Jessica E., and Peter B. deMenocal. 2013. "Abrupt Shifts in Horn of Africa Hydroclimate since the Last Glacial Maximum." *Science* 342 (6160): 843–846. doi: 10.1126/science.1240411.

Tilahun, Chernet. 1990. "Traces of Islamic Material Culture in North-Eastern Shoa." *Journal of Ethiopian Studies* 23:303–320.

Todd, Lawrence, Michelle Glantz, and John Kappelman. 2002. "Chilga Kernet: An Acheulean Landscape on Ethiopia's Western Plateau." *Antiquity* 76 (293): 611–612. doi: 10.1017/S0003598X0009089X.

Trimingham, J. Spencer. 2013. *Islam in Ethiopia.* London: Routledge.

Tripcevich, Nicholas. 2007. "Quarries, Caravans, and Routes to Complexity: Prehispanic Obsidian in the South-Central Andes." PhD diss., University of California, Santa Barbara.

Twiss, Katheryn. 2012. "The Archaeology of Food and Social Diversity." *Journal of Archaeological Research* 20 (4): 357–395. doi: 10.1007/s10814-012-9058-5.

Uerpmann, Hans-Peter, and Margarethe Uerpmann. 2002. "The Appearance of the Domestic Camel in South-East Arabia." *Journal of Oman Studies* 12:235–260.

UN Development Program Technical Report. 1973. *Investigation of Geothermal Resources for Power Development*. Addis Ababa: UN Development Program.

US Technical Project in Ethiopia. 1945. *The Salt Resources of East Africa*. Report no. 33. Washington, DC: US Government Services. https://pubs.usgs.gov/pp/0911/report .pdf.

Valenzuela, Daniela, Isabel Cartajena, Calogero M. Santoro, Victoria Castro, and Eugenia M. Gayo. 2018. "Andean Caravan Ceremonialism in the Lowlands of the Atacama Desert: The Cruces de Molinos Archaeological Site, Northern Chile." *Quaternary International* 533:37–47. doi: 10.1016/j.quaint.2018.09.016.

Vansina, Jan. 1962. "Long-Distance Trade Routes in Central Africa." *Journal of African History* 3 (3): 375–390. doi.org/10.1017/S0021853700003303.

Vikør, Knut S. 1982. "The Desert-Side Salt Trade of Kawar." *African Economic History* 11:115–144. doi.org/10.2307/3601219.

Vilá, Bibiana. 2018. "On the Brink of Extinction: Llama Caravans Arriving at the Santa Catalina Fair, Jujuy, Argentina." *Journal of Ethnobiology* 38 (3): 372–389. doi: 10.2993/0278-0771-38.3.372.

Weldehaweriat, Goitom. 2016. "Archaeological Survey at the Site of Ab'ala, Afar, North Ethiopia." MA thesis, Addis Ababa University, Addis Ababa.

Weller, Olivier. 2015. "First Salt Making in Europe: A Global Overview from Neolithic Times." In *The Archaeology of Salt: Approaching an Invisible Past*, ed. Paolo Bellintani, Olivier Weller, and Marialetizia Carra, 67–82. Newcastle upon Tyne, UK: Cambridge Scholars Publishing.

Wengrow, David, and David Graeber. 2015. "Farewell to the 'Childhood of Man': Ritual, Seasonality, and the Origins of Inequality." *Journal of the Royal Anthropological Institute* 21 (3): 597–619. doi: 10.1111/1467-9655.12247.

Wenig, Steffen. 2006. *In kaiserlichem Auftrag: Die Deutsche Aksum-Expedition 1906 unter Enno Littmann*. Wiesbaden: Reichert.

Wheatley, Paul. 1975. "Satyanrta in Suvarnadvipa: From Reciprocity to Redistribution in Ancient Southeast Asia." In *Ancient Civilization and Trade*, ed. Jeremy A. Sabloff and Carl Christian Lamberg-Karlovsky, 227–283. Albuquerque: University of New Mexico Press.

White, Joyce C. 1995. "Incorporating Heterarchy into Theory on Socio-political Development: The Case from Southeast Asia." *Archeological Papers of the American Anthropological Association* 6 (1): 101–123. doi: 10.1525/ap3a.1995.6.1.101.

White, Tim D., Gen Suwa, and Berhane Asfaw. 1994. "*Australopithecus ramidus*, a New Species of Early Hominid from Aramis, Ethiopia." *Nature* 371 (6495): 306–312. doi: 10.1038/375088a0.

Wilding, Richard. 1976. "Harari Domestic Architecture." *Art and Archaeology Research Papers* 9:31–37.

Wilding, Richard. 1989. "Coastal Bantu: Waswahili." In *Kenya Pots and Potters*, ed. Jane Barbour and Simiyu Wandibba, 100–115. Oxford: Oxford University Press.

Wilk, Richard R., and Lisa Cliggett. 2007. *Economies and Cultures: Foundations of Economic Anthropology*. Boulder, CO: Westview.

Wilson, Richard Trevor. 1976. "Some Quantitative Data on the Tigré Salt Trade from the Early Nineteenth Century to the Present Day." *Annali: Istituto Orientale di Napoli* 36 (2): 157–164.

Wilson, Richard Trevor. 1991. "Equines in Ethiopia." In *Donkeys, Mules, and Horses in Tropical Agricultural Development*, ed. Denis Fielding and R. Anne Pearson, 33–47. Edinburgh: Edinburgh School of Agriculture and the Centre for Tropical Veterinary Medicine of the University of Edinburgh.

Woldekiros, Helina S. 2014. "The Afar Caravan Route: Insights into Aksumite (50 BCE–CE 900) Trade and Exchange from the Low Deserts to the North Ethiopian Plateau." PhD diss., Washington University, St. Louis.

Woldekiros, Helina S. 2019. "The Route Most Traveled: The Afar Salt Trail, North Ethiopia." *Chungara* 51 (1): 95–110.

Woldekiros, Helina S., and A. Catherine D'Andrea. 2017. "Early Evidence for Domestic Chickens (*Gallus gallus domesticus*) in the Horn of Africa." *International Journal of Osteoarchaeology* 27 (3): 329–341. doi: 10.1002/oa.2540.

Wolf, Pawel, and Ulrike Nowotnick. 2010. "The Almaqah Temple of Meqaber Ga´ewa near Wuqro (Tigray, Ethiopia)." *Proceedings of the Seminar for Arabian Studies* 40:367–380. https://www.jstor.org/stable/41224035.

Wolff, Norma H. 2004. "African Artisans and the Global Market: The Case of Ghanaian 'Fertility Dolls.'" *African Economic History* 32:123–141. doi: 10.1353/aeh.2005.0018.

Wolska-Conus, Wanda. 1962. *La Topographie chrétienne de Cosmas Indicopleustès: Théologie et science au VIe siècle*. Paris: Presses Universitaires de France.

Wright, Henry T. 1972. "A Consideration of Interregional Exchange in Greater Mesopotamia: 4000–3000 BC." In *Social Exchange and Interaction*, ed. Edwin N. Wilmsen, vol. 46, 95–105. Ann Arbor: Museum of Anthropology, University of Michigan.

Wright, Henry T. 1993. "Trade and Politics on the Eastern Littoral of Africa, AD 800–1300." In *The Archaeology of Africa: Food, Metals, and Towns*, ed. Thurstan Shaw, 658–670. New York: Routledge.

Wylie, Alison. 1985. "The Reaction against Analogy." In *Advances in Archaeological Method and Theory*, ed. Michael B. Schiffer, vol. 8, 63–111. Amsterdam: Elsevier.

Wylie, Alison. 2002. *Thinking from Things: Essays in the Philosophy of Archaeology*. Berkeley: University of California Press.

Yager, Karina Anne. 2009. "A Herder's Landscape: Deglaciation, Desiccation, and Managing Green Pastures in the Andean Puna." PhD diss., Yale University, New Haven.

Yellen, John, Alison Brooks, David Helgren, Martha Tappen, Stanley Ambrose, Raymond Bonnefille, James Feathers, Glen Goodfriend, Kenneth Ludwig, and Paul Renne. 2005. "The Archaeology of Aduma Middle Stone Age Sites in the Awash Valley, Ethiopia." *PaleoAnthropology* 10 (25): e100. doi: 10.4207/PA.2005.ART25.

Yimam, Kebede. 1994. "Afar Nationalism in the Horn of Africa." Senior essay, Department of Political Science and International Relations, College of Social Sciences, Addis Ababa University, Addis Ababa.

Yoshida, Tora. 1993. *Salt Production Techniques in Ancient China: The Aobo Tu*. Vol. 27. New York: Brill.

Zarins, Juris. 1990. "Obsidian and the Red Sea Trade: Prehistoric Aspects." In *South Asian Archaeology 1987*, ed. Maurizio Taddei and Paolo Callieri, 507–541. Rome: Istituto Italiano per il Medio ed Estremo Oriente.

Zarins, Juris, and John Reade. 1996. "Obsidian in the Larger Context of Predynastic/Archaic Egyptian Rea Sea Trade." In *The Indian Ocean in Antiquity*, ed. Julian Reade, 89–106. London: Kegan Paul International.

Zerihun, Degsew. 2015. "Ethnoarchaeological Study of Wild Edible and Medicinal Plants in Aba'ala Woreda, Afar Regional State, Northeastern Ethiopia." MA thesis, Addis Ababa University, Addis Ababa.

Zewde, Bahru. 2002. *A History of Modern Ethiopia, 1855–1991*. Woodbridge, UK: James Currey.

INDEX

Locators followed by *f* indicate a figure. Locators followed by *t* indicate a table.

foodways: Afar salt trade and, 141–144; agriculture and trade in, 31; Aksumite period, 46–47, 142; *berbere* and *shiro* and, 100; evidence of, 142–143, 143*f*; as evidence of heterarchy, 158; identity and, 141; meat and Afar salt trade, 143; trade relationships and, 161. *See also* bread making

Franchetti, Raimondo, 91

Freidel, David, 20

funerary practices, 8, 35–37, 39, 44, 67–68

Gebrelibanos, Tsegaye Berhe, 94

Geography (Ptolemy), 37

Getachew, Kassa Negussie, 77

godama (salt mining axe), 97, 98*f*, 99*f*, 110

gogo (bread), 109

gold, 18, 50–51, 101

Great Lakes region (Africa), 26

Great Rift Valley, 33

Gulf of Zula, 37

gult (land grant), 72

Guyer, Jane I., 20–21, 29

Habasha, 55

hadeli (lowlands salt miner), 97, 99

Hamed Ela (town), 10, 96, 99, 158

Harar (city), 60, 66–67

Harrower, Michael J., 44

heterarchy: Afar salt trade and, 151–152, 161; Aksumite-period subsistence goods and, 154; *ba'algada* and, 154–155; definition of, 13–16; economic participation and, 51–52; evidence for, 44–45; futures studies of, 162; hierarchy coexisting with, 162; non-elite settlements and, 152; in northern Ethiopia, 160; obsidian trade and, 152; settlement patterns and, 44–45

hidalgo (work cycle), 97

hidamos (house), 73–74

hierarchy: Aksumite state and, 160; *ba'algada* and, 154–155; heterarchy coexisting with, 162; models of, 14; needs for specialization in, 16; in northern Ethiopia, 160

highlands (Eritrean), 12, 14, 31–32, 94, 151

highlands (Ethiopian). *See* north Ethiopian highlands

hodu (salt mining tool), 97, 98*f*, 110

hominids, 55

horizontal differentiation, 153–154. *See also* heterarchy

Horn of Africa. *See* Afar (region); Eritrean highlands; Ethiopia; north Ethiopian highlands

Huntingford, Brereton, 46

Indicopleustes, Cosmas, 46, 50–51, 101, 152–153

informal economies. *See* heterarchy; niche economies

interactions through trade, interregional/intraregional, 19–20

Islam, 60; Afar people and, 67–68; caravanners and, 88; Ethiopian arrival of, 64–68; Muslim immigration to Ethiopia and, 65; present-day Ethiopian practice of, 68; trade and, 65

Jenne-Jeno, 18, 162

Johanson, Donald, 55

Judaism, 31, 58–59, 64

Kebra Nagast, 54

ketema/katma (Afar settlement), 80–81

Khaldun, Ibn, 60

Kidane Mehret (town), 35, 42

kingdoms. *See* Ethiopia, kingdoms of

Klein, Rebecca A., 64

kudu (salt mining assistant), 97

Kusimba, Chapurukha M., 18

Lake Asale, 5, 10, 69–70, 97

languages, 35, 63, 71, 87–88, 157

lithic artifacts, 8, 10, 136, 140, 147–149

lowlands. *See* Afar (region); Afar Desert

Lyons, Diane E., 73

Maria Theresa thalers, 101

markets, regional, 49–51

Matara (town), 9, 34, 38, 42, 146

McIntosh, Susan Keech, 15

Meda Ble'at (Agula), 116; ceramics at, 144; excavation of, 137, 139–141; meat consumption at, 143; site of, 138*f*, 139*f*; stratigraphic sequence of, 139*f*; use phases of, 140

mehabers (social organization), 103

Mekelle, 10, 89, 93–95, 104

Melabdi (town), 79*f*, 100

Michels, Joseph, 40

middle-range conceptual framework, 6

mogogo (griddle), 146

Muhammad, 65

Munro-Hay, Stuart C., 37, 156

Munzinger, Werber, 94

Natural History (Pliny), 27

Negash (town), 65–66, 147

niche economies: Afar salt trade and, 7, 12; Aksumite trade and, 107; caravanners and,

102; caravans and, 29; definition of, 20–22; in Desi'a, 152; economic orders and, 21; function of salt trade in, 110–111; political economy and, 105–107; salt distribution and, 156; salt trade and, 52, 81; settlement and, 114

Niger River, 23–24

north Ethiopian highlands: accumulation of wealth in, 154; Afar salt trade in, 81; Aksumite security in, 157; alternate routes in, 151; architecture in, 73–74; commodities in, 81; economic strategies in, 102–105; home ownership in, 74; identity in, 71; internal variables in, 105–106; landholding in, 72; niche economies in, 160–161; physical environment of, 70; political organization in, 72–73; power in, 150; salt traders from, 84; salt use in, 100–102; settlement in, 114–115; socioeconomic organization in, 73; socioeconomic organization of, 73; state ownership of land in, 72–73, 74; as study area, 89f. *See also* Agula

Nubians, 20, 156

obsidian: at Ona Adi Agway, 119, 124f; role of, 45; significance of, 149, 159; trade of, 9, 45, 151–153, 155; use of, 56, 147–148

Oka, Rahul, 18

Ona Adi Abobay (Desi'a): ceramics at, 144, 147; excavation of, 116, 137, 139–141; map of, 138f; meat consumption at, 143; site of, 140f; stratigraphic sequence of, 140f

Ona Adi Agway (Agula): animal remains and, 143; building phases of, 119, 120f, 122–124; ceramics at, 144; Cherkos Agula (church) and, 136; cowry shells at, 126f, 148; dimensions of, 117; excavation of, 116, 117–124; plan of, 120f, 121f; radiocarbon dating of, 124; role in Afar salt trade, 119; site of, 118f; stratigraphic sequence of, 121f; tools in, 124f; use of, 119, 120f, 122–124

Ona Hahaile (Desi'a): animal remains and, 142; ceramics at, 144, 147; cowry shells at, 148; dimensions of, 127, 130–131; excavation of, 116, 124–132; materials at, 131; plan of, 128f; site of, 127f; stratigraphic sequence of, 130f; use of, 128, 131–132

organizations, social, 102–103

Oromo (people), 63, 67, 154–155

Oromo states, 61–62

pastoralism: in Afar desert, 10; among Afar, 76; in early Ethiopia, 56–58; economic strategies of, 102; niche economies and, 160–161;

parallels with salt trade of, 99; role in Afar salt trade, 151; role in economy, 46; in southern segmentary states, 62; uses of salt in, 100–101

peer networks, 14, 151, 162. *See also* heterarchy

Periplus of the Erythraean Sea, 31, 37–38, 50–51

Phillipson, David W., 45

Pliny, 31, 48, 50–51

political economy: centralized/hierarchical power structures and, 3; diffuse/heterarchical power structures and, 3; early perspectives on, 14; external variables and, 106–107; heterarchy and, 13; hierarchy and, 13; internal variables of, 105–106; role of elite, 18

Punt, land of, 37–38

Red Sea, 30–31, 34, 48, 59, 113, 161

Reilly F. Kent, III, 20

religion, 43, 58, 60, 64, 65–68. *See also* Christianity; Islam; Judaism

rest (Tigray landholding system), 72

Rift Valley (Ethiopia), 56, 68

salt: Afar region sources of, 68–69; Askumite trade and, 5; blocks of, 90–91; caravan systems and, 28; as currency, 24, 91, 101; distribution of, 7, 86–87, 92–93; from Europe, 25; as export commodity, 50–51; focus on, 11; as free, 99; human diet and, 22–23; in *ketemas*/*katmas*, 80–81; Lake Asale as source of, 69–70; in local trade, 22; market quantities of, 94; mining of, 7, 97; present-day prices for, 99; pricing of, 22, 93f, 96, 99, 154; role in Afar region, 81; shop owners sale of, 96; significance in trade, 7; sub-Saharn sources of, 25; symbolic rituals involving, 23; trade in, 23, 63; transportation of, 26; uses of, 21–23, 100–102; West African sources of, 25

salt blocks, 91–92, 93t

salt brokers, 92–93, 104, 105

salt distribution, 86–87, 93–96

salt industries, 23–26, 53

salt market, 92–94, 96, 99

salt miners, 95, 97–99, 98f, 99f

salt mining, 25; practices of, 70; regional methods of, 25–26; wage labor and, 103–104

salt production, 25, 84, 97

salt routes in present-day, 84–86, 85f, 86t

salt shops, 95, 107

salt trade, Afar. *See* Afar salt trade

salt trade, Aksumite, 107, 117

salt trade, European, 28